Why Race Matters in South Africa

Why Race Matters in South Africa

Michael MacDonald

Harvard University Press

Cambridge, Massachusetts, and London, England

Printed in the United States of America

First Harvard University Press paperback edition, 2012

Library of Congress Cataloging-in-Publication Data

MacDonald, Michael, 1952–
Why race matters in South Africa / Michael MacDonald.
p. cm.
Includes bibliographical references and index.
ISBN 978-0-674-02186-0 (cloth : alk. paper)
ISBN 978-0-674-06389-1 (pbk.)
1. South Africa—Race relations—Political aspects. 2. Blacks—South Africa—Economic conditions. I. Title.

DT1756.M32 2006
305.800968′09051—dc22 2005052819

To Richard and Freda MacDonald

Contents

Acknowledgments

I owe thanks to many people and institutions for help on this book, beginning with South African scholars. I first worked in South Africa in 1990–91, when I spent a year housed in the Political Studies Department at the University of Cape Town. I appreciate the hospitality of Mary Simon, Hermann Giliomee, and Wilmot James (then in the Sociology Department). Hermann, characteristically, made suggestions that have improved the book even where he disagrees with it, and Wilmot gave time and ideas unstintingly. In 1995, I taught at the University of the Western Cape on a Fulbright Fellowship. Vincent Maphai, a source of unending insight, introduced me to the department. The late Sipho Maseko was a gracious host, a lively presence, and a serious thinker. Keith Gottschalk was entertaining and encyclopedic in his knowledge of progressive politics, and Bettina von Lieres kept an eye on me in teaching and pointed me in the right direction in my research. When I was in South Africa, Adam Habib, Annette Seegert, Robert Mattes, and Rupert Taylor found time to fill me in on political developments, and Rupert also offered detailed comments on a draft of my manuscript. Raymond Sutter also made helpful comments on drafts of early chapters. I also owe personal thanks to lasting friends I made in South Africa, notably Julia Sloth Neilson and Karl Neilson, Tim and Heather Hughes, and Karen MacGregor. Tim was also an unfailingly fertile source of ideas, information, and insight.

In the United States, Elke Zuern, Robert Meister, and Jason Myers commented on the whole manuscript, identifying weaknesses I had not seen and showing me where I could make improvements. Sung Ho Kim and Russ Muirhead offered constructive comments on particular chapters. Wendy Brown read the whole manuscript and offered excellent suggestions. Mary Dietz and Grant Farred got me through some rough patches and talked through ideas with me. Jim Shepard gave me good advice, great whiskey, and better friendship. Michael Aronson, the editor, supported this manuscript, and I am indebted to him.

I received generous financial assistance from the National Endowment for the Humanities, the Fulbright-Hays Fellowship Program, and Williams College, especially from two excellent Deans of Faculty, John Reichert and David Smith. Josh Earn, a former student, checked the notes and handled my disorganization smoothly. The *South Atlantic Quarterly* published a short version of Chapter 7, and I drew some of Chapter 5 from an article in the *Journal of South African Studies.*

At Williams, I have had the good fortune to talk about South African politics with Brian Levy, Tom Spear, and now Michael Samson, a generous and kind friend. Ingrid van Niekerk and the team at the Economic Policy Research Institute always are ready with a helping hand. Bill Darrow, Craig Wilder, and Stephen Sheppard are valued friends. In the Political Science Department at Williams, where I work, Sam Crane, Cathy Johnson, Jim Mahon, and Nicole Mellow have lively political minds. Mark Reinhardt and my former colleagues, Gary Jacobsohn and Tim Cook, have enriched my professional and personal lives. James McAllister, Marc Lynch, and Darel Paul talk with me every day and make our conversations endlessly interesting.

Mary, my wife, reads my drafts, gives her opinions truthfully, and is generous and gracious. She makes people around her better. My children, Colin and Marichal, who have put up with the project for too much of their lives, give me pride, joy, and purpose. I dedicate the book to my mother and late father.

Introduction

If nationality is consent, the state is compulsion.

—HENRI-FRÉDÉRIC AMIEL

This book addresses three broad questions about why races have come to matter in South African history and why they still matter in South African politics. It begins with the obvious questions: What are "races"? Where do they come from and what do races *do* in South African politics? How do political actors conceive of races and what are the political implications of rival conceptions?

It has become commonplace to deny the old idea that races are biogenetic realities and to portray races as identities that humans, not nature, devise. Almost reflexively, the void that is opened by denaturalizing races is being filled by the idea of "culture." Races, it is thought, are cultural formations, but the culturalization of races raises questions of its own. If races essentially are cultural identities, what differentiates races from cultures? What weight does race carry that cannot be borne by culture, without the assistance of race? The experience of South African whites (to insinuate the racialization that is being problematized) suggests that races are ways of associating different cultural groups, but why do smaller cultural groups combine into larger racial groups? What was gained by assembling into races and what does this say about race? And does it matter whether communities are designated as "races" or some other way (say, as "nations"), given that the membership of the race and of the nation sometimes is the same, whatever the designation?

The white supremacist state obviously classified people on the basis of race and associated all manner of advantages with whites and disadvantages with blacks.[1] But did state power merely confirm, register, and play favorites among races that existed independently of it or did state power actually help to constitute putatively "racial" communities—to make them? Culturalist arguments see white supremacy as favoring whites and disfavoring blacks, not as creating the categories of "white" and "black" in the process. The white supremacist state enfranchised whites as citizens and disenfranchised blacks as noncitizens. Did this merely manifest in politics differences between existing communities that already had developed on the basis of culture, or did enfranchisement and disenfranchisement help constitute the communities themselves? If whiteness originally was associated with inclusion and the benefits conferred by citizenship, and blackness was associated with exclusion and the costs inflicted on noncitizens, should South Africa's "races" be conceived relationally, as mutually constituting and constituted?

The second set of questions revolves around the role played by race and state in making, undermining, and sustaining capitalism in South Africa. What did the state, which had been intertwined with race by white supremacy, do for capitalism and to capitalism? What were the costs, why were they assessed, and what benefits did business get in return? How did the racial state and capitalism shape each other and in what ways did capitalism sustain or corrode the racial state? How did the relationship between them change over time and what changed it? Why did capital reassess its loyalties in response to the township rebellion of the 1980s, deciding that democratic capitalism offered more than racial capitalism? And how was democratic capitalism accomplished, given that white supremacy had prevented much support for democratic capitalism from developing among blacks and had taken extreme measures to prevent democratic organizations from developing?

The rebellion of the 1980s, which was centered in segregated black "townships" on the outskirts of cities, had stalemated apartheid, encouraging negotiations on a new political dispensation. But negotiations on the new political order required the African National Congress (ANC)—as the representative of the township rebellion—to make compromises and bargains binding on civil society, and then to preside over a government that was destined to disappoint the expectations of many blacks, especially activists, who had forced apartheid to negotiate with the ANC in the first place. What made this possible? Was the ANC in actual control of the rebellion? How did it achieve the authority to moderate popular demands, maintain its popularity anyway, and make binding compromises? What role did racial solidarities play in sustaining and limiting democracy in South Africa?

The third set of questions revolves around changes in the meaning of race in democratic South Africa. If white supremacy associated whiteness with citizenship and blackness with noncitizenship, what happens when "non-racialism" becomes the official ideology of democracy? What is non-racialism? What does "non-racialism" mean in principle and how does it work in practice? If races are cultural communities, do "non-racial" political institutions allow Africans, the largest race, to capture control of the state in the name of democracy? But if races are political (as well as cultural) constructs, do they evolve in new directions under new political circumstances, undercutting the electoral prospects of the ANC as the de facto party of Africans? If racial solidarities originated in political experiences, in shared deprivations and shared struggles in the case of blacks, are racial solidarities unmade by the political and economic differences that have developed in democratic South Africa? What is the role of race in sustaining democratic citizenship and the role of democratic citizenship in vindicating capitalism in post-apartheid South Africa?

Democracy is a good in itself, and the whole history of white supremacy vouches for its value. But democracy also is a means to other ends; it rescues, stabilizes, and governs a society that had been brought to the verge of chaos by apartheid. How does democracy do all of this, and how can it retain legitimacy in spite of continuing, even widening, economic inequality and poverty? Are conventional definitions of democracy, which emphasize the procedural nature of democracy, up to the task of explaining why South Africans value democratic procedures, given that democracy has not repaired urgent problems? Perhaps democracy is legitimated for substantive as well as procedural reasons, for empowering those who previously had been disenfranchised. If so, does this suggest that racial solidarities, engendered by generations of dispossession, common oppression and exploitation, and disenfranchisement, now legitimate democracy for many Africans, and that democracy is legitimate because it empowers the "us" that had been forged by white supremacy? And why has capitalism, which was blamed for apartheid by much of the anti-apartheid movement, become taken for granted, unchallenged and unchallengeable by its erstwhile enemies, now that democracy prevails? Is capitalism also availing itself of racial solidarities to reproduce and sustain itself? If democracy legitimates itself via racial empowerment, and capitalism legitimates itself via democracy, what must capital do to turn racial solidarities to its advantage?

The thesis of this book is that South Africa's races originated in political experiences as well as cultural similarities, that the white supremacist state made communities of "whites" and "blacks" by conferring citizenship on the one and denying it to the other. Whites were molded by the political experiences of inclusion, and blacks were branded by exclusion as well as by their respective cultural affinities; but the role of the state did not end there. The racial state gave economic expression to the disparities between the political experiences of belonging and not belonging. Whites became more prosperous, in part because the state subsidized their living standards, insulated them from market competition, denied blacks access to free markets, and organized the exploitation of blacks. Ultimately, the specter of social collapse persuaded capital to entertain democracy as a solution to the disorder of the 1980s and 1990s.

Yet in spite of the achievement of democracy, wealth still is distributed extremely unequally and economic inequality still is expressed racially. Most of the economic elite is white (which is not the same as saying that most whites are in the economic elite), and most Africans are poor. Consequently business, which historically was associated with white supremacy, fears the possibility of racial and economic grievances combining, of the capitalist economy being seen by the poor African majority as just another version of white supremacy. To fend off that danger, business is joining with the ANC government in encouraging the growth of black middle classes and in enlisting racialism, as embodied by the new African bourgeoisie, to support the new political order. The advantage of African economic elites is that they upset the historic equation between blackness and poverty; summon racial nationalism, hitherto the idiom of resistance and revolution, on behalf of capitalism; and legitimate ongoing economic inequalities. Thus South Africa's formula for stable democratic capitalism: racial nationalism legitimates "non-racial" democracy; "non-racial" democracy legitimates capitalism; and capitalism, building an African bourgeoisie along with black middle classes in conjunction with the democratic state, gives material substance to and sustains the salience of racial nationalism. Racial nationalism, not for the first time in South African history, is bending to the needs of the political economy.

1

The Logic of White Supremacy

> There must be no illusions about this, because if our policy is taken to its full logical conclusion as far as the Black people are concerned, there will not be one Black man with South African citizenship. I say this sincerely, because that is the idea behind it. Why should I try to hide it? That is our policy in terms of the mandate we have been given. . . . [E]very Black man in South Africa will eventually be accommodated politically in some independent new state in this honourable way and there will no longer be a moral obligation on [the South African] Parliament to accommodate these people politically.
>
> —CONNIE MULDER, MINISTER OF PLURAL RELATIONS AND DEVELOPMENT, 1978

South Africa counts as a great success for liberal democracy. It now possesses standard liberal democratic institutions—open elections, individual rights, equality under the law, constitutional government, free political activity, and much more—in spite of a history that was neither liberal nor democratic. Apartheid was not liberal because the apartheid state did not respect the rule of law, did not respect individual rights, and did not consider those it governed to be individuals, subsuming them in what the apartheid state designated as "their" ethno-cultural or racial groups. Apartheid was not democratic because the apartheid state restricted the franchise on the basis of race, denied civil and political rights—even citizenship—to many of its subjects as a matter of course, and rejected the sovereignty of the people of South Africa. Ultimately, the illiberal and undemocratic domination of the white minority over the large black majority was unsustainable. But that apartheid was not liberal and not democratic does not prove that it was doomed to fail because it was illiberal and undemocratic.

The failure of apartheid raises a number of issues, beginning with the meaning of apartheid. What was it? Was apartheid just white supremacy with an odd name or did the name signify a distinctive type of racism? Did apartheid, whatever it was, provide the framework for organizing

South Africa's political economy or did apartheid adapt to the imperatives of the capitalist economy? What interests did apartheid represent and which—if any of them—were separable from it? Was apartheid a vehicle for the advancement of other interests or did it impose inviolable rules of its own that both conditioned and constrained the interests of whites?

Apartheid prepared South Africa badly for liberal democracy, and not only because of its racism. Apartheid rightly is identified with racism, but it also was racialist. Often the terms "racism" and "racialism" are used interchangeably, but they carry distinguishable meanings. In the United States, where the word "racism" covers a wide range of meanings, the word "racialism" rarely is used. That both terms are used in South Africa suggests their meanings may differ, that "racism" and "racialism" sometimes refer to different things. Racism has members of one racial group, usually whites, dominating members of a different racial group, usually blacks, for material or expressive reasons. Asserting the superiority of one group and the inferiority of the other, racists prescribe supremacy for the superior population and subordination for the inferior one. Racism deems some people as *better* than other people on the basis of their membership in a race. The "better" people—usually whites—deserve more power by virtue of their superiority, with the sequence being critical for racists. Ostensibly, superiority precedes and grounds supremacy, not the other way around. That is, racists do not regard power as the source of their superiority, but superiority as the source of their power. Whites are more powerful because they are superior, because nature or culture has made them better and more worthy; moreover, whites are superior even when they are not more powerful. It is the putative inferiority of blacks that justifies the subordination of blacks.

Racialists, on the other hand, do not necessarily claim that one people is better than another; they are content to claim that one people is *different* from another. The old segregationist precept in the United States, of separate but equal, affected to be racialist. It did not always proclaim that blacks were inferior or necessarily insist that they were subordinate; it could, and on rare occasions did, make the more modest claim that standards for blacks must be different because blacks were different (from whites), and that they were different because they were black. Of course, racialism usually derives from and abets racism, as the American example shows. Black and white might have been kept separate, but they were not kept equal. Yet even when racialism serves the ends of racism, it elaborates a distinct logic. Racialists regard race as the source of identity and identities as the axes of political institutions, and then urge that government be organized on the basis of race. Thus, racialists agree with racists that race is a critical human attribute, that it plays a constituting role in making people who they are and does not merely comprise one trait among others. But racialists and racists may disagree on what should follow from racialization. Racists require inequality to manifest the superiority of one race over inferior races; racialists, on the other hand, require distinct—but not, they claim, necessarily unequal—representation for the various races.

Apartheid, unlike previous forms of white supremacy in South Africa, was predicated on both racism *and* racialism. Obviously, apartheid was committed to establishing and expanding the absolute and systematic supremacy of whites; but that does not mean that it constituted, or was coterminous with, white supremacy. White supremacy long preceded the advent of apartheid in southern Africa, originating in the Cape colony—the site of the first white settlement—in the eighteenth and nineteenth centuries and spreading in the nineteenth century to the interior of what in 1910 became modern South Africa.[1] Apartheid, by contrast, was not instituted until the second half of the twentieth century, which is why apartheid is not reducible to simple white supremacy. Apartheid was a version of white supremacy, one among several competitors, and what distinguished apartheid from its rivals was not racism, which was common to all of them.

Consider two interpretations of South African "segregation," the system of racial organization that preceded apartheid.[2] The first interpretation was developed by a liberal critic of segregation in the 1930s; the second by an author of segregation and the dominant figure in South African politics for the first half of the twentieth century. R. F. Hoernlé, the liberal critic, portrayed segregation in almost Manichean terms.[3] He took South Africa to have been governed by two principles, mastery and subordination. Whites were masters, blacks were subordinates, and the mastery of whites was elevated into the inviolable principle of social organization. Whites dominated every area of life—government, economy, culture, society—partly because of their stake in each, but also because their commitment to dominate some areas required domination in all areas. Whites did not brook equality anywhere lest domination be undercut everywhere.

The system Hoernlé described was self-perpetuating and interlocking:

"It is contrary to the principle of domination for any White man, let alone a White woman, to be in a position to receive orders from, or to be otherwise subordinate to, a non-European and more particularly a Native. . . . That White domination is incompatible with the subordination of White to non-White is a principle which applies . . . throughout all social relations between the races."[4] Segregation for Hoernlé, rather than being inspired by racial feelings and solidarities, was motivated by considerations of power. Power begat power, and power was the preserve of whites. Color identified who was the subject and who was the object of power, but otherwise did not matter much. Whites acted, blacks were acted upon, and the logic of domination counted for more than racial sentiments. Whites protected all components of their privilege, even those that were trivial, because they considered domination to be indivisible. The pretense, not to mention the substance, of equality in some areas—the economy, say—undercuts the principle of inequality everywhere.

Jan Smuts, the central figure in South African politics in the first half of the twentieth century and an author of the policy of segregation, saw things differently. Smuts, unlike Hoernlé, started with racialized subjects. Racial natures were taken as given. Whites were European, civilized, mature; blacks had the "psychology and outlook" of children.[5] Smuts asserted, "By temperament [Africans] have not much initiative, and if left to themselves and their own tribal routine they do not respond very well to the stimulus for progress. They are naturally happy-go-lucky, and are not oppressed with the stirrings of that divine discontent which have made the European the most unhappy but the most progressive of all humans."[6] Africans and Europeans needed each other, however. Africans provided whites with physical labor, labor being scarce otherwise and Africans being better suited to it; and whites provided the guidance that Africans required, acting as "trustees" for them. Whites were the adults whom the African children needed.

Talk of children and adults helped only so much. It justified white supremacy, in that adults must preside over children. But it did not justify segregation, the purpose of the stereotype. Africans, if the metaphor was extended, could "mature" into adulthood, becoming more like their white teachers. That, however, was precisely what the policy of segregation was meant to prevent. According to Smuts, "Nothing could be worse for Africa than the application of a policy, the object or tendency of which would be . . . to de-Africanize the African and turn him either into a beast of the field or into a pseudo-European."[7] Africans had to be kept different, culturally, politically, and religiously (a position taken without irony by a man whose middle name was "Christian"). To fend off the prospect of Africans assimilating into "European" culture, whites must "evolve a policy which . . . [would] preserve [African] unity with her own past, conserve what is precious in her past, and build her future progress and civilization on specifically African foundations."[8]

The policy of segregation was to allow whites to have their cake and eat it too. It conferred the benefits of control on whites while keeping Africans different. In classic colonialist fashion, segregation had Africans being governed indirectly. As Smuts reported, "The white administration remains responsible for the larger functions of government. . . . But all the purely tribal concerns are left to the chief and his counsellors whose actions are supervised by the white officer only in certain cases intended to prevent abuses."[9] Africans, in other words, were different from whites, and differences had to be respected by and manifested in distinct cultural and political institutions. Different institutions hinged, therefore, on prior differences between white and black, which Smuts tried to impute to nature. But the prospect of Africans assimilating into white culture belied his effort, suggesting the differences were cultural, not natural; and cultural barriers were surmountable, which is why segregation was necessary: in "preserving" supposedly inferior cultures, segregation had the effect of justifying white supremacy.

Smuts, of course, might have advocated assimilating (some) Africans into "white" civilization, because educated Africans resented segregation and were tempted to adopt "European" ways. Instead, he maintained, "It is . . . evident that the proper place of the educated minority of the natives is with the rest of their people, of whom they are the natural leaders, and from whom they should not in any way be dissociated."[10] That is, segregation trapped educated Africans among their "own" people, who were governed by "traditional" chiefs, leaving educated Africans no alternative to being "African" and to being stuck beneath "their" chiefs. With Africans bound by obedience to chiefs and with chiefs bound to the white state, Africans were subordinated indirectly to whites. Whites controlled the chiefs, and the chiefs controlled the people.

Smuts glided over the benefits of white supremacy to whites, presenting segregation as an obligation borne by whites for the benefit of Africans (and the world). Africans, he claimed, were forever children. Yet if Africans were sentenced to a life term as children, Smuts need not have fretted about the danger of Africans adopting the ways of "European" civilization. Obviously, Smuts's problem was that Africans were not children and were capable of assimilating into Western culture, which undercut the justification of trusteeship and the benefits whites derived from it. Consequently, segregationists could not celebrate what they might have claimed as the greatest achievement of white supremacy, the edification of the African race. The dialectics of segregation meant that Africans who thrived in the ways of whites did not validate the "white" order: they endangered it.

Hence the political problem with justifying the structure of domination via racist myths about the indelible inferiority of Africans. Smuts's "happy-go-lucky" children were changed by exposure to Western ways and schools, undercutting the ideological basis of domination. Whites might have accepted that detribalized natives, having adopted "European" civilization, could participate in governing South Africa. But if Africans matured into adults, whites would become unneeded as trustees; and if whites were not trustees, they would forfeit their right to supremacy (since they no longer were *better*). Thus, to the extent whites were committed to preserving the fruits of racism in the face of the increasing Westernization of African elites, it behooved them to reconceive race. Racist power structures could not be defended with silly stereotypes; they required transplanting in less malleable, more absolute conceptions of race. Racism needed augmenting from racialism.

Racism is not what distinguished apartheid from segregation. Both rendered the systematic subordination of black to white as an inviolable principle of public and private relations; both reserved the vast bulk of land for whites, prohibited Africans from leasing land owned by whites, and shunted Africans to reserves—later called "homelands"—to be administered by chiefs who, in turn, were propped up by the white state;[11] both restricted the access of Africans to labor markets, limiting their mobility and reducing their wages; both reserved jobs for whites; both obstructed the urbanization of Africans; both imposed residential and territorial segregation; and both regarded government as the preserve of whites.

The apartheid state went even further in extending and formalizing segregation. It enacted, among other things, the Group Areas Act, mandating residential segregation (to the particular disadvantage of Coloureds in Cape Town and the surrounding areas); the Separate Amenities Act, requiring segregation in public facilities (so-called petty apartheid); the Immorality Act, forbidding sexual liaisons across the color divide; the Prohibition of Mixed Marriages Act; Influx Control, obstructing African urbanization and mobility; and the Population Registration Act, which underpinned apartheid by defining racial categories and the criteria for classifying individuals in them.

But if apartheid deepened segregation and white supremacy, it did not invent either of them. What it did innovate, and what in principle differentiated apartheid from segregation, was a distinct conception of race. Segregation ordained blacks to be *inferior* to whites; apartheid cast them as indelibly *different.* Of course, apartheid openly regarded blacks as inferior for reasons of nature and culture, and systematically subordinated them. But apartheid did not justify white supremacy only in terms of black inferiority.[12] Apartheid did declare African claims in South Africa to be inferior to white claims, but on the grounds that African claims were unfounded. Not belonging in South Africa, Africans lacked standing to claim rights for themselves. They belonged elsewhere, in societies of their own, because their race was different.

Apartheid sought to secure what Hoernlé had described as segregation, the interlocking and absolute domination of white over black, by regrounding domination. Segregation had claimed that whites and blacks possessed distinct cultures and that the twain should never meet (which is why segregation was necessary). Apartheid likewise associated races with cultures, but implicitly addressed the prospect that the link between them was not indissoluble, elaborating a state policy—"separate development"—to prevent Africans from adopting "European" culture. The kernel of separate development was that races are akin to nations, that they engender primary solidarities, organize society, and establish allegiances. It followed that, as combining multiple nations in one state is dangerous (because it associates people with conflicting loyalties), so combining multiple races in one state is dangerous. Throwing multiple racial groups together into one state inevitably thwarts the right of some to national self-determination; inevitably causes friction, breeds disorder, and incites violence; and inevitably prevents conflicts from being adjudicated on the basis shared values (because values spring from groups and each group produces distinctive values).

Apartheid did not apply the multicultural principles of separate development consistently or evenhandedly. It treated the "race" of whites as sufficient basis for a single, encompassing nation, but South Africa was not populated by a generic *white* (or African) culture. Whites identified themselves as "white" and Africans as "African," of course, and they attached these identities to cultural beacons (Europe and Africa). But before apartheid transformed South Africa, cultures were associated more closely with ethno-culture than they were with races. Cultural institutions—churches, marriages, languages, schools, newspapers, popular literature, poetry—were located in ethno-cultural, not racial, communities. Whites, for example, attended either English-language or Afrikaans-language schools, where they were socialized into the worldviews of English- or Afrikaans-speaking South Africans.

The project of building communities of whites, of giving substance to whiteness, was vexed by the history of deep ethno-cultural rivalries between Afrikaans-speakers and English-speakers. The National Party (NP), in addition to instituting apartheid, aggressively pursued the sectional interests of Afrikaners against English-speakers. It reserved state jobs for whites and hired Afrikaners to fill them. It promoted Afrikaner cultural institutions (schools, universities, radio stations, and television broadcasts), openly challenged the ascendancy of English, and made Afrikaans the primary language of the state. It gave public institutions an increasingly Afrikaner cast and did not conceal its project.[13] Culturally, the NP's *volk* was the Afrikaner people, which had nursed grudges against Britain, English-speaking South Africans, and English-language culture since the early nineteenth century.[14] Nevertheless, separate development regarded common race as enough to unify whites politically; but common race was not enough to unify Africans politically.

Separate development nationalized the race of whites; it denationalized that of Africans. Rather than having Africans bound together by race, separate development had them governed by the principle of particularity, by tribe. Separate development claimed to accord due respect to the social reality of tribes, chiefs, and customary law, to cultivate autonomous, independent, and ultimately sovereign states in accordance with African traditions (and not to be reviving indirect rule under new auspices). Actually, the apartheid state appointed, manipulated, and replaced leaders of "independent" homelands[15] and deprived them of viable economies—partly because the apartheid state kept areas with valuable resources for itself, partly because it preferred that homeland governments be subservient and pliable. But the relevant point is not the hypocrisy of separate development, the discrepancy between the stated objectives and the deeds of the apartheid state. The point is that separate development furthered political and ideological purposes.

Separate development sought to contain the contradictions inherent in white supremacy. Having conquered and subjugated Africans, expropriated their land and exploited their labor, and corrupted their traditions through colonization and indirect rule, whites exerted a powerful leveling effect on Africans. White supremacy associated the experiences of Africans with powerlessness and rightlessness, thus building the scaffolding for common African identities and political objectives, the elimination of white racism and racialism. Lest the apartheid state face the consequences of its own policies in the form of a community constituted and unified by shared aversion to white supremacy, separate development sought to fragment the unity of the oppressed that apartheid itself was forging, to offset the homogenizing effect of apartheid on Africans. Separate development was to weaken what unified Africans and to strengthen what differentiated them.

Separate development also justified African rightlessness ideologically. It defined Africans as aliens in South Africa; maintained that they deserved states and societies of their own ("homelands"); and concluded that, as (putative) members of their own states and societies, they could reside in South Africa (their labor *was* necessary) mainly as foreigners and only on the terms set by the host country. Having thus packaged races as nations, apartheid answered Smuts's segregationist dilemma. Where Smuts had struggled to justify the exclusion of Westernized Africans, apartheid succeeded. By nationalizing race, apartheid neutralized African demands for equal rights. Regardless of their cultural practices, Africans did not belong in or have claims on South Africa. Thus, Smuts's nightmare—that educated Africans would claim political rights and undermine white supremacy on the basis of cultural assimilation—was dispelled: because Africans and whites by definition belonged to different nations, Africans were defined out of the nation and out of political rights.

Apartheid created a contradiction of its own, however. It was committed to racializing state and society, and was therefore diminishing particularity among Africans. Yet the apartheid state recoiled from nationalizing Africans in the manner of whites. If Africans were considered to have comprised one nation, they would have constituted the larger nation and presented apartheid with a unified threat. Consequently, power politics pressed the apartheid state simultaneously to nationalize race, creating greater commonalities among Africans, and to denationalize race, disaggregating the racial communities it was promoting through racism and racialism in favor of tribe, particularity, and difference. The white supremacist state was breaking down the very tribal differences that it sought to shore up through indirect rule.

2

The Mother of Identity Politics

> I do not know of any people who really have developed "along their own lines." My fellow white South Africans, enjoying what is called "Western civilisation," should be the first to agree that this civilisation is indebted to previous civilisations, from the East, from Greece, Rome and so on. For its heritage, Western civilisation is really indebted to very many sources, both ancient and modern.
>
> —ALBERT LUTULI

Segregation and separate development represented rival responses to the problems of white supremacy as posed by the African majority. Segregation responded by seeking to reinforce what it took to be "culture," trapping Africans under chiefs and chiefs under the state. Separate development likewise sought to buttress and control chiefs and likewise sought to confine Africans in "their" tribal cultures. But separate development also insisted on translating particular tribal cultures into particular nations, institutionalizing tribes as political units and fragmenting the unity of the oppressed that was immanent in the shared experiences of apartheid. The two modes of white supremacy agreed, therefore, on preserving the trappings of African tradition; on sustaining the practice of indirect rule ("independent" tribal governments—the "homelands"—were subsidized financially and maintained militarily by the South African state); and on reproducing white supremacy. Separate development changed neither the means of segregation nor the end of white supremacy. But it did change the ideological foundations of each.

Segregation and separate development were committed to preserving white supremacy and to installing race as the pivot of social and political organization. But racializing South African society, although knitting whites into a group that contained the ethnic and class conflicts that previously had riven white politics, also set a dangerous precedent. If Afrikaners and English-speakers could bury their differences in common whiteness, African tribes might follow their example. Fearing, therefore, that it might be molding an overwhelming African majority, separate development countered the racializing logic of white supremacy by tribalizing Africans. Whereas Smuts associated races with cultures and left the matter there, separate development appreciated that cultures are permeable, are susceptible to mixing, amalgamation, and contamination. In response, separate development *particularized* the cultures of Africans, then *nationalized* them. Once differentiated into nations and encased in states (real states for whites, fictional ones for Africans), cultures became less permeable. "Blacks" could not become "white" by changing cultures (the fear of all white supremacists) nor could they transcend ethnic divisions (the fear of separate development). Africans were mired in and inseparable from ethnicity, that is, they were tribal.

White supremacy's doctrine of race—in both segregationist and separate development versions—was haphazard, expedient, and implicitly contradictory. It ascribed races to nature, in the fashion of the nineteenth century, declaring that whites were superior because they were innately better and that Africans were inferior because they were innately worse. But the claims of white supremacy were contradicted by reality. Whites were not innately better, and, indeed, made themselves supreme precisely because they were not superior. If whites had been innately superior, they would not have to organize society to elevate them, and they would not have to privilege themselves systematically. Merit would have sufficed.

Consequently, white supremacy associated races with culture as well as nature. Whites had one culture, Africans had another, and white supremacists insisted the two be kept separate. The problem was that cultures are separable from races; people can alter, exit, and surpass "their" cultures. Lest the foundation of white supremacy be undermined thusly, white supremacists took recourse in nature to justify their supremacy. They had races arising from nature *and* from culture, and they studied them through both biology and anthropology.[1] The mix of nature and culture shifted back and forth, but segregation and apartheid alike had races including both nodes. Races were treated as the cultural embodiments of genetic families, a formulation that, interestingly, resembles the whys and wherefores of how nations are thought to originate. By the most influential accounts, nations evolve from ethnic groups, and ethnic groups, like races in white supremacy, are said to evolve from common descent (or the illusion of common descent). White supremacists and conventional conceptions of nations converge on a central point, therefore. Both ground cultural communities in blood heritages and both concede that blood does not really constitute cultural communities.

* * *

Nations are attributed, derived, and explained in terms of factors that precede them temporally and logically. They usually are thought to be refigured ethnic groups. Take, for example, the views of Anthony Smith, one of the most influential scholars on the origins of nations. "Usually," Smith writes, "there has been some ethnic basis for the construction of modern nations."[2] He continues, "Nations require ethnic cores if they are to survive."[3] Over time, Smith's ethnic groups grow into nations. But the transition from one to the other is so slow, so subtle that they are practically the same things. Except for one difference: nations, unlike ethnic groups, press political claims on the grounds they are nations, and political claims are what elevate nations over mere ethnic groups. Smith's nations are ethnic groups that "become politicized and stake out claims in the competition for power and influence in the state arena."[4] Smith, therefore, clarifies two important issues—the source and content of nations—but raises new questions in the process. He now must explain what "ethnic" groups are, where they come from, and what distinguishes them from other kinds of groups.

Smith's ethnic groups are defined by perceptions of common descent. He writes, "Myths of origins and descent" are the "*sine qua non* of ethnicity, the key elements of that complex of meanings which underlie the sense of ethnic ties and sentiments."[5] Members of ethnic groups may share common cultures, may speak the same languages, or may practice the same religions. Their communities of common cultures, languages, and religions are real for Smith. They have names, common histories and destinies, senses of solidarity, common cultural institutions, and attachments to specific territories.[6] But these features do not make communities "ethnic." Communities are ethnic because their members *believe* they are associated by common ancestry, that is, they understand themselves as kin. Ethnic groups, unlike other kinds of "social and cultural" groups,[7] imagine themselves to be constituted by shared decent. But, and things begin getting complicated here, people usually are wrong. It is not the fact of common ancestors that binds members of ethnic groups together and it is not the absence of common ancestors that separates them from outsiders.

Smith is joined in associating ethnicity with perceptions of common descent by Donald Horowitz. Ethnicity for Horowitz is *identified* "by color, language, religion, or some other attribute of common origin."[8] But ethnicity is *defined* by the belief in common descent, in kinship. He believes that ethnicity is "functionally continuous with kinship."[9] Horowitz explains:

> To view ethnicity as a form of greatly extended kinship is to recognize, as ethnic groups do, the role of putative descent. There are fictive elements here, but the idea, if not always the fact, of common ancestry makes it possible for ethnic groups to think in terms of family resemblances—traits held in common, on a supposedly genetic basis, or cultural features acquired in early childhood—and to bring into play for a much wider circle those concepts of mutual obligation and antipathy to outsiders that are applicable to family relations.[10]

The belief in common descent, Horowitz notes, is "putative" and "fictive." Boundaries between groups are in flux; groups are absorbed, amalgamated, and hived off; and groups gain and lose members. Outsiders become insiders, insiders become outsiders, and descent becomes muddled. But the *accuracy* of the belief in kinship is not what matters for Horowitz. What matters is what follows from the belief of kinship, the sense that members of ethnic groups owe special duties—akin to family obligations—to each other.

The perception of common descent is what makes groups "ethnic." The attributes of groups—customs, languages, and religions—merely manifest groups. Confusion follows, as the causes of conflicts between different ethnic groups are misperceived. If groups practice different religions or speak different languages, conflicts between them are seen to be motivated by the religious or linguistic differences. But appearances mislead. Horowitz speaks of the

> accidental determination of attributes of difference. Group A speaks a language different from that of Group B, so language becomes the indicator of group identity in that relationship. But if, instead of Group B, the environment contained only Groups A and C, then religion or color or place of origin might differentiate the groups. In a typical multigroup environment, moreover, different attributes are invoked for differing group interactions. Indeed, it is apt to describe the attribute as belonging to the interaction as much as it belongs to the group.[11]

Horowitz's point is that cultural institutions—religions, languages, customs, and the like—are *indicators* of communities, but that communities exist independently of attributes that "indicate" them. "It is not the attribute that makes the group, but the group and group difference that make the attribute important."[12]

Horowitz's ethnic groups are forged largely by conflicts, and conflicting groups might fight about attributes (language, religion) that manifest differences between them. But ethnic conflicts do not originate in manifestations, attributes, and indicators. They originate in competitions for power. After the fashion of families, ethnic groups are disinclined to trust outsiders. They seek security for themselves by taking power into their own hands, replicating the Hobbesian world of international relations. In seeking power for defensive purposes, they themselves become offensive threats to others.[13]

Horowitz makes important points. He has groups seeking power for themselves and forcing other groups to seek power in response; has boundaries between groups shifting in response to changing political circumstances; and has groups defining themselves in relation to other groups.[14] He makes an additional point, pregnant with implications for South Africa: "ethnicity easily embraces groups differentiated by color, language, and religion; it covers 'tribes,' 'races,' 'nationalities,' and castes."[15] Color, for Horowitz, is just another way of differentiating, similar in kind to other attributes.[16] It marks and identifies; it does not constitute and define. The insight, as will become clear, illuminates much in South African politics, but it suffers a problem too. Both Horowitz and Smith have ethnicity arising from the idea of "birth and blood,"[17] from the perception of common ancestry. Yet both insist that the idea is a "myth," that ethnic groups do not really originate in common descent and are not really constituted by kinship.

It might seem irrelevant whether groups actually are related by descent or merely imagine themselves to be related. Perceptions can count for more than the reality (the "to be is to be perceived" thesis). The problem with this retreat, as Smith and Horowitz imply, is the belief in kinship may define the character of ethnic groups, making them akin to families, but the misperception does not make them groups in the first place. Smith and Horowitz consider groups to be groups because of how they *think* they originated, not because of how they really originated and not because of what they really share ("attributes"). Ethnic groups are groups bound in solidarity by ties of origin and blood—except that they are not. Smith and Horowitz explain that it does not really matter that they are wrong, because what matters are perceptions, but that misses the point. If groups are not defined by attributes and do not share common descent, it is unclear what made them into the groups that could misperceive their origins. Smith and Horowitz explain why ethnic groups differ from other kinds of groups, but fail to explain why they are groups to begin with.

Smith and Horowitz have an out. They could point out that groups can form around misperceptions, that in some sense the group is made into a group because its members are wrong together. The problem is, Smith's and Horowitz's ethnic groups do not seem to be formed by misperceptions. The misperceptions envelop groups that originated prior to and independently of the misperceptions. That is, groups were groups before they misperceived themselves as kinship groups. Smith and Horowitz might retreat again, and argue that ethnic groups are cultural groups that misunderstand their origins. But they foreclosed that response when they denied that cultural institutions were attributes that merely identify groups that exist already.

The problem for Smith and Horowitz is that ethnic groups must exist prior to their (mis)perceptions of ethnicity; otherwise the group would not be able to misperceive itself as bound by common ancestors. Ethnic groups, in other words, must be groups before they make the mistake of identifying their members as kin, before they make the decision that converts them into *ethnic* groups. The misperception explains *post factum* why the group is an ethnic group, but the misperception flashes in groups that are groups already. However, the group can be a group before the misperception only on condition that it is defined by its attributes, which is what Horowitz and Smith expressly exclude by emphasizing perceived origins.

Why does it matter where groups come from, providing they come into existence one way or another? The reason, apart from curiosity, is that groups have come to be vested with political rights by two powerful, and overlapping, traditions: culturalism and nationalism. To the extent groups are thought to possess ethno-cultural integrity, rights are due them. Their political rights reflect natural affinities, shared identities, and felt modes of being, and recognizing them, according to culturalists, does not inflict harm on other groups.

The ideal of universal and culturally unspecified democracy, what the ANC has come to call "non-racialism," is turning out of fashion in much recent thinking. Contemporary multiculturalists deliberately renounce the tenet of most nationalists that their nation possesses special rights and that it is uniquely deserving. Nevertheless, multiculturalists clearly adopt the key claim of ethno-cultural nationalism that groups center personal identities and political loyalties. Multiculturalists posit groups as the axes and identities as the stuff of politics, and they deny liberal claims that states may be neutral in the face of competing ethno-cultural identities. Either states own up to the fact that neutrality is impossible, as politics consists inevitably of representing identities, or states manipulate the fiction of neutrality to enthrone the identities of strong groups at the expense of weaker groups.

Multicultural politics involves expressing identities, and identities crystallize prior to and outside of politics, in ethno-cultures. Cultures are accorded a status akin to that of individuals by liberal theory. They are integral, elemental, and endowed with rights. According to Joseph Raz, "So this is the case for multiculturalism. . . . Cultural, and other, groups have a life of their own. But their moral claim to respect and to prosperity rests entirely on their vital importance to the prosperity of individual human beings."[18] In addition, he points out that "Multiculturalism emphasizes . . . the belief that individual freedom and prosperity depend on full and unimpeded membership in a respected and flourishing cultural group."[19] Multiculturalists often withhold rights from groups as groups but achieve much the same outcome by discerning the right of people to associate with those like themselves. As Will Kymlicka suggests, "Liberals should recognize the importance of people's membership in their own societal culture, because of the role it plays in enabling meaningful individual choice and in supporting self-identity."[20]

Multiculturalists rest their position on the proposition that "individual freedom is tied in some important way to membership in one's national group."[21] "[C]ulture and membership are communal features, whose worth can be fully enjoyed only together with others making similar choices."[22] Multiculturalists are not, at least in their liberal versions, arguing that individuals *must* participate in ethno-cultural groups, or that people *must* remain in the ethno-cultural groups into which they are born and in which they are reared. But multiculturalists are arguing that people are cultured by nature and are able to be intimate only among their "own kind" and that their "own kind" consists of fellow members of the same group. "[I]t is in the interest of every person to be fully integrated in a cultural group."[23] Raz believes that "Only through being socialized in a culture can one tap the options which give life a meaning. . . . [The] sameness of culture facilitates social relations, and is a condition of rich and comprehensive personal relationships. . . . For most people, membership in their cultural group is a major determinant of their sense of who they are; it provides a strong focus of identification; it contributes to what we have come to call their sense of their own identity."[24]

Multiculturalists, in addition to conceiving of humans as cultural and of cultures as tantamount to ethnicity, also have ethnic solidarities trumping other solidarities. They distinguish explicitly "between citizenship and nationhood"[25] and, when the two come into conflict, value "culture, tradition, and language"[26] over the "thin layer"[27] of mutual commitments born of common citizenship. "People from different national groups will only share an allegiance to the larger polity if they see it as the context within which their national identity is nurtured, rather than subordinated."[28]

Multiculturalists, therefore, require states to recognize, respect, and, where necessary, protect ethno-cultural differences from the homogenizing and domineering impulses of strong ethno-cultures. Unable to stand apart from culture, states must abandon ideals of impartiality among competing ethno-cultures, which are only a pretense anyway, and recognize all of the ethno-cultures within them. They must become multicultural themselves.

> A multi-nation state which accords universal individual rights to all its citizens, regardless of group membership, may appear to be "neutral" between the various national groups. But in fact it can (and often does) systematically privilege the majority nation in certain fundamental ways—for example, the drawing of internal boundaries; the language of schools, courts, and government services; the choice of public holidays; and the division of legislative power between central and local governments. . . . Group-specific rights regarding education, local autonomy, and language help ensure that national minorities are not disadvantaged in these decisions, thereby enabling the minority, like the majority, to sustain "a life of its own."[29]

"[C]ulture cannot be restricted to the private sphere, and only those living in a society expressive of their own culture could be oblivious to this fact."[30]

The point is made with particular elegance by Charles Taylor.

> There is a form of the politics of equal respect, as enshrined in a liberalism of rights, that is inhospitable to difference, because (a) it insists on uniform application of the rules defining these rights, without exception, and (b) it is suspicious of collective goals. Of

> course, this doesn't mean that this model seeks to abolish cultural differences. This would be an absurd accusation. But I call it inhospitable to difference because it can't accommodate what the members of distinct societies really aspire to, which is survival. This is (b) a collective goal, which (a) almost inevitably will call for some variations in the kinds of law we deem permissible from one cultural context to another. . . .
>
> I think this form of liberalism is guilty as charged by the proponents of a politics of difference. Fortunately, however, there are other models of liberal society that . . . are willing to weigh the importance of certain forms of uniform treatment against the importance of cultural survival, and opt sometimes in favor of the latter. They are thus in the end not procedural models of liberalism, but are grounded very much on judgments about what makes a good life—judgments in which the integrity of cultures has an important place.[31]

Taylor, in standard multicultural fashion, affirms the importance of political institutions that register ethno-cultural differences. He intimates that subjecting vulnerable ethno-cultures to the same laws as dominant ones violates their integrity, because the fact of vulnerability instills different needs. Strong and weak ethno-cultures should be held to different standards, with the one forbidden to impose its ends on state and society and the other allowed to impose ends in the name of protecting their fundamental right to self-preservation. Minorities, if they are to preserve their culture, may need to use the state to achieve collective ends; majorities, on the other hand, harm minorities if they use states for substantive, as opposed to procedural, purposes. Minorities, in compensation for the insecurity of their position, may deserve state assistance in pursuing collective ends. Note, however, the predicate of the multicultural defense of weak cultures. States, being conceived as subservient to cultures, can express ethno-cultural identities or suppress them; but states cannot develop inclusive identities of their own.

Ironically, the making of ethno-cultural solidarities into the foundation of political identities, the privileging of the cultural, resembles the claims made by white supremacists in South Africa. White supremacists had races as the preeminent political actors, had races enmeshed in and supported by cultures, and had races seeking power for reasons of racial self-expression. Making what now would count as a multiculturalist case for white supremacy, white supremacists claimed political power on the basis of their cultural identity, either because they were superior to or because they were different from Africans. That is, white supremacy, like respectable forms of multiculturalism, had cultural communities, cultural solidarities, and cultural identities composing the core of political identities and the foundation for political interests.

Multiculturalists may resemble white supremacists in their conceptions of the role and source of political identities, but they reject racism categorically.[32] They are motivated precisely by rejection of racial supremacy, hegemonic standards, and cultural imperialism. But multiculturalists do regard identity as the hub of politics, do conceive of ethno-culture as the primary source of identity, and do make politics about respecting and registering communal identities. Happily, white liberals, an influential and not unsympathetic tradition in South Africa, made a better case for recognizing culture. But as their experience shows, recognizing culture can be perilous.

Leo Marquard, a prominent political scientist writing in the early days of apartheid, exemplified the predicament of white liberals in South Africa. Committed to conventional liberal values—the rule of law, toleration, and private property, among other things—white liberals, precisely because of these commitments, were unable to accept the fundamental predicate of most democratic thought and practice: the sovereignty of individuals. People in South Africa, according to liberals such as Marquard, were located inside groups and could not be treated as if their groups did not matter. Unfortunately, democratic institutions that ignored South Africa's different cultures and civilizations would have had the effect of undermining liberal—and, ultimately, democratic—values. Consequently, Marquard drew on the liberal traditions of the Cape colony to argue against racism and for civilization tests, providing that the tests allow for the development of partnership between whites and blacks.

> [T]here is only one alternative to an increasing antagonism—to live in partnership. When the Europeans in South Africa can at last bring themselves to realize this, they will be on the way to solving their major problem. It is obvious, however, that living in partnership must be on the basis of Western civilization. Indeed, in so far as the colonial subjects of the Union are politically conscious, they are unanimous on this. But Western civilization is not acquired in a day, nor will the fears and the self-interested policy of Europeans disap-

pear overnight. Many African are already fit for political citizenship in a Western democratic society; but many of those who think they are qualified will have to learn that admission to the family of Western Europe entails the assumption of responsibilities that are different from those under tribalism. Europeans in South Africa, when they really face this problem, will realize that Western civilization is not a matter of colour, and that it is not preserved by "protecting" it by hot-house methods, but that it flourishes only when it expands and seeks to attract to its ranks on terms of equality all those, of whatever colour, who are imbued with the spirit of liberty, of culture, and of humanity that is characteristic of the greatest traditions.[33]

Marquard represented the political thinking of white liberals. His tradition, obviously and self-consciously, was white, but in a particular sense. Marquard's whites were European, and European civilization was available to blacks. Marquard rejected the main white political traditions—segregation and apartheid—partly for violating liberal values (human dignity, freedom of choice, equality under the law), but also for presuming that liberal values, the values of European civilization, were the property solely of whites. They were available to blacks too. Consequently, Marquard was defending political hierarchies, but was rejecting hierarchies that were racial in origin and intent. Hierarchies based on race were unacceptable; but hierarchies based on and expressing cultural standards and values, even if racial in effect, were different for Marquard. If whites were favored because they were white, Marquard objected; if whites were favored because they were Western, Marquard approved, providing—and this is what differentiated white liberals from white supremacists—Westernized Africans were accorded similar favor.

Marquard parted company with both democrats and white supremacists. Against democrats, he argued that political membership could not be made available to all, but that it must be reserved for those practicing Western values. Opening citizenship to those unprepared for its responsibilities—that is, to Africans who had not been Westernized—would jeopardize it for everyone, making the ideal the enemy of the real. Africans, being unprepared to become citizens, could not be trusted with the vote. But Marquard, rejecting both segregation and apartheid, did allow for the possibility that Africans, by assimilating into Western civilization, could earn the vote and prepare for democracy down the road.

Marquard also rejected white supremacy for conflating race and culture. The logic of white supremacy welds race and cultures together, because if they were separable, Africans could have escaped subordination by switching cultures. Marquard, on the other hand, distinguished culture from race. Culture was something that could be assimilated into and moved out of. Marquard, therefore, could open full citizenship to Africans, on condition they embraced European standards. But to get something, they had to give something: they had to outgrow African culture. Conceiving of rights in the fashion of the Cape franchise, citizenship was reserved for Westerners, for people who accepted European standards and values.

Of course, few Africans were Europeanized, which posed a gigantic problem for South African liberals. Most Western liberals have something lurking behind and ordering society, something that renders the freedom of autonomous human beings as harmonious. For John Locke it was natural law and for Adam Smith it was the invisible hand that established what E. H. Carr called a "harmony of interests."[34] Natural laws and invisible hands are much different phenomena, obviously. But they share the same essential function of ordering the free acts of countless individuals; of squaring freedom with the need for political order; and of sparing states from having to do the dirty work of forging order, as Hobbes had states doing. Blessed with order being immanent in human society, liberal states only had to enforce it, a less illiberal task. South Africans lacked the confidence of their Western brethren, however. The history of South Africa "is the story of strife between the various *groups* composing the political union."[35] South Africans could become liberal only by overcoming their history and reorganizing their society. They had to detach culture, a legitimate source of hierarchy, from race, an illegitimate source.

Marquard regarded Western civilization as liberal and African civilization as illiberal, and he warned that enfranchising illiberal Africans would endanger the liberal bridgehead in South Africa. Liberal values were fragile, which is why liberal equality between those who were and were not Westernized could not be contemplated. But for Marquard, discriminating on the basis of culture was different from discriminating on the basis of race, precisely because culture is separable from race. "Politically conscious" Africans—that is, Westernized ones—could be and should be enfranchised.

White liberals had two kinds of reasons for encouraging African assimilation. First, they took the superiority of Western culture for granted; it embodied higher values than African culture. Assimilating Africans, therefore, had the estimable effect of making a good thing more broadly available. Second, white liberals gained politically from broadening liberal constituencies; it made liberal values more secure. Threatened by white supremacy on one side, which was both illiberal and unsustainable, and by African demands on the other, which would produce illiberal outcomes unless tutored into liberal values, Marquard celebrated African assimilation for reasons of realism as well as altruism. "Partnership" allowed whites and blacks to work together to make South Africa more liberal.

F. van Zyl Slabbert and David Welsh, who were leading liberal intellectuals and politicians in the 1970s and 1980s (Slabbert headed the Progressive Federal Party, the party of white liberals, through much of the 1980s), took up Marquard's banner. They advocated power-sharing (the contemporary version of "partnership"), but with a twist. Generally, South African liberals, like contemporary multiculturalists, argued groups warrant representation because groups are elemental, that they compose society.[36] Slabbert and Welsh, however, discounted the integrity of groups. Racial "conflict in South Africa revolves around its institutionalized inequalities of power, wealth, opportunity and status. . . . [C]olour (or ethnicity) derives its salience because it symbolizes particular positions in a hierarchy, and it is the hierarchical nature of the society that determines its distributional patterns—who gets what, how and when."[37] Slabbert and Welsh's groups, in other words, are made significant by interests, power, wealth. Groups are not important in themselves; resources make them important: "Racial conflict is fundamentally about the allocation of resources (material and non-material)."[38]

Nevertheless, Slabbert and Welsh demanded specific protections for minority groups. "As simple majoritarianism has in no deeply divided society had a democratic outcome, the principle of power-sharing among all groups must be institutionalized."[39] Slabbert and Welsh urged proportional representation, coalition cabinets, federalism, and minority vetoes, "whereby laws can be passed in parliament only if a substantial majority of the members agree to them or, put differently, a minority of between 10 and 15 per cent can prevent the legislation from being passed."[40] The claim, adopted by the National Party in the early 1990s during negotiations on the new constitution, is that multiple sites of power force governments to accommodate minorities, enhancing their legitimacy and unifying society.[41]

Something is amiss, however. Slabbert and Welsh insisted on representation for South Africa's groups; otherwise, they warned, democracy is a charade. But the groups that were to be represented articulated "structural inequalities in racial or ethnic terms."[42] Slabbert and Welsh's "whites" were not defined by race or culture; their color was an "attribute" made salient by economic privilege and political power. Consequently, political protections for minorities, including the right to bring government to a standstill through vetoes, were coded to defend the material interests of the rich and powerful, and to defend them *because* they were rich and powerful. Conservative interests, in other words, are pursued under the cover of group rights. In preserving identities, government is to preserve what produces them. Protecting whites is to protect whiteness, as Slabbert and Welsh imply, and whiteness was a social relationship premised on power.

Inadvertently, Slabbert and Welsh divulged why white liberals need groups. Pleas for special protections for wealth and power are unpersuasive in a society populated largely by poor people. Minority rights, on the other hand, have a democratic ring to them, redolent of defending the underdog. The effect may be the same—inflating the power of whites—but Slabbert and Welsh's conception of race undermined their institutional prescriptions, because the "groups" to be protected were constructed by power and privilege. Slabbert and Welsh, therefore, represent an object lesson in the consequences of dispensing with groups as integral; without groups, liberals forfeit their claim on special privileges.

Ethno-culturalists, multiculturalists, and white liberals disagree on particulars. Smith and the multiculturalists adopt the simplest position. They assume groups as integral actors, and then have them claiming the political prerogatives that are their due as ethno-cultural groups, completing themselves. Horowitz, on the other hand, tries not to assume groups. He highlights the role of differentiating and contrasting in defining groups and, like Slabbert and Welsh, associates groups with conflicts over power and resources. But differences among the three traditions are overshadowed by similarities. All agree that ethno-cultural groups are primary political actors, that their primacy should be recognized more or less formally in institutions, and that values and identities associated with groups set the stakes in politics.

Groups carry a heavy load for the several streams of ethno-culturalism, and sometimes buckle under it. Ethno-culturalists explain the origins of nations by reference to ethno-cultural groups, then ignore the question of where the groups come from. They define ethno-cultural groups in terms of perceptions of common descent, but concede the perceptions are mistaken. They note that ethno-cultural groups share cultural attributes, but refuse to derive the group from the attribute. They end up, therefore, endowing fundamental political rights and powers in groups who define themselves in terms of origins yet whose origins are opaque and whose shared attributes are discounted in importance. The problems facing ethno-cultures are not new; they have vexed the notion of ethnicity ever since Max Weber defined it as the "subjective belief" in "common descent."[43]

Ironically, Weber no sooner defines ethnicity in terms of perceptions of common descent than he concludes that the whole category of ethnicity is misleading, misapplied, and misbegotten. It should be "abandoned, for it is unsuitable for a really rigorous analysis";[44] the "concept of the 'ethnic' group . . . dissolves if we define our terms exactly."[45] It "subsumes phenomena that a rigorous sociological analysis . . . would have to distinguish carefully: the actual subjective effect of those customs conditioned by heredity and those determined by tradition; the differential impact of the varying content of custom; the influence of common language, religion and political action, past and present, upon the formation of customs."[46] Weber's point, be clear, is not that groups do not exist; it is that groups that are called "ethnic" are a motley lot, and that it matters, for example, whether they are based on both common language and common religion or on common language without common religion or on common religion without common language. In collapsing such distinctions, the category of ethnicity has the effect of concealing the actual sources and substance of groups.

Weber's understanding of nationality is essentially indistinguishable from his understanding of ethnicity. Both are based on myths, the same myth of common descent, and both are suspect.

> The concept of "nationality" shares with that of the "people"—in the "ethnic" sense—the vague connotation that whatever is felt to be distinctively common must derive from common descent. In reality, of course, persons who consider themselves members of the same nationality are often much less related by common descent than are persons belonging to different and hostile nationalities. Differences of nationality may exist even among groups closely related by common descent.[47]

Ethnicity and nationality share a second similarity as well. Their illusions of common descent arose from the same source, from political communities past or present.

Rather than taking politics as a field in which ethnicity is expressed, in the fashion of ethno-culturalists, Weber reverses the causality: "[I]t is primarily the political community, no matter how artificially organized, that inspires the belief in common ethnicity."[48] "All history shows how easily political action can give rise to the belief in blood relationship";[49] "the concept of 'nation' directs us to political power."[50] Political power plays a constituting, not just an expressive, role for Weber. Weber's nations, like his ethnic groups, develop from political associations, from being compressed together by organized power. States exert power, establish administrative control over territory, use violence to eliminate rivals, connect life opportunities and experiences to legal statuses they instate, and associate the destinies of discrete individuals into common destinies. They group people together.

Some groups are made up of people who are loyal to states, but loyalty is not a condition for making groups. Some groups are made from people who resist state power, others from those who oscillate in their allegiances. Political power may make national identities in its image, in the sense that states organize together the people who eventually become nations, homogenizing them,[51] or it may organize those who are oppressed and excluded into one identity, overwhelming prior differences among them and defining the new people through its otherness. Weber's identities, in other words, may form either in accordance with or in opposition to states. They develop as sides in power conflicts, then refigure themselves as ethnicities. Weber's ethnic identities are carriers; they are vessels that stabilize the shifting, contingent, and fleeting flux of political experience.

Political power ebbs and flows, changes hands, reverses direction, and is in motion constantly. Groups formed by experiences of wars, states, and colonialism (among other things) may rise and fall, may turn inside out and outside in as the political winds change direction. This is why delusions of kinship play a powerful role in reproducing groups. Weber's ethnic and national groups are contingent in origin, malleable in content, yet, surprisingly, stable in membership. "Ethnicity" and "nationality" fortify groups in the face of shifting political experiences. Feelings of solidarity tend "to persist even after the disintegration of the political community, unless drastic differences in the custom, physical type, or, above all, language exist among its members."[52] Weber's point, then, is that political communities instill solidarities, that solidarities are likely to endure if encased in the durable container of perceived kinship, and that perceived kinship engenders "responsibility towards succeeding generations."[53] It becomes "*proper* to expect from certain groups a specific sentiment of solidarity in the face of other groups,"[54] "a specific kind of pathos."[55]

What, then, is at stake in the different conceptions of nations and national identities and nationality? The answer is that deriving national identities from ethno-cultural identities stumbles into conceptual problems in general and into empirical and political problems in the particular case of South Africa.

Conceptually, ethno-culturalists derive nations from ethnic groups but do not account for the groups that are to account for the nations, leaving both kinds of groups suspended in air. Nations come from ethnic groups, but ethnic groups are just there, unexplainable. They think they originate in common descent, but they do not. They might be thought to develop around shared attributes, and then to misunderstand themselves as kin, but ethno-culturalists explicitly reject that possibility. Ethno-culturalists are left describing how ethnic groups are "mobilized" or "awakened" as nations, the process of nationalism,[56] but do not say how groups that become aware of themselves became groups to begin with. They merely assume away the question.

Conceiving of groups as self-generated, ethno-culturalists—Horowitz is an exception—insulate them from their "other."[57] Focusing on the positive, on the integral, ethno-culturalists discount the negative, the differentiating. National identities, however, elaborate and develop—and do not merely identify—themselves against the backdrop of rival identities, of "them." The "other" defines who is excluded from the nation and, therefore, who is included in it. Nations become by denying, and self-determination for one nation may overwhelm that for another. Groups not only have antagonisms toward rival groups; they also evolve on the basis of antagonisms that are prior to them. "[R]ace creates a 'group' . . . when some common experiences of members of the same race are linked to *some antagonism* against members of an *obviously* different group."[58] That is, the fight shapes the fighter because nations develop relationally, dialectically. Nations are who they are by virtue of who they are not, defining themselves negatively through differentiation and contrast.

Protecting group identities has unadvertised implications, therefore. Ethno-culturalist politics treats identities as self-generated and without relationality; identities exist in and for themselves, wholly. Affirming one identity entails little for other identities (except for providing the precedent of protecting them too). But ethno-cultural identities, insofar as they are established through interactions, involve power relationships. To be specific, white supremacy made power inherent in what it meant to be "white" and powerlessness in being "black." Therefore, classifying identities that are substantially political in origin and content as "cultural," in the fashion of multiculturalists, has the effect of protecting politically inspired prerogatives in the name of cultural rights.

Ethno-culturalist conceptions of groups, in addition to general conceptual and political problems, face empirical problems in South Africa. To the extent nations are seen as arising from peoples already associated into cultural communities by ethno-culture, ethno-culturalists cannot explain the intimate connection between racial and national communities. Black and white ethnic groups advance kinship myths[59] and share language and customs, but the two dominant "races" make no such claims for themselves. Races do not reflect groups with the same attributes; they encompass groups with different attributes. The "white race" spans Afrikaans and English-speakers; the "African race" includes Sotho, Tswana, Xhosa, Zulus, and several other ethno-cultures besides. Lacking common ethno-cultures, whites and blacks might produce no encompassing identity or many parochial ones. But neither should have been able to produce a single identity, because neither spins myths of common descent or shares cultural attributes. That is, ethno-culturalists, having derived nations from particular groups, cannot account for the central empirical fact that racial-national identities encompass different ethno-cultural identities.

3

The White Man's Burden

The strongest is never strong enough to be master forever unless he transforms his force into right and obedience into duty.

—JEAN-JACQUES ROUSSEAU

It is difficult to avoid filtering the role of color in southern African history through the prism of contemporary controversies about race. Our era sees color and thinks race; it thinks race and makes suppositions about cultural identities as sources of political allegiances. But the peoples who met in the southwest corner of Africa in the mid-seventeenth century had world-views of their own. They saw differences in skin color, hair texture, and facial features and noticed the bodies of newcomers from Europe differed from those of people who lived there already. But that says little about what significance they attached to physical differences. It was one thing to register them, a second to conceive of them as "racial," and a third to organize society on the basis of them.

Newcomers to the Cape did not, it is true, look like the indigenes. But that should not overshadow the equally important fact that prior inhabitants of the southwest corner of Africa did not look the same either. The San and the KhoiKhoi ("browns"), hunter gatherers and pastoralists, differed in appearance from the Xhosa ("blacks"), agriculturists who were expanding slowly from the east and intermingling with the San and KhoiKhoi. All of them detected differences in bodies, but none conceived of physical differences as axes of human organization. Race was a European idea, and a nineteenth century one at that.

The origin of the idea of "race" is disputed; by some accounts, it originated in northern Europe, bridged science and culture, and was associated with the emerging discipline of anthropology.[1] Being unfamiliar with European conceptions of science and anthropology, seventeenth- and eighteenth-century whites, browns, and blacks in the Cape did not racialize physical similarities and differences, not even color. They were observed and remarked on by whites and nonwhites alike, but that does not say much about *how* they were seen or conceived. Did perceptions of color constitute communities that would not have existed otherwise or did communities originate independently of the perceptions of color differences? Did color make or did it identify communities?

The historian George Fredrickson has addressed the role played by color in the history that began in the Cape colony. In a memorable book, Fredrickson combined what will be called "culturalist" categories, which posit races as integral cultures, whole in themselves, and prior to interaction with other races, with what will be called a "politicist" narrative. Where culturalism grounds races (and nations) in ethno-cultures, politicism follows Weber in associating races (and nations) with communities that develop from experiences of political power. Fredrickson, in culturalist fashion, begins with races whole and intact. They are present all along, throughout South Africa's history (and prehistory). They do all manner of things, framing communities, motivating behavior, and instilling common institutions, and they do not owe their existence or their significance, as some Marxists have it, to the process of capitalism that developed around the gold mining industry in the late nineteenth century onward. But Fredrickson tells a politicist story through culturalist categories. He begins with culturalist assumptions about the integrity of races, but concludes by having them serve political purposes. The existence of races is given for Fredrickson; their meanings are open.

Fredrickson detects races at the beginning of the process of colonization in 1652. Races do not develop over time, as modes of consciousness. They are forms of being. Fredrickson's whites were inherently "white"; they always had race. But the significance of having race, what it meant to be "white," was not given. It evolved and changed over time. Fredrickson's "whites" were white, yes. But they did not enter southern African history with collective interests *as* whites and did not act *because* they were white. When they established slavery, for example, whites were not motivated by racial prejudices or solidarities. According to Frederickson, "Africans and other non-Europeans were initially enslaved not so much because of their color and physical type as because of their legal and cultural vulnerability."[2] Fredrickson's whites, looking for land and labor, directed their attention to those who had them. It happened that those who had what whites wanted were "brown" (and later "black") and did not want to give them up. To get them, whites required supremacy.

The words "supremacy" and "superiority" can be used interchangeably, but distinguishing between them helps clarify the behavior of whites from the mid-seventeenth through the early twentieth centuries. The opposite of (one definition of) supremacy is subordination, and both supremacy and subordination can be defined in relation to power. Those who are supreme possess power; those who are subordinate lack power. On the other hand, the opposite of (one definition of) superiority is inferiority, and both superiority and inferiority can be defined in relation to intrinsic worth. Superiors are intrinsically better than their inferiors and do not necessarily depend on supremacy for superiority. Using the terms in this sense, white settlers were interested in getting what they wanted, in supremacy, in the Cape colony and were uninterested in debating why they were entitled to it. Until the arrival of Britain in the nineteenth century, Fredrickson's whites did not cast their supremacy as superiority, did not insist that their power reflected their worth. Whites took for granted that they were better than browns and blacks, of course. But prior to British intervention they did not regard their supremacy as something that had to be justified by superiority and did not regard superiority as something that originated in color. In fact, they stumbled onto color as a means of organizing supremacy rather belatedly.

First, they tried religion. In the minds of the early colonists, whites were not enslaving browns and blacks; Christians were enslaving heathens. Justifying slavery on the basis of religion reflected their understandings and the times; plus, it served their purposes. Those who were instituting slavery were Christian and those who were being enslaved were not. The problem was, religious justifications ran the risk of undermining the very interests they were meant to serve. If slavery was permissible because Christians were enslaving heathens, it became impermissible if slaves converted to Christianity, as happened not infrequently.[3]

Fredrickson tells an interesting story, therefore. Whites, having arrived in the Cape colony, were pursuing the bounty of supremacy, not their due as whites. Most of the people who owned property and were free also were white, and a good portion of whites owned property and were free. But race was not the source of economic and political hierarchies. As Fredrickson reports, "Race mattered in the determination of status but was not all-important. The social hierarchy was composed of a white upper class of company officials and prosperous wine and grain farmers; an intermediate group of freemen, mostly white in ancestry, but including (for most purposes) some free people of color; and a servile class, entirely nonwhite but by this time subdivided into chattel slaves and Khoikhoi servants."[4] It may appear, therefore, that Fredrickson was describing a racial hierarchy, but appearances are misleading.

According to Fredrickson, the colony's hierarchy was not recruited on the basis of color. Whites composed the upper ranks, but "some people of color" were equal with whites as freemen. Inequality on the basis of color was not, in other words, the principle of social organization at the outset of the colony. It was elaborated over time, largely for other reasons. Whites took advantage of color, but their power originated largely in "membership in the civil community."[5] As colonizers, whites could make claims on the colonial administration and other colonists for help in seizing land, subduing threats, and garnering labor. They had organized power on their side, both in the sense of the formal colonial administration and of the informal commandos that enacted their interests.[6]

Fredrickson's races, in other words, were given but were empty vessels, to be infused with content by the development of society. By virtue of the hierarchy Fredrickson describes, whiteness—which always was lurking—was saturated with the perquisites of power. Whites craved wealth and status and shunned physical labor, which is why, to be precise, Fredrickson writes about the supremacy *of whites* rather than about *white* supremacy. He does not describe whiteness as having made whites supreme; he described those who were supreme as being white. Trying to reverse the original relationship of power and color, whites later made power the preserve of whites as whites.[7]

The Cape colony was not governed by a state, except for the brief period when it passed under Batavian administration from 1803–6, until Britain assumed control in 1806. Before then, the colony had been controlled by the Dutch East Indies Company, a private company, and, as Timothy Keegan points out, its administration was weak,[8] being understaffed, underfunded, and uneven in scope. It was owned by stockholders and did not articulate the category of citizen. Settlers did not have political rights that could be enforced legally against the colony; but they did have influence and the Company did accommodate them. Settler claims were accepted as legitimate and received favorable answers from the Company because they were issued by settlers, because settlers belonged, and because they had the power to enforce them. The catch is that those who had political voice were identified not only as whites; they also were Christians and burghers. Some whites, Fredrickson notes, used the term "burghers" as "a synonym for white Christians."[9] Conversely, Keegan notes that "it is fair to assume that among the subordinate classes, skin colour or racial identity was not as significant as their shared subordination."[10] Or so matters rested until Britain, about a generation after assuming sovereignty, shook things up. It introduced policies that had the effect of highlighting the value civil membership and political power had come to assume for whites.

In 1828, Britain proclaimed equal economic rights for the KhoiKhoi. Britain did not do much by way of actually implementing them, leaving "the class order virtually intact."[11] Nevertheless, the mere declaration of equality as a principle led whites to demand "*carte blanche* to treat [non-white dependents] in any way that their interests and security seemed to require."[12] Britain refused. In response, many whites "trekked" from the Cape colony eastward and northward, where they formed republics beyond the control of Britain. Although trekkers were influenced by a number of factors (the closing of the frontier, intensifying class conflict among whites, economic changes), Fredrickson emphasizes Britain's policy of equalization between whites and browns *(gelykstelling)*. Equalization, in portending liberal equality under the law, threatened the supremacy that had evolved over the previous 150 years.

Talk of equalization unveiled the substructure of the social order. Whites, without having thought much about it, had achieved systematic supremacy, but had bothered justifying only slavery. Their political thought, as Hermann Giliomee and André du Toit observed, "may perhaps best be characterized as a form of pragmatic realism in which *a priori* moral principles are not much in evidence."[13] Subordinating nonwhites was the linchpin of white society, but whites took the supremacy they had achieved for granted until Britain's talk of reform forced them to clarify what had been implicit all along. Now needing to justify supremacy, Fredrickson's whites took recourse in racial superiority, protesting as *whites*. "[N]ew demands for the abolition of regressive labor systems and for the implementation of basic human rights provoked stronger affirmations of racial differentiation as a governing principle of society on the part of those who were accustomed to ruling despotically over nonwhite dependents."[14] That is, whites adopted racialization as a strategy to justify the supremacy that had evolved more or less independently of racial feelings. Fredrickson is making a politicist point, in spite of his culturalist categories. He is not describing whites as becoming aware of themselves as white; he has them *becoming* white to justify and recast their power.

Whites established supremacy, and later legitimated it by reference to their worthiness as whites. Elevating race into the explicit criterion of membership, calling for "equality for all whites and rigorous subordination for all nonwhites,"[15] had the major advantage of justifying the supremacy of whites, now subject to challenge from Britain, without requiring too many adjustments in the actual allocation of power. It confirmed the inclusion of most of those who already had been included in civil society and the exclusion of most those who already had been excluded. But racializing membership did alter the position of some people. It improved the status of marginal whites because it increased the value of their color, and it degraded that of free browns because it excluded them on the basis of color. When Britain rejected systematic racialization, moving in the direction of formal equality and admitting "civilized" browns to civic society, trekkers left the Cape colony. They founded polities of their own, predicated on the principle of privileging whites *as* whites and exploiting nonwhites *as* nonwhites.

Hermann Giliomee engages similar issues in a major book about Afrikaner history, offering what appears on the surface to be a much different account of the history of whites in southern Africa from 1652 until the mid-nineteenth century. While referring to race, power, and exploitation, the categories that center Fredrickson, Giliomee emphasizes ethnoculture, details differences and disagreements among whites, and interprets *gelykstelling* and the treks differently. Yet at the deeper level, Giliomee, like Fredrickson, confirms the politicist thesis: both describe political power as central to the evolution of whites (or Afrikaners) as a community.

Giliomee's treatment of the period revolves around burghers, but their status was ambiguous. They expected to be treated as citizens, as if they were real burghers. But the Dutch East Indies Company was not a republic; it was not even a state. It was a profit-seeking, privately owned commercial company, and did not have room for citizens. Those who called themselves burghers were not citizens; they were former employees and the descendents of employees who rose to prominence in the Cape's communities, families, and churches. At the beginning of the eighteenth century, most burghers were white and many whites were burghers, but not all whites were burghers and not all burghers were white. But by the end of the century, brown and black burghers were losing status, and poor whites on the expanding frontier were gaining it.

Burghers were mostly farmers and community leaders. They constantly pursued cheap labor, and eventually, Giliomee points out, slavery "penetrated almost all aspects of the burghers' way of life."[16] Political power, in other words, was the predicate of their interests, what enabled them to acquire land and coerce labor. They insisted they "were burghers and citizens, not mere subjects or subordinates. The claim may not have been factually correct, but the burghers never abandoned this aspiration."[17] Lacking citizenship and a state, burghers deployed violence to establish their supremacy. They assembled commandos—"the fighting arm of the burghers"[18]—to expand and defend white settlements, clear KhoiKhoi, San, and Xhosa from their lands, round up labor, and, therefore, make possible the burghers' way of life.

Giliomee's burghers were aware of color from the early years of the colony, but did not develop much racial consciousness or racial animosity until the late eighteenth and early nineteenth centuries. They "conceived of themselves either as Company servants or as burghers," not as whites or as Afrikaners, and the colonial order rested on "non-racial status distinctions."[19] At first, whites sat at the top of the status hierarchy and browns and blacks lay at the bottom, but the middle ranks were ambiguous and fluid in composition, consisting of a mix of whites with less status than burghers and of free blacks and browns with more status than servants and slaves.[20] By the end of the century, the hierarchy was stratified along the lines of what *seemed* to be color, with white burghers on top, white foremen below them, then free blacks, followed by KhoiKhoi servants and, at the bottom, black slaves.[21]

The differentiation of the middle strata between a higher level for whites and a lower level for browns and blacks seems to count as evidence of racialization, but Giliomee argues otherwise. Race was not especially important in the eighteenth-century Cape. Burghers did notice color, did associate color with culture, and did affirm superiority. But they were not preoccupied with color; their racial consciousness was rudimentary, racial divisions were "not rigid," and browns and free blacks "did not appear to suffer any *racial* discrimination";[22] whites associated their superiority not with their color but with their Christianity. How, then, to explain the racial order that Giliomee, like Fredrickson, documents to have evolved in the absence of strong feelings of race?

Whites came to identify themselves in racial and ethno-cultural terms *after* they had established domination, and racialization was abetted by the influx of settlers from Britain, the new colonial power. Not only were English-speakers quicker than Afrikaners to racialize; their arrival also created a market for identities that could encompass the common interests of both Dutch-speaking and English-speaking colonists. As Giliomee explains, "There was more that kept the two white groups together than set them apart. They were, after all, a small minority in a colony with a large slave population and an insecure frontier in the east."[23]

Giliomee and Fredrickson are describing a similar reality. Both have burghers pursuing land and labor; both have whites using the political power of the Company and the commandos to secure land and labor; and both have the supremacy of burghers preceding their feelings of racial—though not of cultural and religious—superiority. They do disagree somewhat on the origins of the treks. Fredrickson points to the loss of political status and the introduction of political equality, whereas Giliomee attributes the treks to "lack of land, labor and security."[24] But Giliomee also recognizes the political determinates of the trekkers, their "loss of patriarchal authority over slaves or servants,"[25] their feeling that "they had been marginalized and disempowered," their loss of political power.[26] The treks for Giliomee were a sort of delayed reaction to Britain's reforms of the 1820s.

Objecting to the loss of status, the trekkers restored domination by regrounding it in political power. Giliomee signals as much in his choice of words. In the main, he refers not to whites or to Afrikaners or to Christians, but to burghers, and Giliomee's burghers pursued the domination of whites in practice, not white domination in principle.

Southern Africans noticed the "white man" and the "black man" from the time whites arrived. But they noticed other things too. Whites thought they were "white." They also thought they were "civilized," "Calvinist" "burgher" "settlers" from "Christian" "Europe" and were more affluent than "black," "savage" "natives" from "heathen" "Africa," who were poor besides. It is anachronistic to assume, therefore, that race necessarily took precedence over lesser identities or that the lesser identities derived from color. The status and the meaning of "whiteness"—and of color in general—were not given;[27] they were ambiguous, contested, and in flux.

Multiple identities overlapped more or less compatibly among whites. Still, it mattered which attribute colonists used to identify themselves, inasmuch as different identities implied different conceptions of themselves. Take, for example, two of the terms colonists used to identify themselves racially, "white" and "European." In describing themselves as European, colonists were identifying with the place their ancestors originated and were intimating that it was more significant than the place of their own personal origin. Most Europeans in southern Africa, after all, were not European geographically, being born, living, and dying in Africa. But they did identify with European culture. They spoke European languages; practiced European religions; and professed European values. In declaring themselves to be "European," they were identifying themselves positively, affirming who they were.

In calling themselves "white," on the other hand, colonists were defining themselves through contrast with others, negatively. Being white—as opposed to being European—said little about cultural traditions, political practices, social and economic arrangements, or who whites were positively. It identified with skin color (or a distortion of skin color: they were not calling themselves "pinks"). But skin color served to identify whites only because other people were not white. Whites were defined by who they were *not* (browns or blacks), a point made clear in Afrikaans. Afrikaans refers to whites not by the word *wit,* which means the color white, but by the word *blank,* which entered Afrikaans from Dutch. The word *blank* in Dutch meant something akin to "light colored" or "uncolored,"[28] not unlike the contemporary meaning of the English word "clear." It was used to mean white in relation to skin color; in other contexts the word *wit* was used to mean white.

Taken etymologically, it was as if whites were saying both that they were lightly colored and that they were without color, that they were differentiated from browns and blacks in part by different color and in the main by the absence of color. It was as if their identity was incomplete until contrast with their opposites completed them. It is not immaterial, therefore, whether colonists understood themselves as *blank* (that is, as white) or as European. The term "white" is embedded in relationality, with whites depending on blacks for collective definition, and resonated politics. Whites were made "white" not solely by cultural affinities or even by contrast to blacks (though these were necessary). They became a racial community in part because of their skin color and cultural affiliations, but not only because of them.

Color and culture, contrary to the sense of ethno-culturalism, did not build political communities and solidarities by themselves. Actual communities in the nineteenth century were not racial, in the sense that full membership in them was not open to all comers from the appropriate race. For example, whites drawn to the South African Republic (also known as the Transvaal, the more important of the two Boer republics founded by the trekkers) by the discovery of gold in 1886 rarely became full citizens. Those arriving in the gold rush, mostly from Britain, were not bothered unduly by their exclusion,[29] but the principle of membership was important anyway. *Uitlanders* were marginalized politically, in part because of their place of origin, in part because of suspect loyalties, and in part because of ethno-cultural differences. One historian explains, "In former days a man acquired citizenship when he acquired his farm. . . . After 1882 Kruger [the president and dominant figure in the Transvaal] proceeded to make . . . the franchise laws . . . so strict that new-comers had hardly more chance of obtaining the franchise than [African] natives of the Transkei."[30] Furthermore, a few years after the discovery of gold (and the arrival of those seeking it), the political assembly of the Transvaal "limited the *uitlander* franchise for presidential and *Volksraad* [the people's assembly] elections to those who, besides being naturalized citizens, had lived in the Republic for fourteen years."[31] That is, citizenship was restricted to whites in principle and to Afrikaners in practice.

Membership in nineteenth-century southern African politics was not allocated by color or culture alone. If the Boer republics had sorted membership solely on the basis of color, British immigrants would have qualified for citizenship. If they had sorted solely on the basis of cultural practices (or even on the basis of actual kinship, since Coloureds were of "mixed" blood and the blood of Afrikaners was "mixed" too), Afrikaans-speaking and Dutch Reform–worshipping Coloureds would have qualified for membership. Coloureds did not qualify as members of the civic community, however, because they were not white. Hermann Giliomee explains why the emerging sense of Afrikaner ethno-culture did not encompass Coloureds: "Whites prided themselves on being a master or 'aristocratic' class. Even its poorest members considered themselves too superior to accept employment in someone else's service, to do manual labour, or to work as artisans."[32] That is, white racism prevented Coloureds from being accepted as citizens, even though they shared common kinship and common cultural institutions with Afrikaners. Whites demanded supremacy as whites and self-determination as Afrikaners; Afrikaans-speaking browns were disqualified because they were not white, and English-speaking whites were disqualified because they were not kin and were not Afrikaans culturally.

African political communities were not reducible to color either, membership in them being sorted ethno-culturally. According to Leonard Thompson, "There was no sense of racial identity among Africans. They knew ties of kinship, of political affiliation, and of cultural affinity such as language; but racialism was not an African concept."[33] African polities were based on clan, lineage, and tribe, on kinship, which is why chiefs did not make common racial cause against whites.

> While African chiefs rarely formed alliances against the whites, and never succeeded in uniting all the Africans in a particular area, time and again specific African groups were prepared to join whites in alliances or in joint campaigns against other Africans. There was no well-developed sense of racial identity among Africans, sectional advantage was placed before wider interests, and views of the most appropriate strategy differed as much as they do among black South Africans today.[34]

Immersed in their ethno-cultures, African chiefs sometimes allied with whites "in their internal power struggles"[35] even though they often were double-crossed.[36] Whites brought superior firepower and organization to their allies and, most importantly, could not become rivals within African politics, because they were alien ethno-culturally.

Color was a necessary condition for political membership, but not a sufficient one. Christopher Saunders notes, "There was no simple, dichotomized white-black frontier with two monolithic, antagonistic blocs facing each other. . . . Both blacks and, in the nineteenth century, whites, were divided among different political units, and different groups competed for power within each unit. The result was that in frontier situations white factions interacted with black factions in a variety of ways."[37]

Racial communities, in other words, were not just there, waiting to be awakened. Something had to give content to races if people were to become conscious of them, to give a "there" to color. Color and culture, obviously, were insufficient to the task at hand, because nineteenth-century polities, except for the Cape, revolved around ethno-cultures and because color, while felt and observed, did not itself define identities or forge communities. What, given the preeminence of ethno-cultures to the nineteenth century, converted color into the foundation of communities in twentieth-century South Africa?

The short answer is that racialization was the doing of Britain and twentieth-century "whites" and that together they installed race as the principle of political and social organization. But the short answer begs a longer explanation. Whites did racialize South Africa, instituting race as the dominant principle of social organization. Saying that "whites" did the racializing is acknowledging, however, that some racializing had occurred already, that some white power and self-consciousness was in place already. Previously, people had been conscious of color, but color consciousness had not created the primary political communities. When whites were ethno-culturally homogeneous, speaking Dutch, Afrikaans, and the dialects bridging them, worshipping in Calvinist churches, and professing similar values, they did not require embracing identities as whites. Parochial identities served nicely, insofar as "whites"—or "Afrikaners" or "Europeans" or "settlers" or "burghers" or "God's chosen people"—were homogeneous culturally. But when British settlers arrived, and whites at once became more heterogeneous and the supremacy of the original ones became more precarious, the grope for racial partnership created the basis for whites as a unified political community. Races were fashioned precisely *because* of ethno-cultural differences, not irrespective of them.

Nineteenth-century whites shared common prejudices against and common interests in exploiting browns and blacks. But that took them only so far. Tensions between Britain and the Boer republics erupted in the South African (Boer) war in 1898–99. Provoked by Britain's quest for gold, the war pitted British imperialism against Afrikaner nationalism. In victory, Britain amalgamated its two colonies (the Cape and Natal) and the two defeated Boer republics (the South African Republic and the Orange Free State) into the Union of South Africa.

The Boer War constitutes compelling proof that color alone had not produced a politically effective and cohesive community of nineteenth-century whites, able to unite in spite of ethnic fissures and state rivalries. Color was not irrelevant, of course. Both sides in the Boer War refrained from arming Africans for combat, attesting that color counted for whites even while they were warring with each other. But what they shared as whites was eclipsed by what divided them politically and ethno-culturally, bequeathing a bitter legacy to the new state. Afrikaner nationalists, having lost what they regarded as an unjust war that Britain had fought unjustly, resented British imperialism. Britain and English-speaking chauvinists, having discharged their imperial obligations, regarded Afrikaners with disdain, as uncultured, troublesome, and essentially Africanized.

Ethnic rivalries were only one source of conflict among whites in the new South Africa. Class struggles between mining houses and (white) mine workers and between subsistence Afrikaner farmers and commercial farmers were equally divisive, and they often were reinforced by ethno-cultural rivalries. At the inception of the state, therefore, the unity of whites was strained to the snapping point. What held whites together in the face of their differences and mediated their conflicts, what elevated race over competing identities and made it the basis of a political community, was self-government. It endowed whites with common interests, common identities, and common threats.

Britain's plan for the postwar order was predicated on unifying whites as a racial group. According to Alfred Milner, one of its authors, "the *ultimate* end" of British policy was "a self-governing white Community, supported by *well-treated* and *justly governed* black labour from Cape Town to Zambesi."[38] The plan subverted itself, however. Britain effectively precluded good treatment and justice for black labor by identifying the community as *white*, which cast blacks as interlopers; by relegating blacks to a subservient role, as laborers for whites; and by vesting whites with self-government, enabling them to govern however they pleased. Britain put the fox in charge of the henhouse. It allowed whites to enhance the value of their votes by determining who could and could not vote. "The question of granting the franchise to natives," as the point was put in the treaty concluding the war, "will not be decided until after the introduction of self-government."[39]

The new state enfranchised most white men from its inception; denied the franchise to all Africans, Coloureds, and Asians in three of its four provinces; and allowed most Coloureds and a few African men to vote in the Cape province, providing they satisfied "civilization" tests (the "Cape franchise"). Historians question the practical significance of the Cape franchise, because the nonwhite fraction of the electorate was small and could vote only for white candidates anyway.[40] But the Cape franchise did have the effect of blurring the state's racial character and of intimating that the state was accountable to some blacks. To sharpen the state's racial identity, voting laws were revised repeatedly from the 1930s through the 1950s. White women were enfranchised in 1930 and the remaining men in 1931, diluting the value of the votes of black men; property and educational qualifications were lifted for white males but not for Africans;[41] African males in the Cape were disenfranchised in 1936; Coloured males in the Cape were disenfranchised in 1956. By the mid-1950s, only whites could vote, completing the identifications of whiteness with citizenship and blackness with noncitizenship.

Citizenship, as Rogers Brubaker writes, may be general and inclusive, extending to all subjects of a state, or it may be "a *special* membership status." In the latter event, citizens are "a privileged subgroup" of a population that includes "categories of noncitizens." That is, people born and bred in the society—even people whose forebears were born and bred there—may be denied the status of citizen. Although subjected to state power, noncitizens are not vested with political rights, as they are not themselves political subjects. They "belong to the state as a territorial administrative unit, but not to the state as a ruling organization . . . Citizenship is constituted by the possession and exercise of political rights, by participation in the business of rule."[42] Denying the vote, therefore, was tantamount to denying citizenship in Brubaker's sense.

Brubaker's definition of citizenship applies perfectly to South Africa under white supremacy. Whites were citizens, with full political rights; blacks were not citizens; and racializing citizenship exalted racial communities over ethno-cultural communities. The state may have seemed merely to have been formalizing custom when it decreed that four "races" (Africans, Asians, Coloureds, and Europeans) populated South Africa, but it was exceeding and changing the status of custom. If the consciousness of being white was to be converted into the consciousness of belonging to the white *nation*, the white supremacist state had to bond whites together, through the medium of citizenship.

Feelings of whiteness demonstrably preceded the common citizenship of whites; indeed, they were the condition of using race as the gatekeeper for citizenship. If citizens were to be identified on the basis of race, they had to have and to be perceived to have color in the first place; the state had to have some way of determining who could and could not participate in the political institutions that soon were to define race formally. Color consciousness had not produced political unity in the nineteenth century, but when Britain allowed Afrikaners from the defeated Boer republics to write their conception of race into the constitution of the self-governing dominion, it empowered them to establish the framework for a community of all whites. Rejecting kinship as the principle of political membership, the South African state declared itself racially. Whites were citizens, regardless of ethno-cultural background, and blacks—with the partial exception of the Cape—were not citizens. The new state, in other words, recast the basis of government; it substituted race for ethno-culture.

Color communities were not ready-made. They had to be built through state activity. Racializing everything it could, the state promulgated and distinguished racial categories, elaborated criteria to ascertain who belonged in which category, and tied racial categories to legal status and life opportunities. On the basis of race, the state specified where people could live; whom they could marry; what jobs they could work and where they could own land; and whether they could vote, own firearms, and move freely within the country. The state could not do whatever it pleased, of course. It could not assign people to racial groups willy-nilly, regardless of the status of parents, siblings, and the force of white opinion. It had to respect the influence of custom and public opinion. But that defers, it does not answer, questions of what was decisive in resolving issues of membership. Whose customs, whose opinions were sovereign? It was the state that answered those questions authoritatively and, in the process, prevented custom from evolving. Racial identities, which had been fluid, now (in the manner of Weber) came to be organized on the basis of their relationship with state power. They were frozen bureaucratically.

The South African state, obviously and undeniably, racialized the country, in the sense of making racial identities the hub of social, economic, and political life. But the state had additional reasons for highlighting race. In dividing society between whites and blacks, it simultaneously was dividing South Africa between citizens and noncitizens. Yes, it was advantaging whites and disadvantaging blacks. But inasmuch as whites were citizens and blacks were noncitizens, it also is true to say that the state was advantaging citizens, who were white, and was disadvantaging noncitizens, who were black. Moreover, color alone did not distinguish between those inside and those outside the protection of the state. What forged the boundaries between the ins and the outs, what differentiated members from nonmembers, what accorded status, power, and material benefits to whites and denied them to blacks, what made "whites" "white" and "blacks" "black" was not solely color (or culture). It equally was citizenship in the state. Citizenship is what gave content to color. White and black were identified by color, but what it meant to be white and black was defined in substantial measure by state power.

Whites valued citizenship for expressive (as well as instrumental) reasons. Expressively, it blessed them with the experience of belonging, validating the feeling that the country was theirs. Their cultures prevailed; their identities were embodied in public symbols, holidays, monuments. Their languages were spoken publicly, published in print, taught in schools, and favored. European manners and customs were adopted and flourished; African ways were snubbed, despised, and invoked as proof of white superiority. Whiteness symbolized belonging. But note what is implied by the symbolic role of color. Color symbolized citizenship, but did not constitute citizens as a club. The state formed the club, the political community, the nation, from the stuff of ethno-cultural and class rivalries by providing preferential access to resources and by associating resources with the collective identities and material interests that whites were coming to share. Citizenship materialized color.

Whites were not monolithic, indivisible, and integral. They were ethno-culturally diverse. Under white supremacy, English-speakers enjoyed greater economic power and higher cultural status, while Afrikaners, more numerous than English-speakers, acquired electoral power. Controlling the highest state offices, Afrikaners split between cultural nationalists, who organized against British symbols and English-speaking influence, and conciliators, who entertained ethno-cultural parity or integration on the basis of racial supremacy. The former tradition was represented by the Hertzog governments (1924–33) and the early National Party governments (1948 through the 1960s) and the latter tradition by the Louis Botha (1910–19) and Smuts governments (1919–24, 1939–48), the coalition government between Hertzog and Smuts (1933–39), and the later National Party governments, which began acting as a white—as opposed to an Afrikaner—party in the 1970s and 1980s.

Afrikaners and English-speakers constituted largely endogenous communities. Each community had its own schools and universities, churches, media, and businesses, and most members married their own kind. Conflicts between the two communities were chronic, occasionally intense, and the stuff of much of white politics. Giliomee even conceived of apartheid as a form of ethnic mobilization. Reserving state jobs for Afrikaners, nurturing the Afrikaner upper and middle classes, making Afrikaans the language of the state, and endorsing Afrikaner symbols, the apartheid state improved the economic and cultural positions of Afrikaners.[43] Understanding apartheid as ethnic mobilization does capture the Afrikaner flavor of apartheid, but it also plays down the backdrop for white politics. Ethno-cultural rivalries, although often intense, presumed and were contained by white supremacy. The racial order expressed the white community it was making. But it also won support for and sustained a particularly virulent form of capitalism.

4

The Politics of the Political Economy

> The native should only be allowed to enter urban areas, which are essentially the white man's creation, when he is willing to enter and to minister to the needs of the white man, and should depart therefrom when he ceases to so minister.
>
> —FREDRICK STALLARD, CHAIRMAN OF THE TRANSVAAL LOCAL GOVERNMENT COMMITTEE, 1922

Apartheid mounted a culturalist argument. It claimed Africans were not entitled to citizenship in South Africa for the simple reason that they belonged elsewhere, in tribal homelands of their own. But apartheid was not really committed to keeping whites and blacks separate. The ideology of separate development was fashioned to justify the rightlessness of blacks inside South Africa while preserving and justifying the domination of whites over blacks. Domination, however, entails involvement, connectedness, and relatedness, not separation and apartness. The whole premise of white supremacy, and the raison d'être for segregation and apartheid, was that whites needed blacks for *something:* that is why Africans were not expelled from "white" South Africa once and for all. The ideology of separate development was not justifying the practice of separation. It was justifying the exclusion of blacks from political and economic rights, from citizenship.

Blacks were the majority of the population, a big problem for white supremacy. They also were indispensable economically, an even bigger problem. Black labor was everywhere in white South Africa—on farms, construction sites, and shop floors; in white homes, as gardeners, nannies, and maids—and whites had no intention of doing manual labor themselves. "Apartheid," as Heribert Adam observed, "can best be understood as the systematic attempt to . . . channel the inevitable political consequences of [economic integration] in the interest of whites."[1] That is, apartheid was designed to balance the contradiction between the reality of economic interdependence, which potentially endowed black labor with political leverage, and the imperatives of white power. As Prime Minister J. G. Strydom put the point in 1952, "Our policy is that the Europeans must stand their ground and remain *Baas* [master] in South Africa. If . . . the franchise is to be extended to non-Europeans, and if non-Europeans are developed on the same basis as Europeans, how can Europeans remain *Baas*?"[2] By nationalizing race, apartheid neutralized the political implications of the dependence of whites on black labor. Declaring whites and blacks belonged to different nations and deserved separate states, it explained why Africans could not take advantage of their indispensability to the South African economy.

Liberals have argued since the nineteenth century that nations are natural nests for political loyalties, that states should be organized on the basis of and around national identities and allegiances, and, in turn, that national identities derive from ethnicity. It was a short step, and a common one until fascism discredited racism, to go on to posit race too as essential to common nationhood. Apartheid, following the example of erstwhile liberals, associated citizenship with nations and nations with races. But apartheid then rejected one of the defining insights of modern liberals, that the promise of political equality is what justifies the practice of other forms of inequality.

Liberal democracies posit citizens as equal, at least formally, in the state and under the law. When actual liberal democracies fall short of achieving full equality, they maintain that the important point is the aspiration that laws apply equally to all citizens. Predictably, liberal democracies are chastised for inequalities that mar the ideal of equality under the law in practice, and the objection is important. But it also is important that emphasizing equality under the law has the effect of funneling the pursuit of equality through the state. If citizens are equal in the state, by liberal logic, they may be unequal outside the state, in society.[3] Apartheid, on the other hand, moved in the diametrically opposite direction. Rather than justifying the practice of economic inequality via the ideal of political equality, apartheid justified economic inequality by rejecting the ideal of political equality in common citizenship. Apartheid rejected the very illusion of equality.

South African capitalism was imbued with racism, for reasons that are contested. Generally, liberals regard business as committed to markets and markets as innately hostile to racism.[4] Markets, they argue, corrode racial privilege and reward merit, which is why racists seek to thwart them. Accordingly, South African liberals of economistic (as opposed to culturalist) bent had apartheid developing precisely "to counter the natural tendency of market forces to substitute cheaper (black) for more expensive (white) workers."[5] That is, the fundamental liberalism of capitalism was perverted by the political illiberalism of racism. The problem with the liberal argument, as one of its more influential proponents conceded, was that leading business interests "supported some major apartheid policies."[6] In particular, mining and commercial farmers favored repressive labor policies that maintained a "plentiful supply of cheap, unskilled black workers," that allowed black workers to be paid submarket wages, and that ensured the compliance of the underpaid labor.[7] The "manufacturing and commercial sectors," on the other hand, balked at labor repression.[8] Preferring stable workforces and free labor markets to nonmarket labor, they chaffed at artificial labor shortages, at overpaying white workers, and at prohibitions from hiring the workers of their choosing. Of course, critics interpret the record differently. Racial capitalism for Marxists was not a blight on capitalism; it was part and parcel of the capitalist system.

Marxists tell a coherent story about white supremacy, with their composite narrative running along the following lines. South African capitalism evolved out of the gold mining industry, whose economics were unusual from the outset. Geologically, the "reef of gold-bearing ore . . . sloped downwards deep underground, and the average grade of gold in the ore was very low," making for high "development and overhead costs."[9] That was half of the problem confronting the mining industry; the other half was that mining houses could not pass exceptional costs onto consumers. Prices were fixed internationally, leaving the industry little alternative to driving down wages, the most elastic cost of production. Through hiring cartels, long-term contracts enforced by penal sanctions, debt inducement, extra-contractual labor, the destruction of alternative employment, pass laws, and, most importantly, migrant labor, the cost of labor was reduced below what would have prevailed in a free market.[10] Moreover, the prevalence of migrant labor, in which male workers rotated between rural areas, where they were born, raised, and died, and urban areas, where they lived and worked in their primes, had the effect of lodging the costs of reproducing labor, of rearing the children and supporting the families of migrants, on villages, where pass laws forced women and children to remain.[11]

Mining houses had two important allies in preventing the development of free markets in labor, the more influential being commercial farmers. Commercial farmers wanted cheap labor, and the cheapest was that which could not explore options in the labor market, that could not escape to cities. This was the attraction of pass laws, the system of internal passports that limited the movement of Africans inside South Africa, and of labor regimes that depended on state compulsion. As Colin Bundy found,

> Both [white] farmer and the mine-owner perceived in the late nineteenth century the need to apply extra-economic pressure to the African peasantry; to break down the peasant's "independence," increase his wants, and to induce him to part more abundantly with his labour, but at no increased price. Implicit in their demands was the assumption that Africans had no right to continue as self-sufficient and independent farmers if this conflicted with white interests.[12]

Commercial farmers made additional claims on the state as well, some conventional and others unconventional. Conventionally, they called for "a massive programme of subsidies, grants and other aid," including "fencing, dams, houses, veterinary and horticultural advice."[13] Regulatory bodies "set prices, subsidized certain foods, and decided what to do with surpluses" and cheap exports were subsidized "with high domestic prices."[14] Farming interests are steeped in pork barrel politics in most societies, of course, and state assistance to farmers is hardly out of the ordinary. But what was extraordinary in South Africa was that white farmers successfully mobilized the state to eliminate rivals, specifically African rivals. To break the self-sufficiency and independence of the black peasantry, the state enacted legislation that "was racially discriminative, and blessed only modernizing white farmers, which of itself conferred important competitive advantages on that class. These were buttressed . . . by legislation (most particularly the 1913 Natives Land Act) aimed at curtailing the possibilities open to peasant production, at preventing the accumulation of capital by Africans and at translating independent squatter-peasants into wage-labourers."[15] The state, in addition to making white farmers more efficient, reserved seven-eighths of the territory for them, expropriated land for them, eliminated black farmers as competitors to them, and, through taxation and compulsion, forced Africans to work for them. A "supportive state apparatus was a precondition for expanding production while holding African workers in the rural areas."[16]

The coalition behind labor control, although dominated by mining houses and commercial farmers, was joined by white unions. The white working classes obviously were haunted by the specter of the large, cheap, rightless workforce that positioned employers to bid down wages, including those of white workers. Lest they too be forced to accept submarket wages and conditions by the artifice of having to compete with those who had been stripped of economic and political rights, white workers were granted explicit protections by law and custom from African competition, were spared the indignity of working under blacks, and were insulated from heavy labor. Demand for their labor was stimulated by reserving categories of employment for whites, by subsidizing state-owned enterprises that absorbed surplus white labor (most notoriously, the railroads), and by enacting import substitution policies that buffered jobs from domestic and international competition. Shielded from market forces, white workers

> were not ultra-exploitable. They enjoyed considerable economic and political power, because of the scarcity of skilled labour, and because as whites they were . . . politically free in the specific sense that they could assert themselves in relation to the employers through such means as trade unions and the vote. These factors placed them in a strong bargaining position in relation to the employers, enabling them to command high wages and making white labor far more expensive than non-white labour.[17]

The mines and farmers dictated labor control and submarket wages for blacks, but white workers got a cut of the surplus generated by blacks.

The economy under white supremacy was capitalist in the sense that the means of production were owned privately and the owners were motivated by the pursuit of profit. But it was capitalist neither in the sense that labor was free nor that markets were competitive. From the beginning of the mining industry, the economy was dominated by large, anticompetitive conglomerates.[18] Soon, the companies that arose in the mining industry controlled the manufacturing and commercial sectors, where they entered into arrangements with each other and furthered their collusive ways.

Marxists, therefore, have a profoundly illiberal form of capitalism driving white supremacy. Steeped in racism and beholden to state patronage, South African capitalism rejected liberal values, including market competition and political equality. That does not mean Marxists regarded the illiberalism of South African capital as necessarily unalterable. The politics of business arose in response to distinct circumstances—the profit squeeze on the mining houses caused by high fixed costs and the dependence of farmers on cheap labor—and, consequently, were subject to change in the event circumstances changed. But under white supremacy, capitalism accommodated racism, domination, and privilege; it did not breed freedom, equality, and democracy.

Marxist accounts of the political economy of white supremacy naturally pounced on the racist exploitation of black labor. But the foremost feature of racial capitalism for Marxists was exploitation; it was not racism. Racism organized and targeted exploitation, identifying who would be victimized by the economics of the mining and agricultural sectors, but the impulse to hyper-exploitation emanated from capitalism.[19] The political economy, as Marxists construed it, was dominated by *classes* of whites, not by *whites* as a class. Race was used to administer things, to identify who was and was not subject to labor control. But classes were organized by their relationship to the means of production and were motivated by economic interests, not by racial identities and solidarities. Marxist conceptions of racial capitalism, in other words, emphasized the role of capitalism and de-emphasized that of race. A few Marxists—Neville Alexander comes to mind—argued that capitalism invented races,[20] but most made the more modest point that capitalism reinvented the significance of races. For most Marxists, races were given by culture, but cultures were molded by relations of production.

The centrality of labor coercion to the political economy of white supremacy begs a question. If differences in color had not been available to organize exploitation, if, hypothetically, gold had been discovered before whites had settled in southern Africa or after independence from colonial rule, would the pressures on mining capital have been any different? The price of gold still would have been fixed, the costs of mining still would have been high, labor still would have been more elastic than most other costs of production, and the mining industry still would have required some ways of underpaying labor. If gold were to be mined, the hypothetical political economy would have had to have been organized by some method for exploiting labor, tribalism perhaps. By the logic of Marxist analyses, mining capital had to intensify the exploitation of labor as the necessary condition of the industry's profitability.

For Marxists, the imperatives of capitalist development were the independent variable and the significance of racial identities the dependent variable. According to Stanley Greenberg, "Capitalist development . . . both preserves and remakes the racial order, extending and reinforcing racial barriers, but also creating new contradictions that paradoxically threaten to dismantle them."[21] Capital took advantage of white supremacy to organize the economy along racial lines, but it was the economic interests of the dominant classes that manipulated racialization. Consequently, the significance of race, racialism, and racism were destined to change along with the interests of capitalist actors. Races are the furniture of capitalism, arranged and rearranged by classes.

Races exist in a common-sense, culturalist sort of way for most Marxists, but Marxists mostly were interested in the connection of race and class under white supremacy, as mediated through culture. In the most influential interpretation, Harold Wolpe argued that mining capital discovered migrant labor while pursuing rightless labor. In turn, migrancy required subcultures for migrants to rotate in to and out of, to raise them when children, to accept them when unemployed, and to shelter them when worn out. "Traditional" African chiefs, having been subjugated by conquest, accepted the life saver capital threw to them in exchange for assuring a steady supply of cheap labor for mines and absorbing the costs of producing the labor force of the future. The uneven economic development of South Africa did not, in other words, result from incomplete capitalism; it was capitalism.[22]

The argument about the political economy of racial capitalism was challenged widely, even by Marxists.[23] But the argument does account for the most conspicuous anomaly in South Africa's political economy under white supremacy, the absence of free markets in labor until the 1980s. The state, as Marxist political economy conceived it, was the instrument of capitalist interests, doing the bidding of mine owners and commercial farmers. Mining capital needed cheap and disposable labor; the state responded with pass laws, oppressive labor systems, the paraphernalia of migrancy, and segregation. White commercial farmers needed land and cheap labor; the state designated most land for whites, forged a landless peasantry susceptible to exploitation, and prevented African peasants from competing with white farmers. Marxist political economy, in other words, saw a clear causal and temporal sequence in the development of racial capitalism. Classes crystallized, amassed the power to make demands on the state, and the state performed the bidding of its masters.

Yet something is amiss. In spite of its elegance, the story Marxists *theorized* oversimplified and distorted the one they *told*. The white supremacist state, in familiar capitalist fashion, did elaborate the legal framework for capitalist development, did obstruct unionization, and did construct infrastructure. It did the things that capitalist economies characteristically depend on supportive states to do. The white supremacist state defined the meaning of property and defended property rights, resolved disputes about property through lawful courts and enforced contracts, educated workforces, printed and backed money, and, generally, secured the conditions of capitalist society.[24] The white supremacist state also feathered the nests of white classes in familiar fashion. It provided commercial farmers with subsidies and price supports and made countless deals with the mining houses. The state also imposed high tariffs, protected domestic industries, and established state industries, again in familiar capitalist fashion.

What was unusual about the white supremacist state was not that it established the framework for the capitalist economy or that it served particular capitalist interests. It was that Marxists describe the dominant capitalist classes as embedded in the state, as dependent on state power for their existence as classes. The state constituted capitalist classes, and without its patronage they would not have developed. Thus, cheap labor not only was something mining houses wanted; it also was something they *required* (until the price of gold was freed in the early 1970s). State power, in compelling Africans to work at submarket wages, is what made the mining industry viable and profitable. Similarly, the white supremacist state secured the conditions that made commercial farming profitable. It destroyed the independent African peasantry, eliminating competition, forcing African subsistence farmers into the cash economy, proletarianizing agricultural workers, and providing white farmers with cheap labor. State power was not merely an adjunct to the dominant capitalist classes; it was the condition of their existence.

Other classes were wired into state patronage too. The Afrikaner bourgeoisie originated in the private sector,[25] but the National Party (NP), which captured the state in 1948, used parastatals and pressure to help the Afrikaner bourgeoisie. The parastatals, which generated a hefty portion of economic activity, came to be dominated by Afrikaners and the pressure induced Anglo American, the leading conglomerate, to sell some of its holdings to Afrikaner buyers, giving the Afrikaner bourgeoisie a stake in South Africa's leading industry.[26] Most importantly, the NP blunted pressure to liberalize labor markets in the aftermath of World War II, assuring its constituencies in commercial agriculture and Afrikaner business plenty of cheap labor.

Capitalist interests, then, depended on the state, but the relationship was complicated by the insurmountable fact that the state was organized as a democracy for whites and that the political and economic commitments of the white electorate had to be accommodated. Of course, capitalists could exert guidance in a myriad of ways, by influencing economic conditions, using mass media, making demands on parties, politicians, and officials, setting agendas, and so forth. But the government also was accountable to the electorate, to whites through elections. Capitalist elites had to accept and work through the general interests of whites as whites, partly because whites were enfranchised in the state as citizens and capitalist elites depended on state power, partly because the white electorate was mostly Afrikaans and capital was controlled mostly by English-speakers, and partly because, in resorting to racism to exploit the vast majority of the population, capitalist classes put themselves in dire need of allies.

Consider, on this score, the experience of the poor whites in Johannesburg shortly after the turn of the twentieth century. As Charles van Onselen tells it, dislocated farmers often provided services or produced petty commodities.[27] Soon they were to be eclipsed by bigger capital and proletarianized. Yet they "were far from being powerless. Indeed, such was the threat posed by them and other unemployed workers . . . that it called forth a significant response from mine owners and state alike in the form of charity and public relief works."[28] Van Onselen regrets the tragedy that "in the succeeding decades the same workers" who had battled for their rights fell "prey to the nets of a narrow nationalism."[29] But in praising the gains of "political muscle,"[30] which is what enabled poor whites to achieve a living wage and what impressed on the ruling classes the dangers of class antagonisms among the "civilized people," van Onselen skates on the two conditions that allowed poor whites to achieve the "civilized" labor policy that protected their jobs, wages, and status.

Van Onselen's lower class whites, like other classes of whites, presumed on their citizenship—their rights to organize, demonstrate, exert moral pressure—to improve immediate living conditions and eventually to elevate their class standing. But their protests were effective only on condition that the state and political society already were organized on the basis of racial exclusion, without which poor whites would have been overpowered by the number of poor blacks, and on condition that the racially exclusive state prized unity, without which the economic interests of poor whites would have been sacrificed to those of white elites. Popular classes of whites, therefore, had to protect their political influence, particularly their monopoly on citizenship, as the condition of satisfying their economic interests. Their economic interests were inseparable from their political interests. The *politics* of South Africa's political economy, in other words, counted as much as the economics: the political monopoly on citizenship and the franchise was the condition of political influence and political influence was the predicate of economic interests.

Whites received all kinds of economic benefits from the state. Their living standards were subsidized by public services that were developed for whites; overvalued currencies exaggerated their purchasing power; tariffs protected their jobs and compensation from foreign competition; the state financed infrastructure; and so forth. The state reserved higher paying, supervisory jobs for them; furnished them vastly better schools at the primary, secondary, and university levels; taught academic curricula in languages they understood; and valued their cultural capital as appropriate. Whites of all classes also lived in neighborhoods with superior services and received much better housing because of direct state investment in housing and the redesignation of black areas as white areas, forcing black—especially Coloured—home owners to sell their houses to white home buyers at a fraction of their value.

The state, then, siphoned wealth from blacks and split it between white society, in the form of higher pay and subsidized services, and white business, in the form of inflated profits. Capitalists captured much of the surplus, with the state showing particular favor to mining houses and commercial farmers. But the state also responded to the political power of whites by enhancing the living standards of whites (or citizens) with resources that were generated through the hyper-exploitation of blacks (or noncitizens).

The class interests of whites stemmed from political power, and political power, for reasons rooted in the nineteenth century, was the preserve of whites. The assumption of British sovereignty over the Cape colony; the migration of Afrikaner farmers to the interior of southern Africa on treks; the establishment of the Boer republics by those who had trekked from the Cape colony; the discovery of gold in one of the republics; Britain's designs on the gold; Britain's victory in a controversial and brutal war against the Boer republics; and the eventual unification of two British colonies (the Cape and Natal) and the two Boer republics (the Transvaal and the Orange Free State) into the Union of South Africa: this history produced the enfranchisement of whites as citizens, irrespective of ethnocultural background, in the new South African state.

The twentieth-century state enfranchised whites from its inception, always denied the franchise to blacks in three of its four provinces, and eventually disenfranchised African and Coloured males in the fourth province. In allocating the franchise racially, the state conveyed that citizenship and its prerogatives—notably, the right to participate in government and to claim the benefits derived therefrom—belonged to whites. Whites were included, blacks were excluded, and the franchise drew a bright line between those worthy and unworthy of belonging in South Africa.[31] More materially, whites were indebted doubly to the state for their class standing. They were propped up by the state, and blacks were made vulnerable to intense exploitation. With blacks pushed down as whites were pulled up, some economic interests were predicated on the different political standings of whites and blacks. Whites could exercise political rights—organizing around interests and identities, establishing political parties, electing governments—and blacks could not.

The benefits conferred by political power helped define what it meant to be white. Political power associated whiteness with both feelings of belonging and material advantages, inflicted feelings of exclusion and material disadvantages on blackness and, implicitly, tied whiteness not only to its positive content, but also to the *discrepancy* between what whites enjoyed *as whites* and what blacks endured *as blacks*. Whiteness became a relationship with blackness, in which whites were devoted to maintaining the exclusivity of their claims, to marking off what distinguished them—the vote, political rights, citizenship—from blacks, and establishing the commonalities that made whites "white." Yes, whites were "white" because of their skin color and their cultural affiliations, but not only because of them. They were white also because *citizenship* converted the consciousness of being white into a *community* of whites.

Actual cultural and political communities did not encompass the majority of whites or of Africans until the founding of the South African state in the twentieth century. Previously, whites had shared common prejudices against and a common interest in exploiting Africans, yet had not become a community unified by race. Color alone had not constituted either political or cultural communities. To convert the consciousness of being white into a white *people,* something was required to give substance to the interests, identities, and cultures of whites *as whites,* to make color the criterion of political membership. The state had to make color into the basis of political community.

When the white supremacist state began cataloging the races of its subjects, it either made the assignments itself or registered memberships that had evolved already, which is what it claimed to have been doing. "Whites" were those who already had been accepted as members of "white" polities, whether the British colonies or the Afrikaner republics, or had been excluded as foreigners—but not as Africans, Coloureds, or Asians—from white communities. It is tempting to conclude that those with political membership and rights before the union of South Africa were designated as "white" and those without them were designated as "black," but the conclusion is complicated by two details. First, some immigrants to the Boer republics, fortune seekers and miners mostly, did not have political rights,[32] yet were accepted as "white" in the new state. Second, some Coloured and African men did hold voting rights in the Cape colony, but did not become full citizens (or "whites"). Nevertheless, political enfranchisement and disenfranchisement became integral to the social meaning of race, which is one reason why Cape Africans and Coloureds were disenfranchised. "[T]he Cape franchise" might have "proved to be innocuous from the white point of view during a half century of operation,"[33] as Leonard Thompson notes, but it committed the grave sin of disentangling membership from race.

Inevitably, blacks resented white supremacy, but effective recourse for their grievances through political institutions was denied to them. By the terms of white supremacy, only whites could act politically. Whites were political subjects and blacks were in the untenable position of being objects of political power. Faced with terrible burdens, they could petition benevolent whites for relief, but could not take direct political action in South African political institutions. As their appeals to the Christian mercy of the white authorities were unsuccessful, blacks tried organizing. But inasmuch as the source of their grievance was precisely that they could not act in institutions, that they were objects of state power, the strategy of pursuing reforms inside institutions was not very promising. Rather recklessly, white supremacy had rendered African demands for enfranchisement subversive of the essential dichotomy between the admissibility of white political demands and the inadmissibility of black demands. Revolutionary transformation, therefore, became the precondition even of minor reforms. Perversely, in shaping Africans into threats to the interests whites shared as whites, white supremacy reinforced the reasons for disenfranchising and disempowering Africans and unified whites against the threat of revolution.

Racializing citizenship was portentous for a number of reasons. First of all, it situated relations between English- and Afrikaans-speaking whites.

The white state, which was controlled by Afrikaners, made Afrikaans into the primary language of the state, sought to build up Afrikaner culture—either to assure the survival of Afrikaner culture, to prepare for the integration of Afrikaans and English culture on the basis of equality, or to promote Afrikaner domination—and increasingly identified the state with Afrikaner ethno-cultural interests, nurturing Afrikaner upper and middle classes and effectively reserving supervisory positions in state employment for Afrikaners. Afrikaners, in other words, used their majority among whites to achieve political power, and used their political power to buttress their cultural and economic positions. But the sequence was conditioned on Afrikaners remaining (more or less) unified politically and on whites retaining the monopoly on political power. Without the racial franchise, Afrikaner preponderance among whites did not amount to much.

Second, the racial franchise allowed the white state to begin constituting a white community. Ostensibly, the state formalized the category of "white" and classified those individuals who were light-skinned and straight-haired and had European ancestors as "white." But defining races was not a simple matter of counting the number of different colors and cultures present in South Africa, formalizing racial categories for each, and then confirming individuals in their rightful categories. Colors were not "pure" and cultures were not equivalent to races. The cultures of whites were diverse (and much Afrikaner culture was essentially African, as far as many nineteenth- and early-twentieth-century English-speakers were concerned), and racialization was motivated by cultural differences among whites. The community of whites, rather than expressing an established racial community, was forged from diverse ethno-cultures.

Third, whites disagreed about genuine and serious issues, especially ethno-cultural ones. But they agreed on the central premise of white politics. Whites could contest the specific terms of white supremacy, could debate the merits of trusteeship versus *baaskap* (brutish mastery) and segregation versus apartheid, and, later, "reform" apartheid versus "grand" apartheid. But white politics was conducted on the basis of and contained by the assumption that blacks were to be disenfranchised and subordinated politically. As David Yudelman explains, "The position of large numbers of black laborers in South African society and their elimination as political actors or even as a contested political issue among whites is absolutely vital. The entire relationship of the state, capital, and organized white labor was wholly based on the premise that blacks were not a politically contested issue."[34] Deborah Posel makes the same point: "All members of the [Afrikaner nationalist] alliance agreed that white political supremacy depended upon the political exclusion of Africans from the white polity. Africans were to exercise political rights in their 'true' spiritual 'home' in the reserves (irrespective of whether or not they in fact resided there)."[35] Thus, custom, law, and political reality forbade whites from appealing to blacks for support against rival whites. Blacks were political objects, and seeking support from them on specific issues would have made them subjects, undercutting the foundation of white interests and identities and weakening the bonds of white unity to boot.

Fourth, business was not happy about subsidizing the costs of racial privilege. But because the political economy was grounded in access to state power and the state was grounded in race, business recognized the imperative of maintaining the racial state. And because blacks were disenfranchised, whites could load the costs of the bargains among themselves onto blacks. "The strategic and ideological imperatives for a white coalition . . . set the terms of official racial domination."[36]

Fifth, white supremacy racialized subordination. Rather than being identified in terms of subjugation, blacks were defined as "Natives," "Bantus," "Africans" (or "Asians" or "Coloureds"), or "blacks." Perversely, organizing domination by race raised the incentive to disenfranchise and disempower blacks. When whites had governed themselves through ethno-cultural particularity, they let the sleeping dog of African solidarity lay. But when apartheid made race politically sovereign, when it subjected blacks to a common racist order and refused citizenship to Africans on racialist principles, apartheid broke the back of tribal communities, amalgamated disparate tribes through common experiences of racism, and invited blacks to organize resistance on the basis of racial identities. Apartheid, having made blacks into a general threat, completed the circle by negating the negation. They particularized Africans tribally, through separate development.

Finally, associating poverty and deprivation with noncitizenship both established the basis of groupness for Africans, Coloureds, and Asians and suggested an obvious solution. If blacks were stripped of land, subjugated, and humiliated because they were denied citizenship, they would seek citizenship. Accordingly, the foremost demand of most black political movements, notably the African National Congress (ANC), was for "nonracial," universal citizenship, in which political rights and citizenship would be allocated without reference to race.

Demanding the universal franchise in the context of apartheid had the paradoxical effect, however, of fusing racial-national and democratic demands. Racial-national interests demanded democracy and democracy appealed to racial-national solidarities. But fusing the national and democratic demands introduced a new risk. After the demise of apartheid, the state might be de-racialized formally without being democratized actually.

5

The Power Politics of the Transition to Democracy

> [The bourgeoisie] compels all nations, on pain of extinction, to adopt the bourgeois mode of production; it compels them to introduce what it calls civilizations into their midst, i.e., to become bourgeois themselves. In a word, it creates a world after its own image.
>
> — KARL MARX AND FREDERICK ENGELS

Citizenship, the predicate of the racial identities and class interests of whites, forged whites into a club. Color identified the club, but citizenship established it. Then grand apartheid converted the aspiration of blacks for citizenship of their own into a demand for revolution. Blacks were forced to defeat the whole political system, merely as a condition of expressing themselves in their own voices. What finally broke the vicious circle, in which blacks were forged into the threat that consolidated white unity, were the increasing political and economic costs of maintaining apartheid being assessed by black resistance. Most forces supporting or opposing apartheid were locked in by the structure of the political economy, but business was in an ambivalent position. As the costs of white supremacy rose and as the risks of democratic capitalism diminished, business reassessed matters.

It had been one thing to defend white supremacy and segregation when most Africans were scattered throughout rural areas and subjected to the control of "traditional" authorities. The African "majority" had not congealed into a real majority because it lacked the common institutions and identities to translate diverse tribes into a single people. But when Africans flowed to cities in search of jobs and excitement and as they became concentrated geographically and indispensable economically, processes that accelerated with World War II, Africans developed the sinews—the racial-national consciousness and the political organization—to convert themselves into a racial majority.[1] Apartheid crystallized in reaction against the potential power of the African proletariat.

The National Party, once elected to government in 1948, pursued ethno-cultural, repressive, and racial objectives. Ethno-culturally, the NP represented Afrikaners;[2] it embodied the Afrikaner, not the "white," nation. The NP favored Afrikaner culture and the Afrikaans language officially; infused legislation and administration with the values and sensibilities of the Dutch Reform Church; built and funded universities for Afrikaners; eventually Afrikanerized the state; and encouraged the economic advancement of Afrikaners. The NP was committed to advantaging Afrikaners twice over, racially and ethno-culturally.

Repressively, the NP expanded the authoritarian powers of the state to deal with the danger that blacks would convert national consciousness and economic indispensability into political power. By the early 1950s, the ANC and other organizations were organizing protests against both particular points of discrimination and the general system of apartheid, causing the National Party government to unloose waves of repressive legislation. In 1960, the ANC and the Pan Africanist Congress (PAC) were banned (the Communist Party had been banned in 1950); the period of detention without bail was increased; whites and blacks were prohibited from participating in political organizations together; newspapers were censored; political organizations were harassed, and so forth.[3]

Racially, the NP preserved, intensified, and justified white supremacy in the face of capital's corrosive pursuit of cheap black labor. Capital generally respected the color bar in employment, reserving better jobs for whites, sparing whites from manual labor, and elevating whites over blacks. But it also paid for the color bar, and its party—the United Party—was preparing to acquiesce to accelerating urbanization of Africans in the late 1940s. The National Party promised to secure white privilege from capitalist subversion.[4]

The NP advanced ethno-cultural nationalism, state repression, and white supremacy. But apartheid was not defined by any of these. Ethno-culturalism was common throughout the world and already had been advanced in South Africa by the Nationalist (as opposed to the National) Party in the 1920s and 1930s; many states were repressive; and white supremacy had been entrenched in the laws and customs of South Africa long before apartheid was thought up. What defined and made grand apartheid truly unique were not its particular elements; it was the theory and practice of *separate development.*

Separate development was not concocted ex nihilo. Its antecedents extended back to the mid-nineteenth century, when Britain developed the methods that came to be known as "indirect rule."[5] British colonialism always had been concerned with minimizing costs while assuring control; and armies, police, bureaucracies, and schools—the standard apparatuses of colonial control—were expensive to maintain, especially for colonies that were regarded as backwaters prior to the discovery of gold in 1886. Seeking control on the cheap, the colonial state recognized—and in some cases bolstered or expanded—the authority of chiefs, who were assigned responsibility for maintaining order in areas under their jurisdiction. Chiefs were secured from challenge from above because Britain needed them to avoid the expense and bother of governing directly and from below because people needed chiefs to avoid the indignity of alien rule. Indirect rule was perpetuated by the apartheid state.

Separate development did not merely rename white supremacy and segregation; it also solidified justifications for both. It did the heavy ideological lifting for apartheid. Taking advantage of the culturalist precept that nations precede and deserve states, it encased African ethno-cultures in pseudo-states. If, according to ethno-culturalism, Africans had their own ethno-cultures, then they deserved their own states; if they had their own states, then they were disqualified from citizenship in South Africa, which represented a different ethno-culture; and if Africans did not have citizenship rights in South Africa, then they were guest workers who had to do the bidding of whites. But the apartheid state did not take ethno-culturalism too literally. If the logic of separate development had been applied consistently, then whites likewise should have been organized ethno-culturally, the same as Africans. One state should have been established for Afrikaners and another for English-speakers. But the apartheid state never contemplated dividing *itself*. The racial logic of white supremacy superseded the ethno-cultural logic of separate development.

Whites exempted themselves from the ethno-cultural logic of separate development for two reasons. First, internal divisions endangered their fundamental interests. Already outnumbered, whites did not want to separate themselves on the basis of ethno-cultural differences. Ethno-cultural tensions did surface in the form of Afrikaner nationalism, but only after blacks had been vanquished and only because the particularistic agendas of white ethno-cultures respected their predicate, white supremacy. Second, the racial unity of whites surpassed the ethno-cultural rivalries of Afrikaners versus English-speakers because the NP answered to *whites* in elections and to *business* in economic policy. Afrikaners controlled the state, in the sense that responsible positions were their preserve, that state policies advanced their sectional interests, and that the NP could pursue parochial advantages. But challenging the essential interests of the English-speaking minority would have threatened both economic stability and white unity (which also was the precondition of achieving the sectional interests of Afrikaners). Politically, Afrikaners were whites first and Afrikaners second, and political imperatives trumped and conditioned ethno-cultural solidarities.

Through the 1960s and early 1970s, apartheid seemed secure. Domestically, the economy was robust, whites were loyal, repression was relentless, and opposition seemed futile.[6] Internationally, the apartheid state was guarded by a belt of sympathetic states, mostly settler colonies (Southwest Africa, Angola, Rhodesia, Mozambique), that buffered it from black-ruled countries farther north. Plus, the Cold War provided the apartheid state with additional layers of protection. South Africa's geographical position at the tip of Africa; its ports and military; its modern economy; and its precious metals made it valuable for the assets that it furnished to the West and denied to the Soviet bloc. Besides, the Soviet bloc backed the ANC-SACP (South African Communist Party) alliance, giving Western governments additional geopolitical reasons for favoring the apartheid state. Even if they harbored moral objections to apartheid, and not all Western governments were moved by them, the dichotomies of the Cold War and the incentives of world capitalism pressured them to engage the apartheid state diplomatically and economically.

In its heyday, then, grand apartheid was supported by a prosperous and growing economy; was imposed by a strong, ruthless, and expanding state; was disorganizing potential opposition by denying blacks the rights of citizenship; was defeating organized opposition via repression and was dominant regionally and recognized internationally; and was unifying whites by converting blacks into their common enemy. But the political economy of apartheid, which rested on disenfranchised black labor, was inherently fragile, because it represented "the systematic attempt to reverse economic integration."[7] It necessarily denied citizenship rights to those who had become indispensable economically and swam against the *zeitgeist* that affirmed democracy and discredited racism. Apartheid, having sowed its own illegitimacy, could not revert to standard strategies of legitimation.

Soweto, the massive African township southwest of Johannesburg, erupted in a revolt in June 1976 that soon spread through much of urban

South Africa. Although the Soweto revolt was repressed easily enough, it was the beginning of the end for apartheid. The revolt was organized poorly, was centered among students and other youth, and had no prospect of overturning the state. Nevertheless, the revolt dashed delusions of apartheid's invincibility, exposed the failure of the state's racial policies, sent apartheid sliding down the slippery slope of "reform," and shattered confidence in the economy. Prices of industrial, commercial, and gold mining shares of stock stagnated through the 1980s,[8] and the currency, which had declined 18 percent against the dollar from 1961 through 1976,[9] was to lose 66 percent of its value from 1976 through the 1980s.[10]

The tone of the official report into the causes of the revolt bespoke the danger. Neither ideological nor dogmatic, it implied apartheid had to be reformed. The report confirmed students planned and organized the original demonstrations, more or less on their own.[11] That is, it did not blame the revolt on outside agitation. The report also confirmed that the direct cause of the disturbances was the imposition of Afrikaans as a mandatory language of instruction in black schools and that the police contributed to the spread of the revolt by overreacting. That is, the report blamed the state for provoking and expanding the rebellion.

The commission traced the revolt to "political" factors,[12] including the homelands policy; influx control; group areas; "discrimination";[13] inadequate housing; disparate salaries; bad transportation; sour relations between the races; weak discipline over the young by parents, teachers, and churches; and, most dangerously, black solidarity. According to the report, "As a cause of rioting, the sense of solidarity was frequently one of involvement with everything symbolised by the name Soweto. And this was Black solidarity. Many of the rioters fully realised that they were thus identifying themselves with the struggle for the Black man's liberation that would come with the overthrow of the existing system of government."[14]

The commission, in other words, insinuated a realist critique of grand apartheid. The imposition of Afrikaans touched off the revolt, but imposing Afrikaans had been inflammatory because blacks already were united in anger. It followed that the state needed both carrots and sticks—what was called "reform apartheid"[15]—to address the crises besetting apartheid.

Notoriously, the apartheid state wielded sticks. It ramped up the repressive capabilities of the army, strengthened intelligence apparatuses, and made itself more responsive to security concerns (Defense Minister P. W. Botha was elevated to Prime Minister and later to State President).

It introduced states of emergency, used torture and conducted state murders, and repressed unwanted political activity. It also responded aggressively to the loss of cordon states in Rhodesia, Angola, and Mozambique with wars, surrogate wars, incursions, assassinations, and destabilization strategies. It invaded Angola, where it fought a prolonged war to overturn the Popular Movement for the Liberation of Angola (MPLA) government; conducted a surrogate war in Mozambique through the Mozambique National Resistance (RENAMO), thoroughly destabilizing the new government; and made incursions, punctuated by assassinations, into Botswana, Lesotho, and Zimbabwe.[16]

But the apartheid state also waved the carrots of reform. It allowed "petty" apartheid—the segregation of restaurants, beaches, park benches, and such—to lapse, partly because it could not be enforced in the face of increasing disobedience and partly because its indignities were not petty. Petty apartheid humiliated blacks and discredited the state, and to no apparent purpose. Most whites could acquire separate facilities "naturally" via market forces because whites were much richer than blacks, which delivered de facto racial segregation without the stigma of de jure controversies. Reform apartheid also sought to make a virtue of necessity by turning black economic advances to its advantage. It acquiesced to trade unions for blacks, expanded property rights and opened the accoutrements of middle-class life to blacks, and abandoned influx control (which was collapsing anyway, due to the impossibility of keeping Africans hemmed in impoverished reserves when urban life beckoned).[17]

Economic reforms were meant to revive growth; rearrange the balance between markets and state in the economy; accede to the demographic necessity that blacks perform more skilled and mental labor, given that whites were shrinking as a proportion of the population;[18] and, most pertinently, muffle the political ambitions of selected blacks. If, the reasoning ran, blacks advanced economically, then they would be diverted from politics. As the Minister of Defense put the point, "The important thing is how many black people are merely interested in satisfying their material demands—housing, education, job opportunities, clothing, bread and butter, etc. There is presently only a limited section that is really interested in political participation. I think for the masses in South Africa democracy is not a relevant factor."[19] Reform apartheid, in other words, reversed the standard strategies of legitimation in democratic capitalism. Instead of using the ideal of political equality to legitimate the fact of economic inequalities, reform apartheid countenanced limited moves toward economic opportunity for blacks in hope of safeguarding what the state embodied and ultimately prized—limited enfranchisement.

Conceding economic rights to blacks was designed to provide labor to business and deflect the ambition of blacks away from politics; it also was meant to engineer divisions between blacks who did and did not benefit from broadening economic opportunities.[20] The idea was that those who benefited from dismantling obstacles would be demobilized as enemies, and maybe even be enlisted as supporters of the system. Blacks in the formal economy—the skilled and new working classes and expanding middle classes—were to be threatened by revolutionary political demands issuing from outsiders.

The logic of dividing opponents and fortifying insiders was made explicit in the centerpiece of reform apartheid, the tri-cameral parliament. Previously, parliament had been the exclusive preserve of whites, restricted to white representatives elected by white voters. Subsequently, parliament was expanded to include three segregated houses, with Coloureds and Indians gaining representation in houses of their own. The house reserved for whites retained real sovereignty, but establishing houses for Coloureds and Indians was supposed to admit the legitimacy of Coloured and Indian political aspirations and to give them responsibility for their "own" affairs (such as schools). Thus, the tri-cameral parliament respected the principle of separate development and recognized demography insofar as it organized, segregated, and stratified representation racially and defended the reality of white supremacy insofar as it reserved effective power for whites. But reform apartheid departed from separate development insofar as it intimated that South Africa was a multiracial mosaic made up of different races and ethno-cultures, not a white society whose black residents were mere sojourners of suspect legal status. Reform apartheid preserved racialism—race remained the axis of political participation—but dampened overt racism.

Finally, reform apartheid pretended to allow some political voice for Africans. It preserved, subsidized, and controlled homeland governments, in keeping with grand apartheid and the tradition of divide and rule, and went on to concede representation in some South African political institutions to Africans. They were named to the President's Council, an advisory panel appointed by the president, and were granted the right to elect councilors to township governments. But in both instances whites decided how blacks were to be represented and how much power they were to be accorded. In an echo of indirect rule, blacks could be allowed a modicum of self-government, provided their leaders answered to whites; but they could not be allowed control over whites. Reform apartheid, therefore, could not address the central demand of black politics, could not succeed in its objective of bringing stability, and could not reassure business.

Usually, capitalist societies invoke equality in the state and under the law to promote stability, to narrow, depoliticize, and institutionalize complaints as far as possible, particularizing them, making them the responsibility of individuals, and, to the extent that the state is involved, adjudicating grievances in its institutions. The apartheid state, on the other hand, generated grievances of all kinds and sizes, and then deprived blacks of the right to try to better things politically. Apartheid not only refused blacks the standing to make government accountable to them, but also created whole categories of noncitizens on the basis of common grievances. Blacks were "black" because they were denied political status due to their color, thwarting standard strategies of capitalist legitimation. It was difficult to make blacks feel personally responsible for suffering that the state had inflicted on them by virtue of their race. Apartheid, in other words, made both state and business, the very political economy, illegitimate, more or less by deliberate design.

It was bad enough for business that apartheid engendered grievances gratuitously, that blacks were antagonized for reasons that brought no advantages to business. But preventing blacks from redressing grievances through legitimate political institutions left them two obvious options. Either blacks endured resentfully, as they had done before the Soweto revolt, or they inflated particular issues into general indictments of the political order, to the detriment of capital. And after forcing blacks to elevate even intrinsically minor grievances into revolutionary demands, apartheid compounded the problem by discrediting capitalism too.

Apartheid, in mandating formal inequality between whites and blacks as the principle of citizenship, prevented capital from legitimating itself through the ideal of equal opportunity. To the extent people are deemed to be equals "before" they enter into economic arrangements, economic inequalities can be attributed to degrees of hard work and pluck. But rather than promoting institutions that depoliticized property, that made property appear as a *private* relationship beyond the purview of politics and the state, apartheid—whether grand or reform—tied wealth to race, highlighting the arbitrariness and unfairness of economic inequalities.

Then, having created an ongoing and irreconcilable legitimation crisis, apartheid afflicted business with a deteriorating economy.

As robust economic growth in the 1960s and early 1970s had assuaged many of the reservations business harbored about apartheid, so the political crises and economic contraction in the 1980s deepened doubts. Certainly, business did not join the antiapartheid movement. It feared politically disenfranchised blacks, but feared politically enfranchised ones too, especially in view of the radical rhetoric of young black activists and the SACP, which stood behind both the ANC and the fledging black trade union movement. Fearing both black disenfranchisement and black enfranchisement, business contemplated the advantages of democratic capitalism as an alternative to social revolution. But until credible black leaders embraced capitalism, business could not do much more politically than signal its willingness to deal.

Business did more economically. It responded to dismal prospects by slashing investment, which worsened the economy and deepened the political crisis. In response to chronic inflation, high interest rates, deepening government debt, prolonged and severe recession, and low profits, capital effectively went on strike in the mid-1980s. Annual investment in South Africa averaged 27.5 percent of GDP from 1981 to 1983; the average for developing countries was 21.9 percent for those years. By 1991–1993, annual investment averaged 16.5 percent of the (shrinking) GDP, in comparison with 19.9 percent for developing economies.[21] The rate of private investment as a percentage as of South Africa's GDP declined by 28 percent from 1981–1983 through 1991–1993, and public investment as a percentage of GDP declined by 57 percent. By comparison, private investment in developing economies increased by about 2.4 percent during the period, whereas public investment declined by 23.6 percent. Private and public investment together shrank as a percentage of GDP in South Africa by 40 percent from 1981–1983 to 1991–1993; it shrank by 9 percent in developing countries over this span. Meanwhile, foreigners also were disinvesting from South Africa. As Stephen Lewis notes, the "net *flow* of new foreign investment has been of declining importance" as foreign investors bought established financial assets rather than making investments that produced new wealth. From the 1960s through the 1980s, "South Africa . . . financed virtually all of its growth from domestic investment."[22]

Apartheid did not cause all of the economy's ills.[23] Some of them derived from dependence on commodities (like gold) at a time when the price of commodities (gold particularly) was plummeting, and some derived from the exhaustion of import-substitution as a mode of economic development.[24] But apartheid was responsible for major economic problems, such as spreading international boycotts and the collapse of the state's credit rating in 1985, and it was responsible for the political crisis.

As the political and economic costs of apartheid were mounting, the interests of capital, including Afrikaner capital, were evolving, becoming separable from state power. When the National Party took over the state in 1948, Afrikaner businesses struggled to compete with bigger English-speaking businesses. But after thirty years, Afrikaner and English-speaking elites alike had acquired the capital and developed the professional expertise to wean themselves from direct dependence on state power. Afrikaner elites still benefited from state largess, of course, but they did not require the white monopoly on political power. Their politics was becoming pragmatic, open to political compromises, as long as economic elites retained enough influence to get what they really needed and to ward off what they really opposed. And as the benefits of white supremacy were shrinking, the mixture that white supremacy had brewed was fermenting.

Black labor had predominated at the lower rungs of production from the earliest days of the Cape Colony; by the 1980s, it was becoming essential at middle rungs too, due to the force of demographics. Whites, a steadily shrinking proportion of the population, were too small a proportion of the population to continue staffing all responsible economic positions, leading business to look to the growing black majority to fill "white" jobs. Yet the incipient black middle classes, even though they were becoming indispensable economically, were snubbed pointlessly (from the perspective of capital), a reckless provocation given the legendary sensitivity of new middle classes to slights to their prestige. By design, apartheid had managed to engineer half of what V. I. Lenin had developed the Communist Party to accomplish.

Lenin designed the Communist Party to bring "closer and [merge] into a single whole the elemental destructive forces of the masses and the conscious destructive force of the organization of revolutionaries."[25] In Lenin's formula for revolution, the revolutionary middle classes—the intelligentsia—provide the strategic vision and organizational skills; the working classes supply the muscle, fire, and numbers. The challenge for Lenin was to find ways to bring the proletariat's preference for mundane economistic reforms—higher pay, shorter hours, unions—together with the revolutionary ambitions of the intelligentsia. Yet through deliberate policy, apartheid had done Lenin's work, achieving exactly what it should have avoided at all costs. It fused different, and potentially rival, classes behind the demand for revolutionary change. But with one difference:

apartheid had created abundant destructive energy, but obstructed the attempts of blacks to organize themselves socially and politically.

In a classic conservative thesis, Samuel P. Huntington identified political institutions as the bulwark against the ever-present threat of disorder.[26] Order for Huntington is not given; it must be achieved, and it is especially precarious when people leave villages and flow to cities, when they are removed from institutions (like chiefs) that had restrained and ordered them and began issuing political demands in their own name. New actors are born and new demands are made. Unable to process and accommodate undeniable social forces, old institutions are overwhelmed, order breaks down, chaos reigns.[27]

Through the 1980s, reform apartheid was enforced by military, intelligence, and police apparatuses, endorsed by a substantial majority of the white electorate, recognized as legitimate by the leading capitalist countries, and sustained by a functioning, albeit faltering, economy. But being congenitally incapable of seeking consent from blacks, apartheid could not contrive institutional solutions to demands that were mounting against it. Actualizing Huntington's nightmare, the demands for political participation, for citizenship, could not be contained, moderated, and channeled in institutions. Institutions for Huntington are supposed to temper demands; in South Africa they became bones of contestation themselves.

The reform apartheid state prided itself for being a stalwart of the world anticommunist mainstream and did receive quiet sympathy from conservatives in Europe and North America. Yet the routine of apartheid subverted the supreme value of conservatives: order. Liberals do not take the establishment and preservation of order particularly seriously, preferring to assume it away as natural and given or as the by-product of society and the market. Conservatives, on the other hand, take order seriously, problematizing it. Order is something that must be made but also must be softened, preferably by embedding it in hierarchies of affect. "To be attached to the subdivision," wrote Edmund Burke, "to love the little platoon we belong to in society, is the first principle (the germ as it were) of public affections. It is the first link in the series by which we proceed towards a love to our country and to mankind."[28] The little platoon most favored by conservatives, the bedrock of society and the school where reverence is learned, is the family. Apartheid attacked African families.

If black labor were to be prevented from organizing and achieving market wages through migrant labor, the family had to be hollowed out. Husbands were separated from wives and fathers from children not as inadvertent by-products of racial capitalism. They were part and parcel of the system that off-loaded costs of reproducing future generations onto reserves and demanded that South Africa be "kept" white. With the exception of those with "section 10" rights, who could live in cities legally, and those with work permits, African men struggled to stay in cities and many African women were consigned expressly to reserves, where they were to rear children. In turn, men working in cities often abandoned their rural families for city women, where chronic housing shortages often forced women to enter abusive and exploitative relationships with men whose jobs provided them with beds in hostels.[29] Even when marriages survived strains of separation and temptation, poor families were burdened by the additional expense of maintaining dual households that were far apart.

The apartheid state humiliated as well as divided African families, as illustrated by an account of a typical police raid one night in the township of Alexandra in Johannesburg in the 1960s. Searching for Africans who were residing in white South Africa illegally, the police caught one particular family unprepared. Mark Mathabane, at the time a young boy, stalled in opening the door to allow his parents time to hide. Then the police barged in, shaking him and shouting questions at him, demanding to know where his parents were hiding. The boy claimed not to know, so the police broke into the bedroom and found the father hiding under the bed. Crawling from his hiding place, the father was stood "naked and head bowed, in the middle of the bedroom."[30] He lied about his wife's whereabouts, saying she was at work. Then the police inspected his passbook, which was not in order.

> My father became speechless. He parted his parched lips and tried to say something, but no sound came. He lowered his bony head and buried it in the palms of his gnarled hands; and at that moment he seemed to age a thousand years, a pitiful sight. The policeman playfully prodded my father's penis with a truncheon. I gasped with horror. . . . The other policeman meantime was still at the doorjamb, revelling at the sight of my father being humiliated. The emotional and physical nakedness of my father somehow made me see him in a different light—he seemed a stranger, a total alien.[31]

One policeman demanded a bribe; but the father did not have the money to pay it and was taken away to do two months hard labor on a "white man's potato farm."[32] Meanwhile, the mother was nowhere to be found. After the police left, the mother called from her hiding place, a wardrobe too small to have been inspected by the police. "My mother, clad only in her underwear, wriggled out from the tiny compartment where clothes would have been hanging, had we had any worth hanging. . . . Afterward she went about the task of restoring a semblance of order to the mess the police had created."[33]

A few years later, the story continues, the father was thrown in jail for a year for the crime of being unemployed in a white area, and the family's poverty deepened.

> My father's long imprisonment began to wreak daily nightmares on everybody in the house. Without income we could no longer afford the rent for our dingy shack. . . . Gradually, my father's absence began to change my mother's personality. She grew irritable and short-tempered, and any slight provocation made her explode in anger. She spent many an afternoon staring blankly through the window while singing songs of sorrow to herself, as though she were going mad or something. She began to drink heavily.[34]

When the father was released from prison, "he was so changed that I hardly knew him."[35] He did not find work, gambled heavily, lost, drank to forget his losses, and fought with his son, with whom he had a thoroughly rancid relationship.

The police, in this story, were oppressive and corrupt; the mother was humiliated, the father emasculated, and parental authority discredited; the father was tossed into prison, which broke him and nearly broke the mother—and these were predictable, inevitable, even intentional, outcomes of official policy. Apartheid, in other words, routinely subverted institutions that that knit society together, routinely sowed disorder, and routinely attacked the self-organization of black society, disrupting the development of informal authorities, of settled communities, of affective ties. Africans, who did not avoid detection in raids, routinely were relocated; over 3.5 million Africans were forcibly removed over the years.[36] Forced removals were meant partly to keep South Africa white, partly to keep labor cheap and rightless, and partly to keep blacks subordinate and disorganized. The weaker the black communities, by the logic of white supremacy, the weaker the challenge they could mount to apartheid. As a system of social (dis)organization, apartheid tried to preempt the evolution of black institutions; as a system of repression, it targeted institutions that developed anyway. But apartheid dug its own grave. Ultimately, apartheid was forced to capitulate by the costs of disorder.

* * *

The ANC often is pictured as orchestrating the movement against apartheid in the 1980s, as controlling events on the ground either directly or indirectly through its front, the United Democratic Front (UDF). By this account, the ANC called for "ungovernability" and South Africa became ungovernable. But this version of events, while serving the purposes of the apartheid state in the 1980s and the ANC since then, is misleading, and not only because it overlooks the contribution of Inkatha (the party associated with Zulu chiefs) and Black Consciousness (BC) to the antiapartheid movement. The ANC did call for the townships to become ungovernable and the townships were ungovernable, but they were ungovernable before and for reasons independent of the ANC's calls. The ANC called for ungovernability in April 1985;[37] the township rebellion broke out in August 1984.

Discontent, which simmered after the Soweto rebellion was suppressed, erupted at the same time as elections to the tri-cameral parliament were being staged. Designed to legitimate racialist representation and to divide blacks along racial lines, with segregated houses for Coloureds and Indians as well as for whites, the tri-cameral parliament backfired on both counts. First, the UDF's call for boycotts of the election was successful; only 18 percent of eligible Coloureds and 12 percent of eligible Indians voted.[38] Second, the elections furnished the occasion for unifying blacks against apartheid, for overcoming the very divisions that the tri-cameral parliament was meant to institutionalize.

African townships in the Pretoria-Witwatersrand-Vereeniging region, the heartland of South Africa, burst into protest and violence days after the boycotted election. Although influenced by the UDF, black resistance "emanated from below, as communities responded to their abysmal urban living conditions."[39] Fueled by economistic demands ("education, rents, housing, township development, evictions, corrupt or unaccountable councillors and repression"),[40] the revolt "swelled up in African townships, swept through schools, and drew in the emerging independent labour movement."[41]

The challenges to political and economic conditions were articulated by the UDF, a front made up of local organizations and "with striking exceptions" were led "by a relatively highly educated, upwardly mobile, petty bourgeoisie."[42] But the township revolt was made by workers, the unemployed, and, especially, the youth. The UDF's "direct role in the initial stages of the township revolt was limited";[43] its "contribution to the revolt was more indirect than direct";[44] and soon its national leadership was "decimated" by arrests.[45] The UDF did not really inspire or lead the revolt, but it did furnish "a broad organisational framework and a symbolic coherence to resistance,"[46] and, most importantly, general political demands. Mark Swilling notes that "the black communities [were] drawn into a movement predicated on the notion that the transfer of political power to the representatives of the majority is a precondition for the realisation of basic economic demands such as decent shelter, cheap transport, proper health care, adequate education, the right to occupy land and the right to a decent and steady income."[47]

Tellingly, the UDF did not articulate symbols and demands of its own. As Jeremy Seekings describes,

> The symbolism of resistance was that of the exiled ANC; the UDF was sometimes incorporated as a symbol in this, but as a subordinate symbol. Thus songs exhorted the ANC, not the UDF; chants praised the armed struggle, not non-violent strategies; and the flags draped over the coffins at political rallies were in the colours of the ANC, not the UDF. Indeed, on the street few people identified themselves as, first and foremost, UDF supporters or members. This was in part the choice of the UDF itself. The UDF never saw its role as challenging the ANC. At a symbolic level, the UDF sought to provide the space for the proliferation of ANC imagery and discourses, for the strengthening of loyalties to the ANC rather than the UDF. In this sense, the UDF was indeed a "front" for the ANC.[48]

The UDF was an intermediary between the popular revolt in the townships and the ANC, but an unusual one. Although almost all UDF leaders identified with or belonged to the ANC, the ANC in exile encouraged but did not command the establishment of the UDF and did not communicate reliably with the UDF.[49] "The ANC simply did not have the capacity to provide detailed direction and co-ordination for political initiatives inside the country."[50] The ANC hinted at much the same point, that its control over its mass base was uncertain and that the semi-autonomous populist organizations were implicit rivals. As the ANC conceded in 1985,

> Without . . . a strong revolutionary organisation, we cannot take advantage of the uprisings. . . . What is missing is a strong underground ANC presence as well as a large contingent of units of Umkhonto we Sizwe. . . . The scope, spread, and intensity of our struggle have also thrown up a large leadership corps of our democratic movement. It is important that we pay close and continuous attention to

> the issue of maintaining close relations with these leaders, educate the masses of our people to understand and accept our own positions, and at all times ensure that we are, as a movement, providing leadership on all major questions, in accordance with our position as the vanguard movement of our struggling people.[51]

The ANC did not control the UDF and the UDF did not control the popular revolt. The insurrection was beyond the control of any organization.

The township revolt drew its objectives from the ANC, but learned some of its methods from Black Consciousness. Through the process of "consciencization," the BC sensibility sought to make ordinary social relations controversial, to show that they were not destined, immutable, and given but were subject to change, to being unmade, and that the institutions and forms of daily life were political. Conflicts over specific issues—housing, land, trade unions, student rights, sports—differed in their particulars, but under the ideological influence of BC they were used to politicize what had been taken for granted, to highlight power relationships that were embedded in daily life, to overcome the passivity that had been implanted by the putative superiority of whites, and to destroy the routines of normality by converting them into sites of struggle. By revealing the power politics of "private" relationships, "conscientizing" demonstrated to blacks that society had been constructed and promised that it could be reconstructed; it showed that blacks were not helpless. William Finnegan explains that

> "conscientization" involved helping people to overcome their fear of the authorities. The "socialization of courage," someone had called it. . . . [Y]ou could almost see it being nurtured and developed . . . [in] rallies and songfests and discussions, in . . . ceaseless talk about "sacrifice." . . . [T]he . . . slogans and catch phrases . . . were the signs and symbols and passwords of a subculture that was flourishing in the boycott atmosphere. It was really more a culture than a movement, because it had no apparent connection to a formal political organization. It was a very potent formation, nonetheless. It was the subculture of revolution.[52]

Synthesizing the methods of BC and the strategies of the ANC, the township revolt "attacked all the visible signs and symbols of the state,"[53] aiming to sweep the state, its agents and its clients from townships. Black councilors, who had been elected under the auspices of reform apartheid, were assaulted physically, burned out of their homes, and sometimes killed; street committees seized responsibility for enforcing revolutionary "justice" and "virtue"; and rival—and shifting—factions of activists competed for control over the institutions of "people's power." Often, the "comrades"—the unemployed, school-boycotting, activist youth—took effective control of townships. They declared boycotts and demanded compliance with their calls and declarations.

> Some people who violated the consumer boycotts were "necklaced" [that is, their hands were tied, a tire that had been drenched in gasoline was hanged around their neck, and they were set afire] or they were forced to eat their purchases—including soap and drain cleaner, which produced severe distress and sometimes death. Young "comrades" would go to the bus stations in the evenings and smell the breath of workers coming home for signs of alcohol. Those who had been drinking were given "Omo treatment," named after a foaming detergent that was forced down their throats until they vomited. Women with permed hair had their heads shaved as a punishment for trying to look bourgeois and Westernized.[54]

Most protests were not violent (the large funerals usually were models of nonviolent discipline), police provoked much of the violence that did occur, and civil society was active and robust. But expelling state power from townships also cleared room for the spontaneous expression of the society that apartheid had disorganized systematically.

The apartheid state lashed out at the ANC and the UDF anyway, further disorganizing opposition. The UDF fell into "considerable disarray"[55] within a year of its formation and the ANC assessed the revolt in terms of its overriding objective, guerrilla war. The ANC "remained committed to . . . the armed seizure of state power, and saw the building of people's power inside the country primarily in terms of political support bases for MK [the armed wing of the ANC and the SACP] and a people's war."[56] That is, the ANC was concentrating on the armed struggle that it eventually would launch from neighboring states and later would extend into South Africa itself, and it was underestimating the township revolt, which was fighting the apartheid state to a standstill.

The apartheid state could not defeat the township revolt, but the township revolt could not defeat the state either. State repression, according to Seekings, "revealed the UDF's lack of a viable strategy for effecting political change. The promise of people's power could not survive intensified repression. And whilst the UDF turned to the ANC for strategic direction, the ANC itself had no convincing answer. Certainly, rebuilding organisation, strengthening alliances, mobilising among white elites—all of these might help, but none could break the stalemate between anti-apartheid groups and the apartheid state."[57]

The cohesion of the state, the strength of the military, the opposition of business to social revolution, and the unity of whites in the face of perceived anarchy prevented the antiapartheid movement from winning. But the inability of the apartheid state to channel black demands into legitimate political institutions likewise prevented the state from winning. Stalemate allowed whites to keep milking the state, but business counted on the state to reduce disorder, not to sow it.

Whites were insulated from many consequences of township disorganization—violence, crime, alcoholism, suicide—by virtue of segregation. But ongoing turmoil—strikes, the deteriorating economy, the crisis in legitimacy, and general disorder[58]—took a steady toll on business, the weakest link in apartheid's coalition. The power politics of reform apartheid, as it was unfolding, was that white supremacy could not survive without capitalism; capitalism could not survive without blacks; and blacks could not abide by white supremacy. But blacks and capitalism might become partners.

Apartheid could not solve the crisis. It engendered vast grievances, preempted legitimate political institutions, and fueled talk of social revolution. But social revolution, although demanded by "comrades" and feared by conservatives, was not in the cards. The more likely prospect was political and social disintegration,[59] and the only viable alternative was a negotiated transition to democratic capitalism, as capital (and soon the SACP too) recognized. Gavin Relly, then chairman of the Anglo American Corporation, South Africa's dominant conglomerate, publicly floated terms for a new political dispensation in the mid-1980s. Conceding that the transition from apartheid was "inevitable," chastising whites for making the trauma "messier and more protracted,"[60] and deploring the divisions being sown among blacks in the futile attempt to cling to a system that was doomed to fail, Relly called for negotiations with ANC leaders on a new political order. Equality of opportunity had to be extended, universal citizenship had to be established, and the "complexion" of business had to be changed through affirmative action.[61] Political leaders would negotiate the specific terms of a "democratic South Africa," with business mediating among them,[62] but Relly was sketching the contours of the new order: a capitalist democracy governed by representative—that is, black—elites. But negotiations require negotiators speaking on behalf of real political forces; the only bet for controlling the township insurrection was the ANC.

The ANC fanned revolutionary expectations from the moment it and the SACP established an armed wing—Umkhonto we Sizwe (MK), "Spear of the Nation"—in 1961 until public negotiations on the new constitutional order commenced in the early 1990s. The content of the ANC's actual demands was ambiguous and contradictory, ranging from calls for democratic nationalism to calls for revolutionary socialism, but it sounded radical. The ANC did criticize capitalism, but its criticism did not guide its actual strategies and tactics. The ANC spoke of the "urban working class as the leading force in the struggle"[63] and hoped the black working class would embrace MK, but it concentrated on fighting the state militarily.

MK was in an awkward predicament. It spoke of a "people's war," which it had little chance of winning (or even waging), and hoped the mass struggle, which was rocking apartheid to its foundation, would provide support for it. MK planned for guerrilla war inside South Africa, along the lines of Cuba, but the bulk of MK's forces remained stationed in Angola, far from South Africa. As a result, "there was to be no People's War in the sense that the High Command [of MK] had conceived of it."[64] That is, from the time it was banned in 1960 until it was unbanned in 1990, the ANC was committed to a strategy that yielded no appreciable military benefits, no territory gained and no victories won, not even substantial engagements (the Cubans in Angola were a different matter altogether). MK never beat, or even fought, the South African army in a major battle (although Angola and Cuba did) and never sustained the people's war in South Africa. It was militarily ineffectual. Because privileging MK crowded out alternative strategies for fighting apartheid, the opportunity costs of armed struggle might have been crippling, diverting the ANC from the decisive task of organizing on the ground in South Africa. Yet when the time for negotiations arrived and the township revolt needed representing, the ANC ironically was not compromised by the failure of its military strategy. Rather, it was legitimated because it waged—or meant to wage—armed struggle. The armed struggle, in other words, served an unanticipated purpose; in establishing the ANC's revolutionary bona fides, it positioned the ANC to negotiate on behalf of a township rebellion that had originated independently of the ANC.

The trade unions were the only plausible alternative to the ANC in negotiating the transition to democracy. Composed mostly of blacks who had been excluded from segregated white unions, the non-racial unions began developing in the 1970s in response to rapid economic growth of the 1960s, vast workplace grievances, and apartheid. At the beginning, important tendencies in the new movement feared that the national-political struggle would divert energy from class struggle. But the political orientation prevailed, abetted by the racial oppression suffered by workers outside the workplace and the resulting incentive for workers to turn their workplaces into sites of political struggle. "Workerists" had a hard time arguing for the supremacy of economic over political struggle when African workers faced repression and deportation to homelands due to their political rightlessness and when the political rightlessness of labor weighed in favor of capital in the class struggle.[65]

The political unions gathered into the Congress of South African Trade Unions (COSATU) in the 1980s, a labor federation that challenged apartheid directly by agitating, demonstrating, and organizing, and indirectly by allying with organizations that were devoted to overthrowing apartheid. Black unions won recognition, increased wages, radicalized black workers, and connected the struggle in the townships to the workplace, thus countering apartheid's plans for splitting the economic demands of black "insiders" from general political demands. Using strikes to press for both political and economic demands, non-racial unions struck at the heart of the bargain between business and enfranchised whites, altering the macro politics of apartheid and raising wages to boot. Reform apartheid had conceded the inevitable and allowed black workers to partake of some prosperity in the hope of quelling their political demands. But the strategy backfired, in large part because non-racial unions attacked apartheid, changed the cost-benefit calculations of business, spread the lessons that had been learned in organizing workers in the face of the hostility of state and business, and worked with the UDF. COSATU contributed substantial organization, guidance, and maturity to the rebellion, and might have pitched a challenge for leadership of the anti-apartheid movement as a whole. Instead, COSATU saw itself as representing the working class, not the nation, and recognized the leading role of the ANC. It provided organization, leadership, and a mass base.

But COSATU did not press for supremacy, leaving the way clear for the ANC.

The ANC's leadership of the township rebellion was secured by the recognition of COSATU, civil society, and the comrades, but that raises a prior question: why did they recognize the ANC in the first place? Part of the answer is Nelson Mandela, who had unrivalled prestige along with immense ability as a leader. As the imprisoned leader of the ANC, "the most famous political prisoner in the world" personified the oppression of blacks (who likewise were imprisoned in their homeland). Moreover, Mandela was imprisoned as a senior leader of MK and the ANC, the oldest liberation organization in Africa, for resisting apartheid. Whereas the ANC's rivals (the Pan African Congress and the Black Consciousness Movement) were unable to develop and sustain themselves organizationally, the ANC had a long history of organized opposition to white supremacy, having been founded in 1912. With its stature ratified by township activists, the ANC did not have to wrestle control from the internal movement; it was conferred voluntarily. Finally, the process of negotiating a transition prescribed some organization—and the ANC had the strongest claim—to serve as the authoritative representative of the township rebellion: the state, business, and the situation required it.

Apartheid, in disorganizing black society, put a premium on organization. Dialectically, the very disorganization that forced the state and business to resort to negotiations also enhanced the value of any authoritative organization. Negotiations were necessitated by the lack of political authority, yet negotiations could succeed only through the efforts of organization that could represent and compromise in the name of the disenfranchised. To produce orderly government, negotiations needed to agree on the new constitutional framework. But negotiations also needed both to legitimate and to moderate the organization that was to lead the move from the old order and to preside over the new order: the ANC.

As the era of reform apartheid coincided with the government of P. W. Botha, the transition to democracy coincided with the presidency of F. W. de Klerk, who deposed Botha in 1989. De Klerk rose from the conservative wing of the NP, but accepted the realpolitik of a point Mandela had made in a letter to P. W. Botha in 1989. "Majority rule and internal peace," wrote Mandela, "are like the two sides of a single coin, and white South Africa simply has to accept that there will never be peace and stability in this country until the principle is fully applied."[66] Accepting that apartheid was untenable and that a negotiated tradition to a new constitutional order was the sole alternative to chaos, de Klerk calculated that his advantages—control of the state, support from business and most capitalist democracies on condition that he negotiated, and an insurmountable military position—rewarded negotiating the transition from apartheid sooner rather than later.

Negotiated transitions from authoritarian to democratic governments are the subject of a large literature, highlighted by the work of Guillermo O'Donnell and Philippe Schmitter. Based on transitions in Latin America and southern Europe, O'Donnell and Schmitter advanced an interpretation that can be boiled down to five essential propositions. First, most transitions are initiated *inadvertently* by "soft-line" authoritarians. Seeking to buttress the regime's legitimacy, soft-liners take steps to regularize procedures, follow law, and redefine and extend rights.[67] They make government less arbitrary and more liberal, but they do not democratize. Soft-liners neither apply "the rules and procedures of citizenship . . . to political institutions previously governed by other principles" nor "include persons not previously enjoying [the] rights and obligations" of citizenship.[68] But the process slips from their control, mainly because conflicts with hard-liners lure them into further reforms that lower the costs of political activity, unleash mass demands for democracy, and "resurrect" civil society.

Second, the transition throws the "very parameters of political action . . . in flux."[69] It removes decisions from established institutions, where economic power usually prevails, and shifts them to political arenas, which are unpredictable. Political organization, imagination, alliances, programs, leadership, flair—plus luck, contingency, and the unexpected—soar in importance as new actors and new institutions are unloosed. "Structural" factors still count, but are not decisive in the short term,[70] providing democrats respect one absolute condition. The "property rights of the bourgeoisie are inviolable";[71] violating them ends the transition, then and there.

Third, liberalizing authoritarians and emerging democrats develop an alliance. Although pursuing different objectives, each needs the cooperation of the other to control its more doctrinaire flanks. The mixture of dependence and competition is expressed in and contained by "pacts," which set forth "mutual guarantees for the 'vital interests' of those entering into [them],"[72] and they facilitate democracy by exerting conservative influences. Pacts promote democracy "on the installment plan," move "towards democracy by undemocratic means,"[73] and infuse democracy with a conservative socio-economic content. Rather than applying the principle of equality to society, as radicals would have it, democracy becomes a procedure for adjudicating disputes.

Fourth, infighting between hard- and soft-liners opens opportunities for "resurrected" civil society, which propels democracy forward. "Trade unions, grass-roots movements, religious groups, intellectuals, artists, clergymen, defenders of human rights, and professional organizations all support each other's efforts towards democratization and coalesce into a greater whole which identifies itself as 'the people.' "[74] Although the "popular upsurge" is "ephemeral," leaving "many dashed hopes and actors,"[75] it "performs the crucial role of pushing the transition further than it would otherwise have gone. But the disenchantment it leaves behind is a persistent problem for the ensuing consolidation of political democracy."[76]

Fifth, the announcement of elections transforms the politics of the transition, installing political parties at the center of political life and exposing the delusions of the "soft-liners." Soft-liners, overestimating their electoral prospects, made themselves dispensable. They had served their purpose by the time elections inaugurate the democratic government. But it turns out that lasting rules have emerged from the thrown-together, expedient deals that carry forth the transition. Democracy for O'Donnell and Schmitter is a process of resolving, containing, and avoiding problems, and it is learned through the process of the transition itself. Therefore, democracy can be achieved without the "preconditions"—middle classes, for example—that often are deemed necessary to democracy. "[P]olitical democracy is produced by stalemate and dissensus rather than by prior unity and consensus. It emerges from the interdependence of conflictual interests and the diversity of discordant ideals, in a context which encourages strategic interaction among wary and weary actors."[77] Democracy is defined procedurally, not substantively, and the procedures can be learned through the departure from authoritarianism (and if they are not learned, the departure is not completed).

South Africa's transition resembled the pattern described by O'Donnell and Schmitter in matters small and large. The process commenced with, and was thought by the authors of reform apartheid to be limited to, economic liberalization and political co-optation. As if following O'Donnell and Schmitter's script, the hard right (Conservative Party) split from the NP in the early 1980s and soft-liners convinced themselves that domination was divisible, that they could countenance de-racializing economic inequalities and institutionalizing token voices for blacks, providing that they retained political control. When reform apartheid failed to restore order, de Klerk's new broom swept unexpectedly clean. De Klerk ditched the fantasy of fashioning a solution with apartheid's clients (homeland leaders, representatives on the President's Council, municipal officials) and set about negotiating a new dispensation with credible black political organizations. Negotiations advanced via pacts between the NP, the old authoritarian party, and the ANC, the representative of civil society.

Yet de Klerk misjudged the situation, wrongly believing that he and his party would retain a share of power over the state. Democracy prevailed because the democratic forces had developed sharper political skills, because the announcement of elections did transform the situation to the advantage of the ANC, because the ANC had a better chance of securing order,[78] because the bourgeoisie regarded the regime as dispensable once it received proper assurances about the status of property, and because the ANC, in accordance with the conservatizing effects of pacts, recognized property rights as inviolable and embraced neoliberal economic policies. Ultimately, the democratic government outgrew power-sharing pacts with the NP, but in the meantime the ANC internalized the limits of political power, abandoned radicalism, and identified with political order and capitalist prosperity.

Every situation is unique, of course. The pursuit of legitimation, which spurs O'Donnell and Schmitter's soft-liners, was a fool's errand for the party of apartheid. Apartheid could not win, could not even seek ratification from blacks without violating its core precepts. Apartheid could reform techniques and strategies of control, but it could not meet the demand for full and equal citizenship. As a result, the apartheid state, unlike the authoritarian ones studied by O'Donnell and Schmitter, could not threaten to restore "the authoritarian *status quo ante*"[79] once de Klerk released Mandela and legalized the ANC.

The NP, therefore, was doomed in negotiations. Once it consented to broadening participation, it had to scavenge the tradition of white liberals (many of whom were in the process of becoming democrats) for ideas. The NP called for power-sharing, vetoes, and inflated representation for racial minorities. But formal and permanent power-sharing was unacceptable to the ANC, because it would have stripped the ANC of the fruits of victory. Furthermore, power-sharing would have weakened the new government, thus defeating the whole point of the transition (and upsetting authoritarian sensibilities): establishing orderly governance.[80]

The NP was vulnerable because apartheid could not achieve legitimation from Africans. But it was vulnerable also because the general increase in political activity and political consciousness, which normally fills the spaces opened by liberalizing authoritarians, *preceded* and *forced* the transition. In other words, the sequence of liberalization and mass protest in South Africa *reversed* that described by O'Donnell and Schmitter. Reform apartheid, the spate of liberalization (the tri-cameral parliament, the President's Council, stronger black municipal governments, rescinding pass laws, expanding property rights for blacks), was patched together *in response* to the Soweto rebellion in 1976, which itself was precipitated not by relaxing domination but by the snub of imposing of Afrikaans on black schools. Democratization in South Africa, therefore, assumed a distinctive purpose in South Africa. It had to *rein in* the "popular upsurge," to establish the integrity of government itself.

When negotiations began, the ANC was the focal point of most hopes, including conservative ones, that South Africa could become a normal capitalist democracy, that order could be established, routines could be depoliticized, civil society could be superseded, and capitalism could be normalized. But if these hopes—as opposed to those of radical civil society, the mass movements, and the comrades—were to come to fruition, the ANC would have to quit flirting with socialism, adopt the politics that was appropriate to governing a capitalist democracy, develop the skills for governing a modern yet deeply divided society, and eclipse and subordinate civil society. Rather than serving as the symbol of a movement, the ANC would have to become a normal political party, one that recognized the political and economic realities of capitalist democracy, that valued realism, and that accepted pragmatically that its full ambitions were unrealizable.

The ANC's leaders, the state, and business agreed on capitalist democracy as the framework of the new order early in negotiations.[81] The details of the deal had to be worked out and the strength of the competitors had to be tested, but eventually the NP and ANC struck a deal. Starkly put, the NP surrendered its demand for power-sharing government and acceded to conventional democratic (or "majoritarian") political institutions, allowing blacks to use their numbers to take over the government. In exchange, the ANC guaranteed property rights, constitutional government, and civil liberties (which became important to the NP about the time it contemplated giving up state power). Essentially, the apartheid state gave up apartheid, fantasies of power-sharing, and vetoes, and the ANC gave up dreams of socialism.

Negotiations changed the ANC. The very fact that the ANC was negotiating implied it would make concessions, which favored the negotiationist tendencies inside the ANC, and the process of negotiating elevated conciliatory, pragmatic figures over maximalists who imagined defeating the apartheid state through armed struggle. By negotiating the transfer of power and the new constitution, Mandela and the ANC came to resemble a president and government, making and implementing decisions of great import on a national, even international, stage. And as it became the government-in-making, the ANC was elevated over civil society. It spoke for and made deals that bound the township revolt.

Many organs of civil society—COSATU, the "civics" that had superseded municipal governments—disagreed with the power relationships that were evolving. They attributed democracy to *their* militancy, thought that they had won democracy, and believed that they had catapulted the ANC into government. But the methods and terms of the transition—pacts, understandings, developing political skills, respect for property, and the primacy of the bourgeoisie—prevented the ANC from meeting central demands made by civil society (for direct political participation, for redistribution of wealth, for more jobs, for immediate socialism). By the terms of the transition, the ANC had to deny key demands of radical civil society; thereafter, it was a small step for the ANC to begin to see civil society as a rival whose independence had to be curbed.

Civil society instigated and propelled democratization. It was not merely "ephemeral" as in O'Donnell and Schmitter's cases. It was inclined to recognize the ANC as the legitimate government but not to defer to government and continued pressing radical demands. Thus when the ANC entered government in 1994, it came to experience civil society much as conservatives experienced it, as a threat. The "messianic socialism, and millennial expectations of revolutionary change,"[82] which the ANC had considered to be revolutionary, just, and expedient during the struggle against apartheid, became dangerous, irresponsible, and counterproductive once the ANC assumed responsibility for governing. Previously, political and economic transformation had been deemed to be inseparable, two sides of the same coin, each backing the other. Now, the ANC government distinguished between and disjoined the two, separating demands for political transformation, which could be satisfied, from demands for economic transformation, which had to be deferred, in accordance to the conservatizing logic of negotiated transitions.

Some public remarks by ANC leaders illustrate the change. Soon after the 1994 election, Tokyo Sexwale, who was associated with the populist left of the ANC and became the first premier of the most important new provincial government (Gauteng), claimed, "We have never encouraged our supporters to create 'peoples' courts. . . . Our position is that they are illegal and should be disbanded. We will implement proper courts to deal with complaints. . . . There won't be any room for lawlessness."[83] Nelson Mandela's speech at the opening of the South African parliament in February 1995—less than a year after taking office—made a similar point. He called for "raising the levels of discipline and responsible action throughout the society"; cautioned that "the government has extremely limited resources to address the many and urgent needs of our people"; criticized the "culture of entitlement," which "results in some people refusing to meet their obligations such as rent and service payments or engaging in other unacceptable actions such as the forcible occupation of houses"; and emphasized that "the government literally does not have the money to meet the demands that are being advanced." He also cast mass action as a threat to stable government. "Mass action of any kind will not create resources that the government does not have and would only serve to subvert the capacity of government to serve the people." Finally, Mandela warned those attempting "to introduce anarchy into our society": "the small minority in our midst which wears the mask of anarchy will meet its match in the government we lead and the masses of the people who put that government into office."[84]

The observations of Mandela and Sexwale reflected the logic of the transition. The ANC, which *had* championed "people's courts" and mass action to render townships ungovernable, became the government; mass action demanding immediate transformation did usurp the government's powers; and government, even if composed of the ANC, does identify with the state. Consequently, the fusion of social and political demands in the struggle against apartheid began fraying as soon as the ANC, having assumed responsibility for a state upholding interests contrary to populist aspirations, began rebuffing demands for radical and immediate changes in South Africa's political economy.

Consequently, the new democratic government confronted a major problem. It had fed the idea that political and social revolutions were two sides of the same coin and had opened government to wider, more accountable participation, yet the democratic government had to respect the fact of capitalist economic power, which revived the need for racial solidarities. Apartheid discredited official, state-mandated racially organized citizenship, but it had regenerated and not necessarily discredited unofficial, voluntary racialist identities and solidarities. Fortuitously, the ANC had spent the better part of the twentieth century developing and refining the perfect ideology for the task awaiting it, an ideology that at once was principled, reassuring to minorities yet respectful of majority rights, inspiring to the opponents of apartheid, and a guide to post-apartheid South Africa: non-racialism.

6

Non-Racialism as an Ideology

Where you sit determines where you stand.

— OLD ADAGE

Apartheid had sliced and diced South Africans, decreeing they were many peoples, establishing separate institutions for the separate peoples, and fighting the consolidation of one people. It does not follow, of course, that democracy need only restore unity lost, or that communal differences were destined to recede if they had not been exacerbated by apartheid. But apartheid *did* fortify divisions among South Africans, *did* encourage parochial ethnic and racial identities, and *did* resist common identities.

The apartheid state posited racial identities as paramount, defined and classified all people on the basis of them, and arranged society accordingly. Races were deemed integral categories and were declared to impress distinctive essences on their bearers. To avoid the friction caused by the rub of different racial essences, apartheid affected to gather like with like and to insulate like from unlike, to keep separate that which was different. As separate development followed logically, so did the antiapartheid movement's challenge to the fundamental precept in the philosophy and practice of white supremacy, that race is the bedrock of political organization. Under the influence of the ANC, the antiapartheid movement called for and made non-racialism the official ideology of South Africa.

South Africa's democratic constitution identifies "non-racialism" as a "founding value,"[1] which raises an obvious question. What is non-racialism, and what does it mean? One point jumps out; "non-racialism" means a number of things, some developed by the ANC and others not, some consistent with alternate definitions and others not.[2] The term originated in the Cape Colony in the mid- and late-nineteenth century, later was reinterpreted by the Communist Party of South Africa (CPSA, later the South African Communist Party [SACP])[3] in the 1920s and 1930s, and was imported into the ANC, where it was modified, recast, and popularized. Befitting its genealogy, the concept is deeply ambiguous.

As the term implies, non-racialism derives much of its meaning from what it is not, from what it negates. Above all, non-racialism is not "racialism," a term with two more-or-less distinct meanings in South African usage. In the first meaning, it is used, much as Americans use the word "racism," to denote racially motivated bigotry, inequality, and oppression. But in the second meaning, "racialism" is not necessarily coterminus with "racism." The word "racialism" insinuates race as a defining human attribute, a central axis of human society and political organization, a fulcrum of political representation and participation.

If racialism may mean either racism or racially organized political participation, the negation—the "non"—multiplies the possibilities. All "non-racial" politics renounces racism, but if that were all that "non-racialism" means, the term "non-racialism" would be redundant. Non-racialists could call themselves non-racists and be done with it. That this is not the case, that the antiapartheid movement and the new constitutional order cast themselves as "non-racial" as well as antiracist, suggests that non-racialism involves more than antiracism, that they are not identical phenomena. To flesh out the differences between racism and racialism, it is well to begin with the most uncompromising definition of non-racialism, which was developed by Neville Alexander.

The most radical form of non-racialism begins by challenging the existence of race altogether and ends by demonstrating the existence of races socially and politically. Although politically marginal, radical non-racialism exposes the practical and theoretical difficulties in sustaining doctrinaire non-racialism. Elaborated by Neville Alexander, an organic anti-Communist Marxist activist and intellectual, it argues races are pure fictions. They are unreal; moreover, they cannot become real. Alexander writes,

> Ethnic groups do not exist: and since "ethnicity" is an attribute reputedly possessed by "ethnic groups," it follows a *fortiori* that it is . . . an "invention." There is no logical reason whatsoever to argue for the existence of entities called "races" or "ethnic groups" simply from the fact of racial prejudice or ethnic awareness of whatever kind. It is anti-scientific . . . to conclude that because a very large number of people in the world believe in the existence of ghosts and hence behave as though ghosts really do exist . . . [that] therefore a category called ghosts has to be invented. Hundreds and even

> thousands millions of people believe in the existence of an omnipotent god and a large proportion of our planet's day-to-day economic, political and cultural activities are still determined by the reality of this belief and of the needs and actions that flow from it but I have never yet been told that this is sufficient reason for anyone to accept the reality of such a deity.[4]

Communal groups for Alexander are illusions, like ghosts or deities. Alexander's problem is that although it is fallacious to deduce the fact of God from the belief in God, that is not the relevant point politically. It is one thing to deny the validity of beliefs, but it is another to deny the existence of *communities* of believers. Christians and Muslims exist whether or not God exists. By the same token, the category of race may make no sense naturally and biogenetically, yet may make sense socially. If believers in God—or, for that matter, in ghosts—are organized, their communities are real, substantial, and politically relevant. For political purposes, to be perceived *is* to be.

Consequently, Alexander cannot sustain his line of argument. He reluctantly concedes that the racial group *does* exist (it is a "social reality . . . a historical phenomenon that comes into being in the process of political, economic and cultural struggle under the aegis of the leading class in the nation"),[5] but he relegates racial and ethnic consciousness to anachronisms that are to be overcome through struggle for "national liberation." The danger, Alexander has come to imply, is not that groups are fictions: they are historical possibilities—reactionary ones—that can be realized. But they are not inevitabilities. Providing racialism is fought non-racially, new "national" communities can replace old communal ones. Progressives must repudiate racialism lest racial consciousness—and, therefore, races—be made rather than unmade by political organizing.

Alexander's position, in other words, is the polar opposite of culturalist conceptions of nations. Culturalists have awareness of groups attesting to the existence of groups, of groups becoming conscious *of* themselves. Alexander, conversely, implies groups exist only because they are believed to exist and not independently of the belief. Racial groups for Alexander are not entities that become conscious of themselves: they are entities created by consciousness, that is, false consciousness. Consequently, Alexander must explain what creates the belief in groups, must account for the reason why people believe in social formations that lack "scientific" foundation. His answer is that racial groups are dependent variables, epiphenomenal, artifacts of the causal force of "racial capitalism."

Racial capitalism entwined fictional racial "groups" with the imperatives of capitalism. Without capitalism racial groups would not have congealed in the first place, and without artificial racial groups capitalism would not reproduce itself. "A non-racial capitalism," Alexander promised while writing under apartheid, "is impossible in South Africa."[6] Having conceived of South African capitalism as indelibly racial, Alexander not only rejected the SACP's two-stage conception of South Africa's transformation—moving in discrete stages from apartheid to democracy and then to socialism—but also, á la Leon Trotsky, telescopes the repudiation of racialism into the transformation into socialism. As non-racial capitalism is unsustainable, the break from racialism is, perforce, tantamount to the rejection of capitalism. Racialism is the *necessary* corollary of capitalism, without which capitalism cannot reproduce itself. By the same token, Alexander ultimately has racialism serving as a mode of capitalist organization, bending to the imperatives of capitalist development.

If Alexander ultimately reaches the end point of most South African Marxists, with racialism being relegated to an adjunct to capitalism, and if he cannot efface race from South African political discourse, he nonetheless makes a crucial contribution. Trying to deny the integrity of racial groups and warning that racialism insinuates itself into the thought and politics of professed "non-racial" organizations, Alexander ultimately demonstrates the implausibility of conceiving of South African politics without racial groups. Alexander makes a valiant effort but ultimately cannot sustain the most radical version of non-racialism: denying the existence of race runs afoul of basic South African social realities.

Alexander admits as much when he describes racial consciousness as an "invention." It is one thing to say that inventions are not natural, but it is quite another to say that they do not become real. Once invented, inventions do exist. Thus, Alexander establishes one way of defining non-racialism. It means not that racial groups do not exist, but that they *should not* and *need not* exist, that racial consciousness and, therefore, racial groups can be abolished. Races, because made through social practice, can be unmade through systematic and militant counter-racialism. Rigorous non-racialism means that races, even if real, can be made unreal, providing progressive politics undermines racial consciousness. Principled rejection of racialism converts non-racialism from an ideal into social reality.

The term "non-racial" developed to describe the liberalism that developed in the Cape Colony in the mid-nineteenth century (after the treks). Its hallmark, the "non-racial" franchise, was instituted in 1872 and granted votes to African and Coloured males who met "nonracial property qualifications and, after 1892, educational tests."[7] The non-racial franchise was not racially neutral, as intimated by the criteria voters had to meet. The vote was restricted to Westernized blacks, privileging European over indigenous cultures. Whites were not required to satisfy "African" standards; but Africans (and Coloureds) were required to satisfy "European" standards as the condition of participating in political institutions that originated in Europe (state, citizenship, elections). Having established European culture as the norm, Africans voted on condition they escaped their race by becoming like Europeans.

The Cape's non-racial franchise was much more inclusive than those in the two Boer Republics and Natal, where the vote—and, therefore, citizenship—was allocated expressly or effectively on the basis of race. Whites voted; Africans did not. Racialized citizenship, the inclusion of whites and the exclusion of Africans, flowed from the idea that race was tantamount to skin color, essentially physical in nature. The Cape's non-racial franchise, on the other hand, cast race culturally, allowing for a more inclusive conception of citizenship. Citizenship—or, more accurately, partial citizenship, as Africans were forbidden to sit in parliament—was open to men who were deemed to possess the cultural accouterments of Europeans. To qualify for the "non-racial" franchise, to become "non-racial," was to meet European standards, if not necessarily to reject African culture altogether.

The meaning of "non-racial" changed dramatically as Cape liberalism withered in the decades after the unification of South Africa in 1910, as blacks were stripped of the vote in the 1930s (Africans) and 1950s (Coloureds), and as the ANC adopted, propagated, and carried "non-racialism" to its current perch. The ANC did not, alas, substitute one fixed definition of non-racialism for that of Cape liberals.[8] In its hands, the term's meaning became layered, the first being laid in the period between the inception of the ANC in 1912 (then named the South African Native Congress) and the advent of the ANC Youth League in the mid-1940s. At the time, the ANC was neither cohesive organizationally nor coherent ideologically. Challenged from both the right and the left of African politics, with chiefs defending their prerogatives and Communists pushing socialist politics, the ANC's politics occasionally swung to one or the other. But pronounced swings were uncommon; generally the ANC's politics was centered by a few principles and a number of specific struggles. The struggles generally were defensive in nature, protesting the land acts that prohibited Africans from owning land in most of the country, the pass laws that regulated the movement of Africans, and the repeated attempts to revoke the vote from Africans in the Cape, which were consummated in 1936. The ANC's principles were anchored in liberal ideals of legal and political equality, suffused with Christianity taught in missionary schools. For the early ANC, South Africa was made up of interdependent racial groups bound together by mutual respect, Christian brotherhood, and liberality of spirit.

The ANC in its Christian liberal phase denounced racial inequalities bitterly, but other kinds of inequalities passed largely unchallenged.[9] The ANC did not demand political equality for all South Africans, partly because it preferred petitions to demands, but mostly because it petitioned for *racial* equality. It sought to eliminate race as the basis of inequalities, which was not the same as seeking full equality under the law. The explanation for this is partly pragmatic. It made strategic sense for the ANC to concentrate fire on specific inequalities rather than inequality in general because its white allies were committed unalterably to certain forms of social inequality. But there was more to the ANC's moderation than that. Not only did the ANC respect the line white liberals drew between enfranchisement for some Africans and disenfranchisement for the bulk, but it also pursued racial equality without defining equality racially. That is, African opinion did not counterpose African to European standards; it did not argue that African ways deserved equal treatment with European ones.[10] What it argued, after the fashion of Cape liberalism, was that Africans who met standards set by whites ought to be extended the rights and privileges due whites. If Africans succeeded at the white game, they earned the rewards accorded whites.

Thus, the African franchise was critically important to the ANC. Imposing a racial franchise not only deprived Africans of influence, but questioned the achievements, and particularly the Christianity, of Westernized Africans. Political Africans had qualified for the vote by virtue of what they learned through and accomplished because of Christianity; depriving them of the vote, therefore, implicitly cast aspersions on their Christianity. It even debunked Christianity itself. Christianity forged a common brotherhood of man and created a united nation through the performance of Christian duty. As one African leader protested,

> The pessimistic expectation of a division on race lines . . . either betrays a lack of faith in Christianity, or amounts to a confession that Christianity as we know it in South Africa is bankrupt. . . . [The non-

> racial] franchise is ethically moral because it places a premium on merit rather than colour. It is Christian, indicating the white man's humanitarian duty towards the black. . . . This franchise is thus nothing less that the noblest monument of the white man's rule, emblematic of his genuineness in practicing the precepts of Holy Scripture towards the subject races.[11]

The vote, then, assumed vast significance for African public opinion. Voting not only affected state policy, something critically important at a time when the state was conducting sustained attacks on Africans. It also indicated that Africans were educated, civilized, Christian. Disenfranchising Cape Africans, the project of various white governments until finally accomplished in 1936, thus was tantamount to pulling a bait and switch, expelling Africans from the world they were entering on the grounds they were barbarians or children or heathens, no matter what their achievements by European standards. One prominent African spokesman argued, "The franchise is valued not merely because it gives potential influence, but because, as in Native government, it is a symbol of manhood. Those Natives who have the franchise feel that they have a status in the country."[12] As another leader stated to one of the advisory institutions that had been set up by the government:

> It would take too long to recapitulate the privileges due to the franchise. [Native] progress was largely due to this. They told their children to learn, to build better houses and to be thrifty, all with the object of getting the vote so as to escape the curfew regulations, be able to walk on pavements, and gain the respect of others. The Bill [to disenfranchise Africans] would kill all these incentives to progress.[13]

Attacks on the "non-racial" franchise asserted the incorrigible Africanness of Africans and posited civilization as the property, the singular property, of Europeans. Africans, according to the logic of disenfranchisement, must "develop on their own lines," regardless of their preferences and accomplishments. They could not choose their lives or benefit from their interactions with whites because their race was indelible. Africans could not become "European."

The non-racial franchise, in addition to recognizing and granting influence to Africans, served another purpose for the ANC. It signified the interdependent and inseparable fates of blacks and whites and built bridges between them. The ANC was not arguing that blacks and whites constituted a single nation, though occasionally individual members approached that position. As a journalist closely associated with the ANC put the point, "In regard to the principle of separate representation [proposed by the government] the idea seemed to be that the people of South Africa—white and black—were not one nation. . . . It was impossible to evolve a Nation within a Nation. They could not have a separate Bantu Nation and a separate European Nation in South Africa so long as the two races live side by side."[14] This thesis, arguing that a common state creates a single people, anticipated the ANC's eventual position. It did not, however, represent the predominant view in the ANC at the time, which took the country's population to be made up of racial groups, preached interracial cooperation, and rejected segregation as a principle of political organization without concluding that South Africans were a single people.

Providence for the ANC had associated South Africans but had not combined them, which is why non-racial institutions constituted a moral imperative: they embodied the brotherhood of man. Brotherhood, of course, implies interconnectedness, not identity. Brothers are bound together and are different. Accordingly, non-racialism in its Christian version did not maintain the oneness of South Africans. Quite the contrary, South Africans appear as the composite of integral peoples. People come together as brothers, in spite of differences, much as the ANC at the time had the various African tribes coming together as Africans.

In its 1919 constitution, the then South African Native National Congress declared its intention

> To encourage mutual understanding and to bring together into common action as one political people all tribes and clans of various tribes or races and by means of combined effort and united political organisation to defend their freedom, rights and privileges;
>
> To discourage and contend against racialism and tribal feuds or to secure the elimination of racialism and tribal feuds; jealousy and petty quarrels by economic combination, education, goodwill and by other means.[15]

Note the wording: the Congress spoke of bringing tribes together, of combining efforts, of discouraging feuds. Its constitution not only did not suggest getting rid of tribes; it spoke as if the "people" was composed of tribes, as if they were its constitutive units. The African people was conceived as standing above, but as made up of, particular tribes. The ANC's job was to join the various tribes into a united political organization.

The early ANC's idea was to eliminate tribal rivalries, not tribes themselves. Tribes were to remain centers of life, culture, and community, but they were to be removed as loci of political loyalties and activities, superseded by the African people for the purpose of promoting "common action as one political people." Tribes were to lose only political responsibilities; they were to retain their distinct place in the lives of the African people, providing cultural identities. As the point was made by Pixley Ka Izaka Seme, one of the founders of the ANC and its president from 1930 to 1936, "The demon of racialism, the aberrations of the Xosa-Fingo feud, the animosity that exists between the Zulus and the Tongaas, between the Basutos and every other Native must be buried and forgotten; it has shed among us sufficient blood! We are one people. These divisions, these jealousies, are the cause of all our woes and of all our backwardness and ignorance to-day."[16] The problem for Seme was not the fact of tribes, which he took as given, but the conflicts among them, which he characterized as "aberrations." The solution was to resolve political divisions among tribes by affirming political unity, by constructing one people that encompassed particular tribes without dissolving them.

This conception of the nation is striking for a couple reasons. First, the ANC did not understand its nation in essentialist terms, making it an exception to the rule for nationalist organizations. National consciousness was not there to be "discovered" or "awakened." It had to be invented, deliberately and through *political* means. Africans were to be fashioned into a nation, into *Africans* (as opposed, say, to Natives), by a political organization, the ANC, which was antecedent to the conception of the nation. What is remarkable about this is not that the nationalist organization was engaged in the process of creating a nation, which has become a commonplace in scholarly literature about nationalism,[17] but that it *understood* itself to be creating a nation long before the insight occurred to scholars. The ANC presented itself as author, not as midwife. Second, the ANC's nation developed through interaction with others. It did not fulfill a telos, like an acorn growing into an oak of its own nature, but became through interaction with others. The nation for the ANC was an outcome made by historical experiences, including encounters with the whites who introduced the notion of "nation" to Africans. The ANC's nation, in other words, came to exist through the participation of the (white) "other." Thus, the original ANC nation necessarily repudiated notions of racial purity: even the African people, a hybrid of clashing histories and peoples and consisting of those subjugated to the South African state, were mixed.

These elements—constructing a nation from tribes, assimilating African into European standards, and protesting racial while acquiescing to others kinds of inequalities—constituted the core of the ANC's Christian liberal politics. It was a patient politics, advancing moderate proposals, working with and often deferring to white liberals, and accepting the values of British liberalism. As shown by their flexibility on the franchise, where they sought to give Africans the vote on the same basis and with the same restrictions as applied to whites, Christian liberals were not dogmatic. They wanted equal opportunity under a common legal order but were willing to forego democracy and to proceed slowly and temperately, partly in deference to the sensitivities of their white allies, but also out of forbearance. The ANC's Christian liberalism was tame, pragmatic, nonviolent, and, in conception as well as strategies and tactics, a function of what seemed feasible in a rapidly racializing and increasingly racist political order. The commitment to non-racialism was sincere and abiding; but what, precisely, it entailed was flexible and fluid. The substance of the ANC's non-racialism was contingent on other forces.

The Christian-liberal tradition predominated in the ANC until the late 1940s, its hold ultimately being loosened by developments in white politics. African patience and deference were predicated on faith that goodwill eventually would pay off and specifically that white liberals would win elections and dismantle white supremacy. But the white electorate refused the role required of it. As Albert Lutuli, later to become president of the ANC, put the point when the government divested him of his chieftaincy,

> Who will deny that thirty years of my life have been spent knocking in vain, patiently, moderately and modestly at a closed and barred door?
>
> What have been the fruits of my many years of moderation? Has there been any reciprocal tolerance or moderation from the Government, be it Nationalist or United Party? No! On the contrary, the past thirty years have seen the greatest number of Laws restricting our rights and progress until today we have reached a stage where we have almost no rights at all . . . [18]

The white electorate, as Lutuli noted, divided between supporters of segregation (the United Party) and apartheid (the National Party), both racist. Against this background, white liberals either went along with the flow, defending segregation and aligning with business interests that were ambivalent about recognizing the economic rights of Africans, or doomed themselves to irrelevance in white politics. When the NP won the 1948 election and began enacting apartheid, the Christian-liberal objective of interracial cooperation and the ANC's strategy of working with white allies was dashed. Bereft of viable objectives and strategies, Christian liberals were vulnerable to challenges from the new generation of leaders that had congregated in the ANC Youth League (ANCYL).

Three challenges were particularly influential. First, the Youth League forced militant methods onto the ANC, convincing it to pursue objectives directly and not to rely on white liberals to accomplish their ends for them. The ANC, while remaining committed to nonviolent methods (until the 1960s), began organizing mass actions (boycotts, civil disobedience) and breaking the habit of deferring to and acting through white benefactors. Second, the Youth League caused the ANC to ditch liberal conceptions of the franchise that had disqualified most Africans through "civilization" tests. The ANC, which hitherto had dampened democratic impulses lest white liberals be embarrassed, called for full political equality and yearned for social equality too. In particular, it pressed for a universal adult franchise. Finally, the Youth League reinterpreted the ANC's conception of tribe and race, with fundamental implications for its sense of political membership and obligation.

Under the leadership of chiefs and Christian liberals, the ANC accepted tribes as building blocks of the nation: the nation was what encompassed tribes and made them one politically. Races, in this view, were regarded as meaningful human associations, but not as foundational; races were composites of tribes. The Youth League, on the other hand, accorded tribes a lesser status. According to A. M. Lembede, "Out of the heterogeneous tribes, there must emerge a homogeneous nation. The basis of national unity is the nationalistic feeling of the Africans, the feeling of being Africans irrespective of tribal connection, social status, educational attainment or economic class."[19] As the Youth League declared, "Our stupendous task is to organise, galvanise and consolidate the numerous African tribes into one homogeneous nation."[20] Clearly, the ANCYL was not describing what it believed to be true; it was not claiming that the African nation actually had replaced tribes in the hearts of Africans. What the ANCYL was describing was its vision of what it wanted to make true.

Departing from ANC tradition, it wanted feelings of African nationality to dispel customary tribal sentiments. For the ANCYL, Africanness was to become the primary identity of those who were to become Africans, and it was either to eclipse (the first quotation) or to extinguish (the second quotation) traditional affections. "National unity," hitherto a construct of tribes, now derives directly from nationalist feeling. The nation lives independently of tribes, which no longer serve as intermediaries between the nation and the individual. The ANCYL, in other words, redefined the place of tribe and nation in South African politics.

The ANCYL, in intimating that tribes were to forfeit their individual identities, that they were to merge into a single African nation, transformed the ANC's thinking. Previously, the ANC had treated tribes as sites of essential commitments and tribal leaders as natural leaders of the African people, a prestige recognized by their special representation in the ANC.[21] Africans, in the old view, were connected with their "political people" through particular tribes. The Youth League, however, took the "nation" as the fount of collective identities, as the source of "nationalistic feeling," and suspected tribal loyalties of endangering racial unity. Prior to the ANCYL, tribes were allowed to generate important solidarities and limit what the race could demand of its members; the "nation," essentially, specialized in political affairs, leaving other concerns to tribes.

The ANCYL not only worried that tribes interfered with the allegiance due the "nation," but considered the existence of tribes to be a blight on the nation's integrity. Tribes, whose politics previously were to have been coordinated through the ANC, now were to "consolidate . . . into one homogeneous nation." No longer were tribes composing the nation; hereafter, the nation must dissolve tribes in pursuit of "national" homogeneity. Of course, the ANC could not change its thinking about tribes without also changing its thinking about race, which it was coming to conceive more nationally. The ANC presented races as "nations," an association made matter-of-factly in the Freedom Charter (where the term "national group" is used) and one laden with fundamental political implications.

It is a commonplace of 20th- and 21st-century politics that nations have rights, including to self-determination. Circumstances may prevent them from enforcing their rights and rights to self-determination may clash with each other (in multi-national states, for example), requiring compromise by one or more of the "nations," but nations are agreed to possess political rights of one sort or another. The claim that *races* have rights, on the other hand, is seen as suspect, having been discredited by white supremacists and fascists. Races are seen as exclusionary, and preferences offered in racial solidarity are considered racist. If, however, races are characterized differently, as nations, benefits associated with them become appropriate. Calling a people a "national group" or a "nation" dignifies and elevates its claims, attributing rights to the group. For example, if Africans are designated as a "national group," they are credited with some right to self-determination, potentially even the right to a state of their own. Clearly, both the ANC and the ANCYL scrupulously avoided this inference, partly because it reeked of separate development and partly because it implied the right of all four "national" groups to secede. Nevertheless, talking of races as "nations" does associate them with claims to sovereignty and does allow for the suggestion that they ought to control states. Calling races "nations," in other words, not only names them differently; it allows them claim on the ultimate loyalty of their members and makes supreme the identities that now are designated as "national."

The ANC did not push the implications of its new vocabulary to the point of urging separate states for separate nations. But it did diverge from Christian liberals in characteristically nationalistic fashion. Christian liberals, remember, had deferred to European standards, which they generally accepted as superior to those of Africans. Hence their position on the franchise: Africans with property and of education had earned the right to vote by meeting white standards. Youth Leaguers, by contrast, celebrated Africa, which is not to say they rejected Europe. Not only were most leaders of the Youth League products of missionary education, usually faithful ones, but their core political values—liberal democracy and nationalism—did not develop in Africa indigenously. They were imported, from Europe. The Youth Leaguers did not, in other words, reject the lessons they had learned from Europe; what they rejected was *deference* to Europeans. Thus, the Youth League observed, "The African regards Civilisation as the common heritage of all Mankind."[22] Accordingly, the Youth League did not justify claims to national and democratic rights in terms of the Europeanization of Africans. Europe was not the source of rights for the ANCYL, and Africans did not derive rights from becoming like Europeans; they had rights *naturally*, as taught by British liberalism, and did not need to defer to whites. Thus, in casting races as national groups, the Youth League rejected paternalism and positioned itself to reject the content of Europeanism in South Africa.

Youth Leaguers, in equating races with "nations," took for granted both that South Africa's population consists of four races and that races—now called "national groups"—were constitutive units, that is, focal points of political organization and participation. As the ANCYL stated matter-of-factly, "South Africa is a country of four chief nationalities."[23] Because nations organize political participation, "cooperation can only take place between Africans as a single unit and other Non-European groups as separate units. Non-European unity is a fantastic dream which has no foundation in reality."[24] The ensuing politics, adopted by the ANC in due time, was *multiracialist*. It was *racialist* in accepting race as the source of political identity (hence, for example, the ANCYL expected each racial group to have a political organization of its own) and was *multi*-racialist in trying to abolish the white character of the state and to open it to *all* racial groups. In that respect, the ANC had been multiracial all along: it always had urged the state to dismantle racial barriers to political participation, while organizing itself on the basis of race (membership was restricted to Africans) and casting itself nationally (it was the African *National* Congress). But the Christian-liberal tradition did not take the implications of its name literally; it did not equate race with nationality. The Youth League, by contrast, vested races with political rights, thus stumbling into racialism through the back door of nationality.

The ANCYL did not introduce multiracialism to the ANC. Multiracialism had been implicit in and sometimes explicit for the ANC from its inception. It had taken as an article of faith that South Africa was made up of racial groups, with each requiring its own mode of representation (hence the rationale for the ANC). But the ANCYL changed the texture of the ANC's multiracialism permanently, raising it from an intuition to a principle. Christian liberals thought races were important communities in South Africa, but had them pinched from below by tribes (the site of cultural identities) and from above by the brotherhood of man. For the ANCYL, however, races were bedrocks of political participation and identity, the equivalent of nations. Accordingly, it criticized Coloureds for lacking a "national" organization of their own ("Coloureds . . . will never win their national freedom unless they organise a Coloured People's National Organisation to lead in the struggle for the National Freedom of the Coloureds").[25] With freedom having to be pursued nationally—or, alternately, racially—the logic of the ANCYL suggested two destinations: official recognition of race-nations in political institutions (essentially the culturalist position of white liberals) or official non-recognition of race-nations (the predilection of national majorities in most societies).

In the event, the apartheid state spared the ANCYL the responsibility of having to decide on the institutional implications of non-racialism. But the ANCYL's leaders did blend into and assume leadership over the ANC, making it more militant in means and more radical in ends. The refashioned ANC rejected "civilization" tests for the franchise and demanded standard liberal democratic institutions, especially universal adult franchise. The new liberal democratic commitments did not take account of and square with the ANC's old multiracialism, however. If South Africa really was made up of distinct racial groups that, as the ANCYL had it, required political organizations of their own, it is unclear how liberal democratic institutions could fit into South African circumstances. The analysis of and prescriptions for South Africa thus seem at odds, something the ANCYL did not address and the ANC subsequently absorbed unreflectively.

Liberal democratic nationalism became the primary outcome of the interaction of the ANCYL and the ANC, but not the only one. It also produced an exclusivist Africanism, which insinuated that only Africans really belonged in South Africa (or anywhere else in Africa, for that matter). But Africanism exerted much less influence than the democratic nationalism exemplified by the likes of Albert Lutuli and Nelson Mandela. They spoke of democracy, "non-racialism," and an inclusive South African nation, which became the third—and current—meaning of "non-racialism" for the ANC.

If the first sense of the ANC's non-racialism revolves around liberality of spirit and the brotherhood of man and the second involves designating racial groups as national groups and divesting the state of its exclusive racial character, the third entails negating the negation of racism and racialism. In this understanding, "non-racialism" is defined largely by what it is not, by the "non." It is not racism and not racialism, creating a double negation at its heart. "Non-racialism" means, depending on the context, rejecting racism, rejecting racialism, or rejecting both. But non-racialism, especially as the term has been used since the 1950s, is not a purely negative concept. It also affirms liberal democratic ideals.

Rejecting racism is an essential part of "non-racialism." But different terms bespeak different referents; racism and racialism may be overlapping phenomena, but they are not identical ones. Racism is associated with racially motivated inequality and oppression. It installed whites over blacks economically, politically, and culturally; established whites as subjects and blacks as objects, as whites acted and blacks were acted upon; acclaimed the humanity of whites and demeaned that of blacks; and justified power and privilege for whites on grounds they were naturally and culturally *better* than blacks, more *civilized.* For racists, supremacy flows from superiority: domination attests to moral right.

Racism is *necessarily* invidious. Racialism, on the other hand, maintains that races are different and are sites of political identity and participation. As a version of culturalism, racialism locates individuals in races, makes races into foundations of political identities, and regards racial identities as the stuff of politics. Politics for racialists is not primarily about doing things; it is not about governance. It is an expressive activity, enacting who people *are.* Politics is a field, a stage on which identities, already having been formed by culture, are displayed. Collective identities for racialists are not constructed through political participation or power; they are pre-political, originating outside and prior to political interactions, in culture, and confer the stakes in politics.

Racism and racialism are distinguishable, therefore. Racialists conceive politics expressively; racialism declares who people are, presenting benefits conferred on them as tokens of respect for "their" communities. Wanting state power to express the identities of racial groups, racialists may diverge from racists in their political objectives. Where racists must insist that their group deserves more power because it is better than others, racialists must insist only that groups, because they are *different,* require representation as groups. What matters for racialists is that *races* are respected as the wheel of political organization; what matters for racists is that power and benefits are distributed in accordance to the superiority of whites. Of course, racist and racialist politics usually are joined in practice, with racists insisting on racially organized politics as a condition of their supremacy, and racialists insisting that their superiority be expressed through supremacy. But the difference between them is that *hierarchy* is the necessary organizing principle of racism, and *difference* may be the organizing principle of racialism.

In South African usage, apartheid was both racist *and* racialist. It was racist in systematically installing and privileging whites over blacks; it was racialist in defining political participation racially. This is why the "non" in non-racialism may reject racist domination and racialist political organization or racist domination but not racialist political organization, which eventually was to leave the ANC government plenty of room to choose what, precisely, it would have to reject on the basis of non-racialism. "Non-racialism," as the negation of the negation, is an ideal, an aspiration, consisting of three objectives: overcoming racism, eradicating official racialism, and propounding universal citizenship.

The first two objectives of the ANC's non-racialism, attacking racism and racialism, are defined by the evils they intended to get rid of; the third is positive, determined by the purposes it means to realize. "Non-racialism," in this thrust, is the constructing of a universal nation, based on political equality and belonging. South Africans, whatever their backgrounds, must be guaranteed equal citizenship under the law without regard to distinctions of race or ethnicity. The nation, now formally dissociated from race and blood, includes all South Africans by virtue of common citizenship. The argument is characteristically democratic in aspiring to build an inclusive nation and characteristically politicist in arguing that membership in the nation flows from citizenship. The non-racial nation must be invented, which summons the importance of the state in the ANC's thinking. The state becomes necessary as the source of the non-racial nation, drawing heterogeneous groups into one people and makes them into South Africans. The nation is to form around the democratic state.

Democratic institutions are what define the ANC's "non-racial" state. The ANC spoke of an inclusive and embracing national identity, but it pursued it through racially denominated political parties. "The Congress Alliance," observed the ANC in 1959, "formed of separate organisations, has raised a whole generation of South Africans of all races and colours in a new mould—in the mould of equality and brotherhood, in the mould which alone of all South African patterns can claim, 'Here there is no racialism.'"[26] Consequently, the ANC had to answer one compelling question: how was racially organized politics compatible with non-racialism? It offered essentially three answers in response.

First, the ANC claimed that African nationalism is inclusive, democratic, and predicated on rejecting privilege for any group. Professor Z. K. Matthews, best known for calling for the process that produced the Freedom Charter, associated African nationalism with "co-operation with other sections of the population strictly on the basis of equality. The nationalism which we express is not the narrow nationalism which seeks to exclude others from South African nationhood as we are excluded today but a broad nationalism which is all-inclusive, with no position of special privilege for any group such as we find is the case in this country today."[27]

Lutuli made the same point:

> The African National Congress, having accepted the fact of the multiracial nature of the country, envisaged an ALL INCLUSIVE AFRICAN NATIONALISM which, resting on the principle of "FREEDOM FOR ALL" in a country, UNITY OF ALL in a country, embraced all people under African Nationalism regardless of their racial and geographical origin who resided in Africa and paid their undivided loyalty and allegiance. Congress should not be ashamed to tell the African people that it is opposed to TRIBALISM but for obvious practical considerations it must gradually lead Africans from these narrow tribal loyalties to the wider loyalty of the BROTHERHOOD OF MAN throughout the world.[28]

Matthews and Lutuli envisioned African nationalism as inclusive; they invited whites, Coloureds, and Asians into the nation along with Africans on the basis of cultural respect and interaction. To be sure, Africanists make the same claim, even denouncing the very idea of race (what better proof could they present of their "non-racialism"?). But Africanists exclude whites and Asians—Coloureds occupy an ambiguous position for them—from the nation in practice. Where Africanists have Africans embracing the authentic Africa, the primordial Africa unsoiled by European contamination, Lutuli insisted on the "multiracial nature" of South Africa. Africanists pretend only one race exists (the human race), then dismiss whites and Asians as interlopers, taking with the right hand what they offered with the left. The tradition of Lutuli and Mandela, however, actively and expressly welcomed all South Africans.

Having been embraced in the nation, minorities would hold political rights in the state. Mandela argued in court that the ANC stands for political equality, no longer countenancing legal inequalities based on "civilization." All South Africans are equal under the law, are entitled to equal political participation, and are able to consent to government (a departure from the thinking of Christian liberals).

> In its proper meaning equality before the law means the right to participate in the making of the laws by which one is governed. . . . That the will of the people is the basis of the authority of government is a principle universally acknowledged as sacred throughout the civilised world, and constitutes the basic foundation of freedom and justice. . . . The African National Congress . . . believed that all people, irrespective of the colour of their skins, all people whose home is South Africa and who believe in the principles of democracy and of equality of men, should be treated as Africans; that all South

> Africans are entitled to live a free life on the basis of fullest equality of the rights and opportunities in every field, of full democratic rights, with a direct say in the affairs of the Government.[29]

In calling for citizenship for all South Africans, for the universal franchise and full political equality for all citizens, Mandela believed the ANC was affording the greatest possible protection to racial minorities: democracy.

Second, the ANC dissociated culture from race. It proclaimed that South Africans were produced by the interaction of various cultures, including European ones. Europeans undeniably belong in South Africa, according to the ANC, and Lutuli even announced his preference for "Western" culture: "[T]he African has accepted the higher moral and spiritual values inherent in the fundamental concepts of what, for lack of better terminology, is called 'Western Civilisation.' "[30] Lutuli elsewhere went even further. He declared cultures themselves to be amalgams. No civilization is pure, integral, elemental. Lutuli proclaimed, "I do not know of any people who really have developed 'along their own lines.' My fellow white South Africans, enjoying what is called 'Western civilisation,' should be the first to agree that this civilisation is indebted to previous civilisations, from the East, from Greece, Rome and so on. For its heritage, Western civilisation is really indebted to very many sources, both ancient and modern."[31]

Lutuli, in other words, undercuts the very foundation of culturalism, the assumption that cultures are constitutive. Cultures have values—they do not have unique souls—and individuals may adopt, alter, and amalgamate values. Lutuli continues, "What is important is that we can build a homogeneous South Africa on the basis not of colour but of human values. . . . [I]n trying to build a new homogeneous democratic South Africa, colour and race should not come into the scene. . . . The main thing is that man is my brother not by blood, but because we cherish the same values, stand for the same standards."[32] Democracy creates something new, distinctive, and inclusive—*South Africans*—by mixing and synthesizing old cultures and values. "And so can develop a true South African culture, built up of the best of all our cultures."[33]

If the first reason why the ANC rejects institutional recognition of South Africa's multiracialism centers on its promises of cultural rights for minorities[34] and the second reason involves the dissociation of culture and race, the third follows from its understanding of the origin of the nation.

The ANC—in particular, Lutuli, Mandela, and Oliver Tambo, head of the ANC during Mandela's imprisonment—made conventional democratic claims. Democracy was good and democracy required equality in citizenship. But the ANC also made an unconventional claim. The nation it envisioned was a *political* construct, formed *through* common citizenship. That is, the non-racial nation assumes and supersedes racial differences, furnishing another reason for Mandela, Tambo, and Lutuli to attach such a premium to non-racial political institutions, especially the franchise. In the absence of democratic institutions that engender a common nationality and a common loyalty and that treat South Africans of all racial and ethno-cultural backgrounds equally, the South African people could not be born.

As Govan Mbeki, a senior member of both the SACP and ANC, put the point, "The ANC is struggling to form one people, to be represented in one parliament in one country. In spite of various ethnic groupings in the country, black and white, the ANC is seeking to forge one nation, building a non-racial democracy in a unitary state."[35] Mandela made a similar observation: "We were inspired by the idea of bringing into being a democratic republic where all South Africans will enjoy human rights without the slightest discrimination; where African and non-African would be able to live together in peace, sharing a common nationality and a common loyalty to this country, which is our homeland."[36] Common citizenship, then, unites four racial groups and a dozen or so ethno-cultural groups into one nation. It follows that the "non-racial" people could not demand the non-racial state, because the non-racial nation does not precede—and, therefore, cannot demand—the non-racial state. Democracy cures racialism and produces the non-racial people, but it does not express cultural nations.

The ANC's nation was to be the (more or less) direct outcome of instituting democracy. As Lutuli put the point, "I stress that the question of 'colour' and 'swamping' will not be relevant in . . . a non-racial democracy."[37] By the logic of non-racialism, racialism is destined to wither away once the racial state quits buttressing it. To quote Mandela's speech from the Rivonia trial, "It is not true that the enfranchisement of all will result in racial domination. Political division, based on colour, is entirely artificial and, when it disappears, so will the domination of one colour group by another."[38] The ANC's hope was that racialism would wither without the sanction of the state. Lutuli predicted, "The government, mainly through education—directly and indirectly—will discourage the attitude of thinking and acting in racial categories, as racialism, and all forms of discrimination shall be outlawed. The question of reserving rights for minorities in a non-racial democracy should not arise. It will be sufficient if human rights for all are entrenched in the constitution."[39]

The ANC's democratic, "non-racial" nationalism, then, advances several key promises. All citizens would have the same political rights; race would not be recognized by the state; universal guarantees for all citizens would render specific protections for minorities unnecessary; and non-racialism would prevail, mostly because race would cease to matter formally. Note, however, the predicate of the ANC's thinking about non-racialism: real democracy would dissolve the appeal of racialism. Unfortunately, the ANC's reasoning verged on the circular: non-racial institutions would dispel racialism by ignoring race officially and ignoring race officially would prove that racialism had been dispelled. The catch is that the ANC could not and can not prevent South Africans from harboring racial affinities. It can demand only that the state keep racialism in its place.

An important corollary flows from making non-racial citizenship the source of the nation: the nation is real only to the extent that citizenship is genuinely equal, genuinely non-racial. If non-racial citizenship is what establishes the universal nation, the universal nation would be undermined by de facto particularism. The problem, as white liberals have stressed, is that non-racialism can be rejected in name yet enacted in practice, that political power that is organized on the basis of racial identities may come to be dignified by non-racial discourse, and that the largest racial group—Africans—may consecrate a racial agenda with democratic pronouncements. Racially blind institutions are not racially neutral, liberals argue; they load the dice in favor of the largest group, then allow the winners to claim a democratic halo. What matters are not the formal properties of South African institutions, not democratic intentions and promises of individual rights, but the circumstances that endow institutions with content and purpose. Contexts and particulars, not proclamations and rights, are decisive in producing political outcomes.

The tensions between form and substance were debated inside the Communist Party of South Africa (CPSA) in the 1920s and 1930s.[40] The CPSA originally was based among white workers, with many of its leaders having emigrated from Britain or Lithuania. It denounced the ravages of early industrialization, organized against capitalists, and sided with white workers as they sought protection from African competition. Indifference to African interests, the implicit predicate of white politics, was assumed as a matter of course upon the foundation of the CPSA in 1921. But this soon changed, as a minority faction of the CPSA joined forces with the Communist International (Comintern) to recast the party's politics. Previously, the CPSA had championed white workers as the vanguard of the working class, emphasized socialist over democratic demands, and discounted the importance of formal political institutions. Subsequently, the CPSA reversed itself, urging formally democratic institutions as a springboard for socialism.

The CPSA's original politics ran counter to V. I. Lenin's dictum that national liberation movements must attack the most vulnerable links in the capitalist chain. Lenin had argued that capital had responded to deepening contradictions in Europe by achieving super-profits abroad, through imperialism.[41] Accordingly, the Comintern advised Communist parties to unite subject populations in pursuit of national rights. If, the Comintern reckoned, oppressed nations were to liberate themselves from colonial domination, they would eliminate the super-profits captured in colonial societies that sustained world capitalism and would expose the capitalist heartland in Europe to challenges from its own proletariats. To that end, the Comintern called on Communist parties to ally with national liberation movements, the goal being to bring together oppressed people, regardless of class, behind the demand for national self-determination. At the Comintern's behest, the CPSA revamped its political program, now calling for equal political rights for all South Africans and repudiating white supremacy. But the Comintern did not stop there. Over the objections of most of the South African leadership, it insisted on what it called the "Native Republic."

The demand for the Native Republic, controversially, cast democracy racially. The CPSA did not treat democracy as encompassing all South Africans fully and equally. In calling for an *African* republic, it identified who would and would not feel at home in it. Racial—or national—content was made part and parcel of democracy. Democracy did not stand above races and nations, blunting, integrating, or surpassing them. It highlighted them. The CPSA's democratic demand was, at bottom, a *racial-national* demand, a demand for self-determination for Africans. With the democratic demand coded racial-nationally, the CPSA sought alliance with national liberation organizations (including the ANC).

The Native Republic cast what Lenin called the "democratic-national" revolution as distinctively national. It was a Native Republic, an *African* Republic. In this respect, the CPSA's Native Republic resembled other nationalist movements gathering momentum at the time, Zionism for example. Zionism was not seeking abstract liberal democracy, one that would treat Jews in the same fashion as it treated other citizens. The state was not understood as a vessel whose content was to be defined by citizens; the Zionist state was conceived as a *Jewish* state, and it screened members accordingly.[42] As the Zionist state was to be organized on the basis of prior solidarities, so the Native Republic insinuated race as the condition of full membership and genuine participation. The Republic was implicitly racial.

The demand for a Native Republic turned the CPSA topsy-turvy; the CPSA ended up forfeiting its political base in the white working class and removing leaders critical of the Comintern's preferences. But after the fallout, which critics claimed was produced by the formulation of a *Native* Republic, the CPSA trimmed the excesses and de-racialized its conception of democracy. The CPSA accepted a key objection made by Communist critics: it was provocative to specify the Republic's "native" character a priori and was unnecessary to boot. Adult suffrage, full democratic rights, and universal citizenship for all residents of South Africa would produce much the same effect, if that was what the African majority wanted. Enfranchising Africans enabled them to define the ethos of the "nation," to define symbols and set the tone of the democratic republic. Because sloganeering for a Native Republic ventured much and gained nothing, the CPSA adjusted its line. It sought to achieve the same outcome without demarcating the republic racially. It called for full democracy, which is what it meant to say the republic was "national," and opened participation to all citizens equally and without regard to race. All South Africans were to receive equal political rights, but nothing was to prevent the majority from conferring a de facto African character on the state. The communal identity of the state could be rendered as the outcome of the democratic state, not as its premise.

The CPSA was describing the non-racial state. It did not coin the term, but the import of the CPSA's new line was to strip racial-national requirements from citizenship, without preventing the majority from choosing an African character for the state. Communal connotations were permissible; it was denotations that were forbidden. The new conception, in other words, was essentially liberal democratic; the state would prescribe formal equality, but would allow actors motivated by "private" concerns—cultural affinities, for example—to pursue public support. It seems ironic, perhaps, that Communists pressed for liberal democratic institutions while professed liberals recoiled from them, but both twists made sense politically. Distinguishing between a "Native Republic" and "non-racial democracy," as both Communists and liberals realized, was to draw a distinction without a difference. The Native Republic set membership terms at the outset: the communal character (Native) was stamped a priori on the political form (Republic). But theoretical differences between the Native Republic and non-racial democracy were overshadowed by the practical probability that the heavy majority of African citizens, following its cultural predilections, would impress an African character on the state and society through democratic methods, a posteriori.

The ANC's non-racialism picks up where the CPSA left off. It affirms classically liberal democratic values (the primacy of individual merit, the right to self-definition, equal rights for all citizens) and rejects the right of the state to impose group identities on citizens. It opens participation in the state to all South Africans, aspires to the universalistic "civic" nation, repudiates group definitions as ethically unworthy and politically unwise, and eradicates white supremacy. But the non-racial state does not challenge groups. It declares a common national citizenship above ethnic and racial groups, but does not aspire to abolish groups. "Non-racialism" posits political equality as a supreme value, assigns communal identities to the private realm, and allows the public state to represent private interests and identities.

Non-racialism, initially one commitment among others for the ANC, became shorthand for the ANC's defining project in the 1970s. Featuring "non-racialism" highlighted the ANC's objections to apartheid, of course. Apartheid was racist and racialist; the ANC, to negate the negation, declared itself antiracist and non-racialist. But the ANC had additional reasons for accentuating non-racialism, as was indicated by the timing of its redefinition. The ANC popularized the idea of non-racialism in the 1970s and 1980s, not because apartheid's racialism intensified then, but because of the emergence of Black Consciousness (BC) as a major force in black politics. The ANC and its allies emphasized non-racialism to contrast themselves with BC.

The Black Consciousness movement grew out of student politics in the late 1960s and early 1970s to become the central ideological influence on the 1976 Soweto rebellion. The specific demands made by BC resembled those of the ANC—it called for an "open society, one man, one vote, no reference to colour"[43]—but its general analysis of and redress for racism was much different. Steve Biko, BC's founder and most influential voice, had white supremacy being constituted by the interaction between the modes of mastery and subjugation. Drawing on the work of Frantz Fanon,[44] Biko conceived of domination as psychological in origin and content. Blacks for Biko were subordinated because they accepted in their hearts and minds that they were inferior to whites, not, as the ANC and the SACP had it, because whites had more economic, military, and organizational power.

The ANC had envisioned black liberation largely in formal terms. Freedom consisted of the right to participate equally in common institutions and was to be achieved politically, by changing laws and institutions. Biko's equality, on the other hand, could not be achieved merely by equality under the law because domination was not motivated by and did not inhere in institutions. The ANC, Biko believed, construed the causes of white domination too narrowly. Where the ANC's whites acted instrumentally, Biko's whites subjugated blacks for expressive reasons, humiliating, emasculating, and dominating for the thrill of it. "[W]e recognise the existence of one major force in South Africa. This is White Racism," he wrote, which "works with unnerving totality."[45] Attributing inequality to the needs of whites to master and the acquiescence of nonwhites to subordination, Biko envisioned liberating "the black man first from psychological oppression," from his "inferiority complex."[46]

To establish meaningful equality, to overcome feelings of inferiority and powerlessness, blacks must act by and for themselves. From his political debut in the South Africa Student Organization (SASO), an organization of black students, Biko criticized white liberals.

> What I have tried to show is that in South Africa political power has always rested with white society. Not only have the whites . . . kicked the black but they have also told him how to react to the kick. For a long time the black has been listening with patience to the advice he has been receiving on how best to respond to the kick. With painful slowness he is now beginning to show signs that it is his right and duty to respond to the kick *in the way he sees fit*.[47]

Biko's bite might give the impression he accepted racial definitions and ennobled racial solidarities, making a virtue of the necessity imposed by apartheid. As apartheid prescribed racially distinct political organizations and identities, insisting people must be associated with their own kind, so Biko seems to agree blacks must avoid political associations with whites. "[B]lacks are beginning to realise the need to rally around the cause of their suffering—their black skin."[48]

On these grounds, Biko rejected what passed for "non-racial" politics in South Africa. It does not necessarily follow, however, that he rejected non-racial politics in principle. Biko objected to "non-racialism" for producing predictable and pernicious outcomes in practice; he left open whether it was a good or bad thing in principle.

> The integration [non-racialists] talk about is first of all artificial in that it is a response to conscious manoeuvre rather than to the dictates of the inner soul. In other words the people forming the integrated complex have been extracted from the various segregated societies with their in-built complexes of superiority and inferiority and these continue to manifest themselves even in the "nonracial" set-up of the integrated complex. As a result the integration so achieved is a one-way course, with the whites doing all the talking and the blacks the listening.[49]

Biko was arguing that non-racial politics is illusory in the context of white domination, that the objective—and, especially, the *subjective*—fact of white power preempted the prospect of equality. By corollary, if the project of Black Consciousness is achieved and equality is established, non-racial politics would seem to become possible, because equality must abolish domineering whites and acquiescing blacks. But Biko did not predict happy endings. He did not affirm the predicate could obtain in fact, that black and white really can be equal. He wrote during the peak of apartheid, but spoke to postliberation, postcolonial concerns.

Biko's conception of race was specific and unusual. Most South African political traditions—certainly white supremacy, white liberalism, the SACP, and, sometimes, the ANC as well—take race as a given. They battle over its significance, but they agree race is *ascribed,* that it is impressed on people (either by nature or culture) who lack much say in the matter. Of course, people may be more or less conscious of their race, but race is there to become aware of and to be embraced. Biko took exception to the South African consensus: blackness was not ascribed for him. (Whiteness may be another matter.) It was achieved, earned. Biko's racial consciousness was not a process of self-discovery and self-awareness;

blackness did not exist inertly, waiting to be found. It must be made first, must be invented by blacks before they could become aware of it, a proposition with powerful political ramifications.

Biko's racial categories are "black" and "white"; they are not "African," "Coloured," "Asian," and "European," and his "whites" and "blacks" are not attributable to "nature" or "culture." Race for Biko, as for Neville Alexander, is a contrived consciousness. But whereas Alexander conceives racial consciousness as an artifact of capitalist domination, Biko had white domination creating the possibility of blackness. He preserved the category of race, but dissociated it from nature and culture. Thus, Biko's first axiom: people may become "black" without first being "African," an opportunity that was embraced by many Coloured and Indian students at the time. As Biko put the point in a SASO statement,

> We have . . . defined blacks as those who are by law or tradition politically, economically and socially discriminated against as a group in the South African society and identifying themselves as a unit in the struggle towards the realisation of their aspirations. This definition illustrates to us a number of things:
>
> 1. Being black is not a matter of pigmentation—being black is a reflection of a mental attitude.
> 2. Merely by describing yourself as black you have started on a road towards emancipation, you have committed yourself to fight against all forces that seek to use your blackness as a stamp that marks you out as a subservient being. . . . Black people—real black people—are those who can manage to hold their heads high in defiance rather than willingly surrender their souls to the white man.[50]

Thus, Biko's second axiom about blackness: as people may be black without being African, so they may be African without being black.

To be black was to satisfy two requirements: it was to suffer from *and* to fight against racial oppression. Those who were discriminated against but did not resist were not really black, because blackness is not ascribed. They were defined negatively, as "nonwhites." Blackness, on the other hand, was a positive racial consciousness that opposed racial oppression. To be black was to be *militantly* black, openly, proudly, and defiantly.

> [T]he type of black man we have today has lost his manhood. Reduced to an obliging shell, he looks with awe at the white power structure and accepts what he regards as the "inevitable position". Deep inside his anger mounts at the accumulating insult, but he vents it in the wrong direction—on his fellow man in the township, on the property of black people. . . . In the privacy of the toilet his face twists in silent condemnation of white society but brightens up in sheepish obedience as he comes out hurrying in response to his master's impatient call. . . . The first step therefore is to make the black man come to himself; to pump back life into his empty shell; to infuse him with pride and dignity, to remind him of his complicity in the crime of allowing himself to be misused and therefore letting evil reign supreme in the country of his birth. This is what we mean by an inward-looking process. This is the definition of "Black Consciousness."[51]

Black emancipation, therefore, was largely an internal psychological process. It involved nonwhites freeing themselves from feelings of inferiority, unworthiness, and powerlessness and asserting themselves as actors, as subjects, as efficacious, as *black*. The catch is that emancipation could not be solely personal, that is, solely psychological. Lest they remain in the toilet, blacks must conquer the dragons within by slaying those without. They could not call whites *Baas* (boss or master), partly because deference reinforces powerlessness, partly because it reinforces white power. Slaves, in other words, must challenge the master's power *in the world* if they were to free their souls. Otherwise, they were mere stoics, denying the importance of the world that enchains them.

Blackness for Biko could not be conferred or ascribed on the basis of color. It must be accomplished by transforming "nonwhites" into subjects, into actors. This conception of race—or of blackness, as Biko's whites operate according to a different logic—departed dramatically from most of South Africa's other traditions. Biko's blacks arise politically and historically, not naturally and culturally, through processes of subjugation, colonization, dispossession, and violence. With racial selves constructed, racial consciousness did not merely become aware of the historically created race; it did not merely register that races were constructed. Biko also had race inhering in consciousness and not, as others have it, in the self that is the object of consciousness. In other words, Biko's races did not exist until they were asserted consciously: there was no racial group to be conscious of until consciousness created the racial group.

It might sound as if Biko was splitting hairs, as if it does not matter whether racial consciousness is consciousness of existing race or is itself what creates race; but pivotal political consequences actually flow from the distinction. Because Biko's blacks exist in and through consciousness, only certain consciousnesses—those originating in the *experience of* and *response to* oppression—were suitable, were really "black." To be black was not to be African and was not even to be conscious of being African. It was to achieve a specific consciousness, a particular subjectivity about race and power, to recognize that blacks, because oppressed by reason of their blackness, must affirm themselves as black.

The logic of Biko's position, therefore, is that blackness includes all who meet its admission standards and none who fails them. As blackness is available to Coloureds and Indians, it is not ascribed for Africans. Like the others, "Africans" have to adopt militant politics to make themselves black, which was another reason for the resonance of BC among Coloureds and Asians: blacks were not Africans renamed. Nevertheless, the consciousness that made blacks was associated with color ("the greatest single determinant for political action").[52] This produced Biko's third axiom about blackness: whites could not become black. It was "impossible" for whites to identify totally with blacks when they "enjoy privilege and . . . live on the sweat of another."[53] Racial privilege, in other words, bound whites to their racial group, whatever their predilections; the parameters of whiteness were fixed and given. Whites, having been spared discrimination and protected by racism, could not become black, whatever choices they took as individuals: blackness was not that elastic; it could not be constructed that inclusively. What made the exclusion of whites from blackness interesting is that it implies Biko was working with contradictory ontologies of race; belonging was not ascribed, but exclusion was. Lacking the searing brand of racism and the catharsis of rejecting it, whites could not switch sides. Blackness, presuming objective determinates, was not universal in scope. It could not integrate whiteness.

So where does Biko stand on non-racialism, on what it means and whether it is possible? Inevitably, his views were affected by his times. Writing in the heyday of apartheid, Biko had very specific opinions about what "non-racialism" really involved for whites. "Non-racialism" was a dishonest way for white liberals to reinforce their control and inculcate black quiescence. It was a *white* politics, one that sought to foreclose the use of racial consciousness and solidarities to resist racism.

> The liberals set about their business with the utmost efficiency. They made it a political dogma that all groups opposing the *status quo* must *necessarily* be non-racial in structure. They maintained that if you stood for a principle of non-racialism you could not in any way adopt what they described as racialist policies. They even defined to the black people what the latter should fight for. With this sort of influence behind them, most black leaders tended to rely too much on the advice of liberals.[54]

As white liberals were decreeing how nonwhites should oppose apartheid, they were nestled in the bosom of apartheid, accounting for Biko's contempt. "[N]o matter what a white man does, the colour of his skin—his passport to privilege—will always put him miles ahead of the black man. Thus in the ultimate analysis no white person can escape being part of the oppressor camp."[55] White liberals, Biko accused, hid behind and fed off the very racism they claimed to fight. Benefiting from racism, they dictated how their victims should respond to indignities they visited on them.

If Biko's whites are given their race by their privileges, blacks must struggle to acquire theirs. Blackness is steeped in and develops out of white racism. "We are oppressed not as individuals, not as Zulus, Xhosas, Vendas or Indians. We are oppressed because we are black. We must use that very concept to unite ourselves and to respond as a cohesive group. We must cling to each other with a tenacity that will shock the perpetrators of evil."[56] Two implications follow from Biko's proposition. First, blacks must *choose* their racial identities and solidarities. They do not arise from an incipient identity, as culturalists have nationalism developing from ethnicity. Blackness must be created by "nonwhites," who become black by acting *politically* on the basis of blackness.

Second, Biko's blacks come into being only because of and through interaction with whites. Biko's dictum that "we are oppressed because we are black" is more complicated than it seems. Biko had blacks being oppressed because they are black, but he did not have them as black *until* they were oppressed. Blackness was not innate and incipient. It must be prepared *by whites,* in a double sense. On the one hand, whites made black consciousness possible by asserting skin color as the basis of oppression, without which blackness lacks political and psychological resonance. On the other, blackness consists of blacks affirming themselves against and in the presence of whites. Because Biko's blackness must cancel whiteness, whiteness serves as the midwife of blackness. Whites make blacks possible, but blacks determine what it means to be black.

Biko's whites and blacks are related dialectically, therefore; each exists only through the other. As blacks develop through interaction with whites, their identities developing through the suffering from and rejecting of white racism, so whiteness requires blacks to establish the domination that constitutes it. The interdependence of whites and blacks is asymmetrical, however. Ultimately, blacks can become independent of whites, needing whites to become but not to stay black. Whites, like Hegel's former masters, can be undone by their dependence on their subordinates; they can be shed once blacks purge the white brand from their souls. White power, inhering "in the mind of the oppressed,"[57] evaporates once blacks dispel feelings of inferiority. Whites, however, are wedded to their dependence on blacks. Without blacks, whites cannot dominate; and without domination, whites are not white.

Biko's blackness is self-affirmation; his whiteness is domination. Blackness becomes independent of whiteness; whiteness, though, requires the existence of nonwhiteness. Where Biko's blacks become independent of race, his whites require it. Biko's whiteness is necessarily and unalterably racialist as well as racist; his blackness, however, can outgrow race. Black Consciousness, in other words, is implicitly non-racial in the full sense of the term. It forges people, black people, who define themselves without reference either to whites or to the concept of race. In eliminating power disparities between blacks and whites, Biko ultimately dissolves the race of blacks and abolishes the condition of whiteness. It is like a teeter-totter: as blackness ascends, whiteness must descend, because it is predicated on the domination that nonwhites overcome when they create themselves as blacks.

Biko's point is not that whites must be abolished. They may participate as individuals in a free South Africa; but whites may not be *racial* because the soul of their race is to oppress blacks. Blacks, on the other hand, may assert racial pride, racial consciousness, and racial solidarity, even as they boast of rising above racial definitions. Biko, therefore, can be used to justify a kind of racial inequality, where individuals have equal rights but races have different standing in society, and not just because one makes up a majority and the other a minority. Obviously, this implication was moot at the time Biko was writing. White power was supreme and the prospects of black liberation appeared distant. But he did insinuate a "non-racial" basis for treating racial claims differently, some being worthy and others unworthy.

Biko's BC unconsciously spoke for the aspiring middle class that was being thwarted by racism. BC's activists, especially in universities, were not, in the main, poor or working class in their class trajectory; they were preparing to become future elites.[58] (Biko was a medical student.) Biko did not see himself as the voice of an emerging black elite, yet his ideas on racial solidarity, racial consciousness, and racial empowerment are a godsend for interested actors seeking patronage from the post-apartheid state. They have the effect—whatever the original intention—of sanctioning racially conscious assertions by blacks as good things in themselves and serve the purposes of important tendencies in the ANC.

Black Consciousness activists were absorbed by the ANC in the aftermath of the Soweto rebellion. BC had ideas, but the ANC had organization,[59] mostly in exile, and the ANC incorporated BC into it. Its ideas already were layered, made up of different and inconsistent elements. New definitions of non-racialism had superseded old ones not just because they were intrinsically superior and not just because they had offered sharper insight into the essence of "non-racialism," but because they spoke more usefully to the needs of the moment, offering direction about where to go and how to get there. Liberal democratic definitions of non-racialism prevailed over Christian-liberal definitions not because they are truer—both make plausible claims on the term—but because liberal democratic definitions provided a more telling indictment of and offered a more powerful alternative to apartheid as times, opportunities, and constraints changed.

By the same token, racial empowerment and the construction of black elites, the implicit objectives of BC, have come to answer the needs of the ANC in government. "The quintessence" of black consciousness, Biko observed, "is the realisation by the blacks that, in order to feature well in this game of power politics, they have to use the concept of group power and to build a strong foundation for this."[60] The ensuing politics, which affirms specifically racial interests as it disclaims race and which deracializes the interests of blacks while racializing those of whites, is very useful for a government making racialist appeals while professing the ideology of "non-racialism." It explains that blacks, even when acting racially, have progressed beyond race.

7

The Political Economy of Identity Politics

For where your treasure is, there will your heart be also.

—LUKE 12:34

Liberal democrats are coded to debate the relationship between "freedom" and "equality." Valuing both, they forever are arguing about what each means,[1] about how to balance them, and about what it means to speak of political equality when freedom allows the rich to bring more resources to bear on political affairs. Does the influence of wealth in making and enforcing law expose liberal democratic talk of equal opportunity as hollow or is it the necessary outcome of freedom? Can opportunity be equal in societies in which wealth is inherited and can freedom be meaningful in societies in which equality reigns supreme? These theoretical debates and practical conflicts among liberal democrats are spirited, but they also are conducted within parameters. Liberal democrats of all stripes agree in drawing a principled distinction between the "public" and the "private"; in regarding the "public" as the realm in which members are equal and the "private" as the realm in which inequalities emerge as the inevitable consequence of freedom; and in treating equality in the public realm—in citizenship and under the law—as providing important justification for inequality in other realms, notably the economic. Equality under the law performs the indispensable service for liberal democrats of proving that economic inequality is legitimate, that it is the by-product of freedom and equal opportunity.[2]

Consider, therefore, the problems that awaited the ANC when, along with some junior parties, it was elected to govern South Africa in 1994. Democratic states are suited to justifying economic inequalities, much better suited than apartheid had been, but South Africa's economic inequalities are especially difficult to justify. They did not result from the interplay of freedom and equal opportunity or even from the failure to level playing fields for of all the players. Fields never are perfectly level, of course, but that is not the problem facing the ANC government.

The problem is that South Africa's inequalities were made intentionally and systematically, as the raison d'être of white supremacy. The standard justification for the higher living standards of some citizens—that they prove merit, that they are just deserts—do not work for whites in South Africa. Economic inequalities are difficult to explain away and difficult to rectify.

Capital holds the same advantages in South Africa that it holds in most developing societies. It is scarce and mobile, whereas labor is plentiful and stationary. Recognizing these as facts of life, the ANC, after some hesitation, opted in favor of capitalist democracy during negotiations on the new constitutional order. Economically, the ANC government ditched the anticapitalist rhetoric of the antiapartheid struggle, adopted in principle and upholds in practice the institutions of capitalist society, and is implementing orthodox neoliberal economic policies. Politically, the ANC government respects the constitution and observes democratic forms, promotes stability and enforces order, responds to private interests of various sorts, manipulates racial politics, and calculates party and personal advantage. But the most difficult challenge facing the ANC government is neither to accommodate the demands of capital nor to respect the requirements of democracy. It is to mediate between them.

The ANC sees the fate of capital, in the form of mostly white-owned businesses, and democracy, in the form of mostly poor Africans, as linked by a quid pro quo. As the ANC put its part of the bargain, "The democratic state has to attend to the genuine concerns . . . of private capital if it [is] to ensure industrial stability, sustainable economic growth and a secure political democracy."[3] In exchange, "private capital must recognise that the democratic state offers the best possible environment for the realisation of the interests of capital. So the partnership between the democratic state and capital is mutually beneficial."[4] In other words, capital requires political stability, which can be provided best by democracy, and democracy requires economic investment, which only capital can offer. But business also wants high profits, the poor also want better living conditions, and conflicts between them might become embittered by the past marriage between business and white supremacy and their surviving offspring, inequality in the living standards of whites and blacks. The democratic government, therefore, is in an unenviable position not because it must defend economic inequalities, but because the economic inequalities it must defend stem from white supremacy and are, therefore, illegitimate in terms of liberal democratic values.

The transition to democracy disentangled citizenship from race, opening citizenship to all South Africans irrespective of race, but it did not disentangle class from race. Business still is owned overwhelmingly by whites and still is mostly unreformed. Lest the racial resentments of Africans fuel the economic grievances of the poor, infusing demands for economic re-distribution with the passion of racial nationalism, the ANC is endeavoring to break down the associations of prosperity with whiteness and poverty with blackness. In principle, the ANC could divorce class from race by driving down the class status of whites, so that whites would become poor too. But that would be counterproductive economically and would not help Africans anyway. The ANC prefers to raise African economic elites, with the effect of detaching class from race but without threatening the essential interests of business and without preventing the ANC from using racial appeals for its own purposes. The ideology of non-racialism comes in handy here.

The ANC's conception of non-racialism follows the example of liberal treatments of religion; essentially, it privatizes race. Liberals classically distinguish between what they call the private sphere, where religion is allowed to flourish, and the public sphere, where religion is to be stripped of official standing. Separating church and state serves several important purposes. It protects religion from the state and the state from religion; it also keeps each in its place. Along the same lines, non-racialism locates race in the private, the unofficial, sphere. Officially, the non-racial state is universal. It sees blacks and whites as South Africans only, relegating race to the private sphere (save for the important exception of affirmative action). But making race a private matter not only preserves race; it also keeps race available for purposes of political mobilization. The non-racial state is a liberal democratic state, and liberal democratic states represent "private" interests in "public" institutions.[5]

South Africa's government is democratic and non-racial. It protects civil liberties, guarantees free elections, recognizes individual rights, denies official status to race, and does the things expected of democratic governments. For obvious historical reasons, Africans are especially appreciative of the dignity of democracy, of the rights, voice, and experience of political belonging. But Africans also value democracy for instrumental reasons, because they are the majority of the electorate. The catch, of course, is that Africans constitute the electoral majority only on condition that they conceive of themselves racially and only on condition that their peoplehood as Africans is supreme over their other identities. Democracy, therefore, is legitimated by racial nationalism, because it has the obvious and predictable effect of empowering Africans. But it legitimates only if racial nationalism is valued in the first place, only if empowering Africans *as* Africans is taken by Africans as the preeminent political good.

South Africa's formula for democracy does not stop there. After using racial nationalism to legitimate democracy, democracy is used to legitimate capitalism. Democratic governments in capitalist societies usually accept capitalism in practice and in principle; usually bless it with democratic consent; and usually exclude controversies about its status from the give-and-take of ordinary politics, routinizing capitalism.[6] Legitimating capitalism via democracy in South Africa presumes, however, that racial nationalism is legitimating democracy in the first place. If nationalism is to legitimate democracy and democracy is to legitimate capitalism, it behooves both state and capital to give Africans nationalistic reasons for favoring democracy and capitalism, to give them an African bourgeoisie. South Africa's version of capitalist democracy, as advanced by business and the ANC under President Thabo Mbeki, uses racial nationalism to undergird democratic government; uses democratic government to ratify capitalism; and completes the circle by using capitalism to materialize the significance of racial nationalism, the predicate for the strategy of legitimating democratic capitalism and capitalist inequality.

The relationship between the ANC and capital had not been cozy before the preliminary stages of the transition. Without declaring itself socialist, the ANC left the clear impression that capitalism was to blame for apartheid. It trafficked in anticapitalist rhetoric during the antiapartheid struggle, but, preferring the atmospherics of anticapitalism to explicit calls for socialism, the ANC did not reject capitalism in principle. Its views remained ambiguous.

Consider, on this score, Mandela's interpretation of the Freedom Charter in his "I Am Prepared to Die" speech: "The Freedom Charter . . . calls for redistribution, but not nationalisation, of land; it provides for nationalisation of mines, banks, and monopoly industry, because big monopolies are owned by one race only, and without such nationalisation racial domination would be perpetuated despite the spread of political power."[7] Mandela interpreted the Freedom Charter as calling for nationalization of mines, banks, and monopoly industry. But, read carefully, Mandela called for nationalization as a means to the goal of achieving racial, not economic, equality. Mandela called for nationalization because mines, banks, and monopoly industries were the exclusive property of whites. But Mandela's logic implied a subtext. Implicitly, he allowed for the possibility that mines, banks, and monopolies could escape nationalization provided that they shed their racial character, that they ceased to be the preserve of whites. That is, the problem as diagnosed by Mandela could be corrected by nationalization, as he stated directly. But the problem also could be corrected, as he implies indirectly, by more modest means: by changing the racial complexion of capital. Mandela was not necessarily demanding an end to capitalism, an end to monopolies, or even an end to white-owned monopolies. He was demanding an end only to the monopoly of whites on monopoly capital. Black-owned monopolies would satisfy the criteria Mandela was setting forth.

Mandela opened the way for a capitalist response to the problem of racial capitalism. He did not explore the opening, he and his comrades being on trial for their lives at the time, but during and after the transition thirty years later he put the prestige of his party and his person squarely behind the capitalist alternative. Upon his release from prison, Mandela invoked the Freedom Charter as calling for nationalization, but he soon retreated in the face of unsettling economic news. Foreign exchange reserves were low and budget deficits were high.[8] But the positions of Mandela, Mbeki, and those who were being groomed to become the ANC's senior economic policy makers were shifting even before the ANC became privy to important financial details. Mandela became convinced by business leaders that nationalizing key industries would be imprudent and that adopting neoliberal economic policies would be prudent; the ANC government would have to respect "the opaque mechanics of financial markets, the profit-maximising migration of transnational corporations, and the strictures and interventions of transnational institutions such as the International Monetary Fund, World Bank, and World Trade Organisation."[9]

Mandela and Mbeki's position on nationalizations and economic policy accorded with the larger project of depoliticizing capitalism. They took private property for granted, courted business, and, eventually, instituted their neoliberal economic regimen without consulting with party or government leaders,[10] thus providing capital with an indispensable service that could be provided only by the ANC. The ANC is invincible in national elections, having won 63 percent of the vote in the first election in 1994, 66 percent in 1999, and 70 percent in 2004, and can absorb the political costs of maintaining neoliberal economic policies because it draws on racial solidarities, appealing to Africans *as* Africans. It might be thought that white liberals, who cannot legitimate capitalism and implement neoliberal policies themselves, would regard the manipulation of racialism as the necessary price to pay for extricating capitalism from its compromising past and gaining a government that has the legitimacy to legitimate capitalism. But that is not so. Liberal intellectuals—especially those of a culturalist bent[11]—criticize what they see as the original sin of South Africa's corruption of democracy. They fault the new constitution for conceiving of citizens—no irony is intended here—in classically liberal terms, as autonomous, whole, and integral individuals.[12]

South Africa, according to the culturalist critique, is not made up of individuals who act individualistically, who choose allegiances and associations for themselves. It is made up of groups, and culturalists argue that prudence and justice require that groups should compose the hub of government, that groups, in good Madisonian fashion, should be made to check and balance the power of other groups, formally and institutionally. It is prudent to recognize groups formally because they exist whether or not they are recognized and because small groups must be enfranchised formally if they are to counter the power of large groups politically. It is just to represent groups formally because groups identify people to themselves and affirm who they are. Some culturalists even identify themselves by reference to their group. They are not mere "liberals"; they are "*white* liberals."[13]

In most societies, liberals proclaim their universality, speak of human rights, and incur criticism for ignoring the particular, for abstracting people from the specific conditions that locate and define them. Many—although not all—of South Africa's white liberals, on the other hand, are proudly culturalistic and defiantly particularistic. They take groups as whole and intact before they come to be involved in politics and take group identities as the stuff of politics. It follows, since culturalists have identities developing independently of political activity, that non-racial political institutions do not make South Africans less racial. South Africans, according to the culturalist critique, are racialized by culture, and pretending otherwise merely favors the largest group. It allows the ANC, as the party of Africans, to win election after election, to consecrate the racial majority of Africans with a democratic halo, and to prevent other groups from offsetting the majority group, which does not even admit its groupness. "Majoritarian" democracies merely tabulate the population of each group. They reduce elections to an ethnic "census,"[14] and the party of the largest group wins irrespective of how it governs.[15]

As one liberal wrote of the inaugural democratic election in 1994, "The

ANC's enormous victory was founded less on the non-racialism that it preached than on the reverse, with the election constituting to a large extent a mere 'ethnic census', a worrying notion not only because of the persistence of such strong racial cleavages but because of the difficulties it presents for the development of a properly competitive multiparty system."[16]

Nelson Mandela put a similar point somewhat differently: "It is clear that the majority within these national minorities continue to believe that the ANC represents the interests of the African majority and that their own perceived interests stand opposed to those of the African majority."[17] The problem, according to the culturalist critique, is that voters vote for the party of "their" group; because voters do not vote for the parties of other groups, parties do not compete for swing voters; because parties do not seek swing voters, they do not broaden their base of support; because they limit their appeal, parties remain legitimate only within their own groups; and, because the party of the majority group marginalizes and ignores losing minorities, the minorities turn to subversion.[18]

Liberals rightly appreciate that competitive elections turn the wheel of democracy. Electoral competition makes parties accountable to electorates; causes parties to patch together majorities in each election; bridges insiders and outsiders; promotes pragmatic, problem-solving government; and reconciles losing parties to their defeats, insofar as losers reckon on turning the tables the next time around. If, however, elections become mere formalities, the ins always remain in and the outs always remain out, and minorities are consigned to irrelevance. Consequently, culturalists indict democracy in South Africa as an illusion, pleasing garb disguising the indelible reality of racial domination by the African majority. "It is for this reason," writes Hermann Giliomee, "that we speak of ascriptive voting and . . . of elections that are little more than a census, telling one more about respective sizes of the population groups than about the voters' policy preference. Floating voters form an insignificant part of the electorate, and the result is foreordained by the race and/or ethnic affiliations of the electorate."[19]

Culturalists make a powerful point, and not only because expanding the electorate has not intensified electoral competition. South Africa's political institutions also serve to curb political competition. Elections to the lower house of parliament—the important one—are conducted on the basis of proportional representation, without constituencies. Parties receive seats in proportion to their share of the total vote. A party with 60 percent of the vote gets 60 percent of the delegates in the parliament, with winners being selected from lists ordered by parties. Seats effectively belong to parties, with the party leadership being able to "redeploy" members of parliament and assign seats to members of their own choosing (although in some circumstances, members of parliament switch sides, to the advantage of the ANC). Whoever controls the assignment of seats—in practice, the party leadership—controls the parliamentary delegation,[20] centralizing power at the top, collapsing legislative power into executive power, and stifling "open debate and dissent."[21]

The tendency toward centralized control is accentuated by the control exercised by the central party organs of the ANC—that is, by President Thabo Mbeki—over provincial governments. Leadership of provincial parties has been separated from leadership of provincial governments, preventing provincial figures from concentrating power and allowing the central party to choose provincial leaders.[22] Meanwhile, Mbeki has strengthened and enlarged the president's office, reorganized the cabinet, and asserted direct control over senior bureaucrats, who sign contracts with the presidency rather than with their own ministers.[23]

The centralizing tendencies of the constitution and the state are reinforced by the political culture of the dominant party. The ANC's culture, especially as it developed in exile, responded to the dangers of repression and infiltration by putting a premium on hierarchy, secrecy, and unaccountability.[24] The movements that operated inside South Africa, on the other hand, developed differently. Even though they were more susceptible to penetration and repression, being located inside the apartheid state, they stressed democratic methods of organizing. Following the example of black trade unions, leaders were authorized to act only by democratic mandates after exhaustive debate and were held accountable to their mandates. Inevitably, the cultures as well as the ambitions of the internals and externals clashed once the exiles returned in the 1990s to claim their due as leaders of the liberation movement.

Arrayed behind Thabo Mbeki, the exiles confirmed their control of the party and the party's control over the internal movements. They replaced the culture of debates and mandates—and the unending controversies about who was mandated to represent whom in which debate—with more centralized, less accountable methods of governance. Increasingly, power percolates to the top of the ANC, to the president; the power and independence of parliament shrink commensurately; leaders with power bases of their own are undercut and removed from influential positions (in several cases to run black empowerment corporations); and power is concentrated in a party that, as culturalists stress, manipulates race to shield itself from electoral competition.

Culturalists in South Africa rightly point to the significance of racialism to politics, but miss the significance of economics to politics. Politics for them centers on identities, which are to be expressed and represented, not on interests, which compete for power and resources. Culturalists do not register, therefore, that the ANC's economic policies favor economic elites, or, in other words, that they favor whites disproportionately.

Living standards—nice houses with swimming pools, gardens, and security walls; travel abroad; expensive cars—are not what culturalists mean by "culture"; they mean ethnicity, color, blood. But South African whites generally take prosperity to be part and parcel of their way of life, of what they have in mind when they speak of "white" culture. The point is understood by the Democratic Alliance (DA), the successor in the democratic era to the Progressive Federal Party. Whereas the Progressives embraced culturalist conceptions of politics, the DA stresses conventional liberal individualism, which it deploys, among other things, to attack affirmative action policies.[25] Having made individuals into the bedrock of the social order, the DA recognizes that cultural concerns do not necessarily center on the ethno-cultural identities of groups; they also center on the ways of life of members of groups, that economic policies that have the effect of allowing whites to live the lifestyles of "whites" are cultural in impact. Thus the first problem with culturalist treatments, and one sensed by more individualistic and economistic liberals, is that culture is rendered too narrowly. Culture is reduced to ethno-culture (and ethno-culture, of course, is notoriously difficult to define).

The second problem with the liberal critique of post-apartheid politics, and this point holds for individualistic as well as culturalist liberals, is that it discounts the significance of other forms of power, particularly economic. Capitalist societies vest power in financial markets, corporate boardrooms, and economic discourse. In South Africa, all of these theaters remain under the control of whites. Of course, that does not mean the whites who control them necessarily act *as* whites, that they are concerned with furthering racial objectives. But it does mean that whites have power at their disposal, that their powers are not necessarily limited to economic affairs, and that the government is competing for their confidence; it means that whites, whatever their electoral prospects, have *political* influence, that they have economic power that can be deployed in defense of their "cultural" identities, and that they can check and balance the majority's power.[26]

Besides, the "cultural" identities of whites are reinforced by consumerist, secularizing, postmodernist globalization. The medium of globalizing culture is, of course, the English language, no small advantage to bilingual whites in general and English-speaking ones in particular. Presenting whites as a vulnerable minority on grounds that the parties they support fare poorly in elections denies, therefore, the potency of their cultural and economic power. Focusing on the importance of representing ethno-cultural identities symbolically, culturalists overlook the conspicuous fact that private power remains predominately the preserve of whites and that liberal democratic institutions represent private—including white—power. Yet culturalists have these benefits to whites paling beside the towering fact of the ANC's electoral success. South Africa's constitution is undemocratic, they argue, because it is illiberal (and it is illiberal because it does not recognize identity).

The culturalist critique of South African politics, then, narrows both the ends of politics, making them about expressing identities, and the means to the ends, group empowerment. Having construed influential minorities as vulnerable, they worry that members of disaffected groups will turn against the political system. They expect political instability to follow from conventional liberal representation,[27] regardless of what policies are implemented by the state, on the grounds that representing identities in the state is tantamount to controlling the state and that controlling the state is tantamount to controlling the society. Ignoring the constraints confronting the ANC and the powers remaining with whites, liberals misinterpret the import of their greatest insight.

Racial solidarities *do* influence elections, in spite of formally "non-racial" political institutions, and the ANC does trade on racial identity, representation, and politics. But what white liberals, whether culturalist or individualist, do not see is that the material interests of whites—at least of prosperous ones—benefit from the emphasis on representing African identities. Africanizing state leadership serves as the condition—the camouflage—for stabilizing the state, recognizing the power of business, and instating the material interests of prosperous South Africans (who are disproportionately white). Emphasizing racial identities represents poor Africans symbolically, while putting them off economically.

South Africa is what the World Bank was calling an "upper-middle income" country around the time of the transition to democracy. The wealth of the South African economy, divided by the total population, was somewhat above average for the world as a whole. The per capita GDP of South Africa, the total production per person, was $2,980 (in 1993 U.S. dollars), about the same as Brazil or Malaysia and a cut above the $2,480 per capita GDP for "middle income" countries.[28] White supremacy did leave a reasonably developed infrastructure, financial system, and many of accouterments of the first world (including a medical system that had staged the first human heart transplants). The achievements it bequeathed in some areas, however, were offset by shortcomings in others.

The new democratic government inherited the standard problems of developing economies: poverty, unemployment, shacks, informal settlements. But South Africa was not riding the familiar seesaw of middle-income countries, in which strengths and weaknesses cancel each other to produce middling living standards. Although prosperous for a middle-income country, South Africa fared substantially worse on most development measures than countries with comparable or less wealth. "Among comparable middle-income developing countries, South Africa has one of the worst records in terms of social indicators (health, education, safe water, fertility). . . . Indeed, its social indicators are not very different from those of some low-income sub-Saharan African countries."[29] For example, South Africa's infant mortality rate was 52 per 1,000 live births compared to an average of 35.8 for other "upper-middle" income countries; its mortality rate for children under five years of age was 69 per 1,000 live births compared to 42.6 for middle-income countries; and its life expectancy was 63 years—this is before the AIDS pandemic hit with full force—compared to 69 in middle-income countries as a whole.[30] It follows, inasmuch as average living standards are lower than those of comparison groups, that some South Africans were living especially well. Income inequality, as quantified by the "gini coefficient," was vast, 0.61 in 1992. Only Brazil had a worse score, 0.63.[31]

Low living standards for the many in South Africa were the condition of high living standards for the few. It was too simple to equate the many with blacks and the few with whites because the equation of race and class was breaking down in the twilight of white supremacy. But the correlation between wealth and race remained strong. At the time of the transition, "nearly 95% of South Africa's poor [were] African, 5% [were] Coloured; less than 1% [were] Indian or White. Africans [had] nearly twice the unemployment rate (38%) of Coloureds (21%), more than three times the unemployment rate of Indians (11%), and nearly ten times the unemployment rate of Whites (4%)."[32] Thirty-three percent of Africans had running tap water in their dwellings, 46 percent had electricity or gas as their main energy source for cooking, and 42 percent had flush or chemical toilets; the figures for whites were 97 percent, 99 percent, and 99.8 percent, respectively.[33] Democratizing South Africa, in other words, did not have a lot of wealth to distribute, although it did have a little more than most countries; it distributed what it had very unequally; and economic inequality correlated strongly with race.

South Africa generated extreme inequality in income throughout the era of white supremacy, but it was narrowing toward the end. A state survey on household income in South Africa's twelve main urban areas found the gini coefficient was decreasing in them (from 0.63 in 1990 to 0.55 in 1995),[34] and the mean annual household income in the twelve largest urban areas was increasing rapidly, by 140 percent for Africans, 93 percent for Asians, and 68 percent for Coloureds between 1990 and 1995.[35] "The most affluent 20% of households earned 60% of all household income in 1995 [as compared to] 70% in 1990" and "the middle . . . 50% of households were earning 13% of income in 1995" as compared to 10 percent in 1990. Meanwhile, the household income of whites shrank by 3 percent. Still, "the poorest 20% of households earned 2% of all income in 1990 and the same 20% earned 2% in 1995."[36]

Africans (and Asians) were recording large gains; the percentage of Africans in the highest quintile increased from 2 percent in 1990 to 6 percent in 1995, crowding out whites (51 percent of whites were in the top quintile in 1990, 33 percent in 1995).[37] As many Africans were prospering, more were stagnating or slipping. Thirty-four percent of African households were in the bottom quintile of household income in 1990, increasing to 38 percent in 1995.[38] In other words, the number of Africans in the poorest or the richest quintiles was increasing before the ANC took power. Some were becoming comfortable (by the standards of South Africa), but 65 percent of Africans remained "poor" by the reckoning of the World Bank.[39] "Despite [its] relative wealth, the experience of the majority of South African households is either one of outright poverty, or of continued vulnerability to becoming poor."[40] Put differently, the Human Development Index (HDI), which measures "a country's economic and social wellbeing,"[41] had whites living about like Israelis (ranked nineteenth in the world), whereas Africans were living a little worse than Swazis (ranked one hundred and seventeenth).[42]

Income inequality was declining between racial groups, but was widening within them, especially among Africans. As a group, the gini coefficient among Africans in the twelve main urban areas soared from 0.35 in 1990 to 0.51 in 1995,[43] a stunning increase. With some blacks becoming substantially more affluent and whites becoming slightly less affluent, the racial character of economic inequality was changing. Economic inequality within racial groups, according to a World Bank study, had become "at least as important as between group inequality in explaining South Africa's overall inequality."[44] A black middle class—which included a substantial African component—was emerging as apartheid was disintegrating, as both a cause and an effect of its collapse.

Around the time of the transition, in other words, income inequality was diminishing among South Africans as a whole; income inequality was narrowing among racial groups, as the position of whites was slipping and those of Asians and Africans were improving; and inequality within racial groups was becoming "at least as important" as inequality among groups. That is, inequality within groups, especially Africans, was increasing as inequality among groups was decreasing, and income inequality among Africans came to rival that among South Africans as a whole. The share of income going to Africans rose in the early 1990s; but "almost all of this increase occurred among the top 10% of black earners, while poorer blacks actually experienced a decline in income."[45] These trends, moreover, were pronounced before the ANC commenced using the state to construct an African elite.

The incoming ANC government was stepping into a sensitive economic situation. Capital had been effectively on strike since the early 1980s; per capita GDP had diminished by 19 percent from 1981 to 1993;[46] blacks expected relief from deep poverty and extreme inequality; and business feared economic mismanagement. Moreover, the ANC had devoted little thought to economic issues during the struggle against apartheid. Some tendencies in the ANC had extolled the command economies of the USSR and East Europe, especially East Germany, but that model had been discredited by the time of the transition. In the absence of other alternatives, the ANC campaigned on the Redistribution and Development Programme (RDP) during the 1994 election, even as its leaders were being converted quietly to neoliberal orthodoxies. Developed mostly by the Congress of South African Trade Unions (COSATU), the RDP identified "attacking poverty and deprivation" as "the first priority of a democratic government."[47] The government promised to "make substantial public investments so as to meet the basic needs of all citizens and in particular the disadvantaged."[48] To achieve the objective of reducing poverty, the RDP proposed what it said was an integrated program of economic development and social democratization.

Economic development was to focus on developing South Africa's infrastructure, which was to yield two kinds of benefits. On the one hand, it was to improve directly the quality of life of the poor in South Africa, to "provide access to modern and effective services like electricity, water, telecommunications, transport, health, education and training for all our people."[49] On the other hand, developing the infrastructure was to ignite what was essentially a Keynesian logic. Meeting basic needs was to "open up previously suppressed economic and human potential in urban and rural areas. In turn this will lead to an increased output in all sectors of the economy, and by modernising our infrastructure and human resource development, we will also enhance export capacity."[50] In other words, the RDP promised to promote economic growth by eradicating poverty; the slogan was "growth through redistribution." The RDP states:

> The Government's central goal for reconstruction and development is to meet the social and economic needs of the people and to create a strong, dynamic and balanced economy which will
>
> - create jobs that are sustainable, and increase the ability of the economy to absorb new job-seekers in both the formal and less formal sectors
> - alleviate the poverty, low wages and extreme inequalities in wages and wealth generated by the apartheid system to meet basic needs, and thus ensure that every South African has a decent living standard and economic security
> - address economic imbalances and structural problems in industry, trade, commerce, mining, agriculture and in the finance and labour markets
> - integrate into the world economy utilising the growing home base in a manner that sustains a viable and efficient domestic manufacturing capacity, and increases the country's potential to export manufactured products

- address uneven development within the regions of South Africa and between the countries of southern Africa
- ensure that no one suffers discrimination in hiring, promotion or training on the basis of race or gender
- develop the human resource capacity of all South Africans so the economy achieves high skills and wages
- democratise the economy and empower the historically oppressed, particularly the workers and their organisations, by encouraging broader participation in decisions about the economy in both the private and public sector.[51]

The core economic precept of the RDP was to grow the economy by redistributing wealth and alleviating poverty; the core political precept was to empower the people, to use "civil society" to democratize society as well as the state. "The empowerment of institutions of civil society is a fundamental aim of the Government's approach to building national consensus."[52] The ANC also pronounced that

> Thoroughgoing democratisation of our society is . . . absolutely integral to the whole RDP. The RDP requires fundamental changes in the way that policy is made and programmes are implemented. Above all, the people affected must participate in decision-making. Democratisation must begin to transform both the state and civil society. Democracy is not confined to periodic elections. It is, rather, an active process enabling everyone to contribute to reconstruction and development.[53]

In principle, the logic of the RDP collided with the "growth oriented" policies recommended by the International Monetary Fund (IMF).[54] According to the IMF, businesses will invest more if investments are profitable; businesses will create more jobs if they invest more; and poverty will be curtailed, to the particular benefit of blacks, if more jobs are created. As the IMF put it, "[S]ubstantive gains in income for the nonwhite sections of society will principally depend on their ability to enter skilled employment, and on the ability of the economy to grow more rapidly than has been the case in the past two decades."[55] To that end, the IMF dispensed its customary advice for promoting higher rates of domestic savings and rates of investment; discouraging government spending, deficit financing and tax increases; narrowing budget deficits; liberalizing trade; restraining growth in wages; and rewarding capital.[56] State intervention in the economy—as exemplified by the RDP, which ostensibly guided the economic policy of the first ANC government—loomed as the problem, and private investment appeared as the solution.

In practice, the ANC's commitment to the RDP was tepid from the beginning, amounting to only 2–3 percent of state budgets, even before the government adopted the IMF's advice in 1996 in the form of a neoliberal economic package called "Growth, Employment and Redistribution," or GEAR for short. GEAR reflected the supply-side, monetarist, "Washington consensus" policies advocated by the IMF. Because "sustained growth on a higher plane requires a transformation towards a competitive outward-oriented economy,"[57] it called, among other things, for increasing "non-gold exports," "brisk expansion of private sector capital formation," "a faster fiscal deficit reduction programme to contain debt service obligations, counter inflation and free resources for investment," stable exchange rates, anti-inflationary monetary policies, tariff reduction, and "tax incentives to stimulate new investment in competitive and labour absorbing projects."[58] The proposal concurred with some of the RDP's objectives, such as developing infrastructure and investment in labor intensive projects, but the thrust of GEAR shadows the IMF's assessment of South Africa's economy. It endorses "supply-side industrial measures," "wage moderation," "greater flexibility in the labour market regulatory framework," and promises that "deficit reduction releases the pressure . . . on the capital market, . . . facilitates the accelerated flow of domestic resources into industrial investment and contributes to the overall financial stability of the economy."[59]

GEAR was supposed to do all kinds of things. By the year 2000, for example, the fiscal deficit was to be 3 percent of the GDP, average real wage growth in the private sector was to be 1.4 percent, real bank rates were to be 3.7 percent, real private investment growth was to be 7.1 percent, GDP growth 3.3 percent, employment growth 1.3 percent, and gross private saving was to be 20.6 percent of the GDP; only the goals for deficit reduction have been met. Annual growth rates, for example, have ranged between 0.69 percent and 3.0 percent. Of course, disappointing growth rates might be caused by factors, domestic or global, beyond the control of the government's economic policies. But neoliberalism has a spotty and controversial record in general and carries the additional risk in South Africa of rent-seeking, that is, of businesses pocketing the incentives offered to them without doing what is expected of them.

Critics challenge the IMF's policies for increasing deprivation, dampening growth, failing to narrow income disparities or generate growth, and ignoring local particularities.[60] Neoliberals counter that supply-side policies, by turning to the private sector, promote markets; that markets motivate business; and that business, taking advantage of market opportunities, generates employment as firms compete with each other. Whatever the validity of the IMF's logic, it is predicated on a central premise. Market competition is what makes business create jobs in pursuit of profit, a point so obvious that it passes unsaid. But rather than being market-sensitive, consumer-satisfying, and demand-meeting entrepreneurs, South Africa's conglomerates are cross-owned, rent-seeking, competition-evading oligopolies. They recoil from market competition.

South African business originated in the mining industry. From the outset, as Frederick Johnstone notes, "Groups, as they were called, came to establish common central organisations and to implement common measures in order to eliminate competition between the mining companies for factors of production, especially labour, and to rationalise the process of production."[61] Its profits having been inflated by collusion, coerced labor, and anticompetitive practices, mining houses established and bought companies throughout the economy. As a team of economists describes,

> A small cluster of families and institutions control a large proportion of South Africa's core mining, manufacturing, and financial assets. The institutions through which these concentrations are represented are the large and highly diversified corporate groups that dot South Africa's industrial landscape. These corporate centres, in turn, control groups (themselves extremely large and diversified) that represent the conglomerate's interests in broadly defined economic activities—mining, manufacturing, and financial and other services.[62]

As of the year 2000, the five largest conglomerates were reckoned to control—not to say own—61 percent of market capitalization on the Johannesburg Stock Exchange (down from 83 percent a decade earlier).[63]

The conglomerates—including Anglo American, Sanlam, and Old Mutual—compound their influence through holding companies, subsidiaries, and pyramids. The team of economists went on, "If Company A owns 51% of the voting stock of Company B, which in turn owns 51% of the voting stock of Company C, then A will have acquired control of C but will, through its 51% commitment to B, have contributed only some 25% of C's equity capital."[64] The effect of concentrated, pyramided business structures is exaggerated by pervasive cross-ownership and joint ownership. Consider the most important example: Anglo American, South Africa's dominant conglomerate. A few years ago, the Oppenheimer family, which had held controlling interest in Anglo American, sold most of its holdings in Anglo American and increased its holdings in De Beers. But before these transactions, Anglo American owned 32.2 percent of the shares of De Beers and De Beers owned 28.7 percent of the shares of Anglo,[65] making them cross-owning oligopical partners, whose watchword was *collusion,* not competition.

The arrangement was criticized by investors for depressing the value of their shares, and eventually was altered. The Oppenheimer family reduced its holdings in Anglo American, and together with Anglo American acquired 45 percent of De Beers apiece, then delisted it. While Anglo and De Beers no longer are cross-owned—the Oppenheimers own about 3.5 percent of Anglo but do not control it, and Anglo owns 45 percent of De Beers—the practice remains common. Cross-owning, moreover, coexists with joint ownership, which likewise exerts a depressing effect on competition. To give a few examples, Sanlam, a leading (Afrikaner) institutional investor, owns 4.9 percent of Old Mutual, another leading institutional investment house, and each owns parts of other leading companies. Sanlam owns 6.8 percent of South African Breweries and Old Mutual 5.6 percent; Old Mutual owns 20.8 percent of Standard Bank and Sanlam 6.3 percent; and Old Mutual owns 51 percent of Nedcor, another banking firm, and Sanlam 3.5 percent. Just to cover its bets in the banking industry, Sanlam also owns a portion of FirstRand and a controlling interest—22 percent—of ABSA Group, giving it little reason to encourage competition in the banking sector.[66]

Monopolies and collusive oligopolies, according to neoclassical economic theory, "restrict output and charge a higher price."[67] Liberal economic theory has the fact of competition making capitalism work, encouraging full production, exerting pressure for lower prices, and preventing capitalists from maximizing profits by underproducing. Competition is what forces producers to increase production beyond the point at which monopolists maximize their profits, and employment expands commensurately to meet the increased production. By the same token, the benefits that are said to be accorded by market capitalism evaporate without competition. Absent competition, producers can get away with cutting off production when the marginal unit reaches the profit maximizing point and need not extend production to the unit at which the average profit is zero.

Therefore, illiberal capitalist economies—economies in which the means of production are owned privately and production is for profit, but in which colluding capitalists muffle competition—restrict production to the disadvantage of the economy as a whole.

The consequences of South Africa's collusive uncompetitive capitalism are pretty much what liberal economists would predict: inefficiency, underproduction, low investment, high unemployment, and avoidance of risk. Domestic and foreign investors alike shy away from investments in new productive capacity[68] and instead they steer investments to established financial assets.[69] The exceptions, moreover, prove the rule: most foreign investments are in mining and were made in the early years of the industry. Subsequent investments mostly are returns on earlier investments.[70] Collusion is common,[71] exports are centered on raw material, the domestic market is difficult for outsiders to enter,[72] and competitiveness and foreign investment are low. According to the *World Investment Report* in 1997 by the United Nations Conference on Trade and Development, "Market dominance by a few major players is one of the main reasons why foreign investors have avoided South Africa after the end of sanctions."[73] Unemployment is high, but profits are good. Anticompetitive measures, in other words, have accomplished their purpose, raising profits by restricting output.

Note the implications of the structure of South African business for the economic policies that the IMF advocates. The IMF champions supply-side policies because, it says, they generate jobs. But collusive capitalism neutralizes market competition; market competition is what forces firms to increase production; increasing production is what increases the number of jobs; and increasing the number of jobs is what cures poverty. Take away the competition and, liberal economics says, companies will generate profits at the expense of jobs.

So why was GEAR adopted? Austerity packages usually are forced onto governments that are sinking in debt and running out of options. Needing hard currency for imports, governments look to borrow money abroad, where they find that banks are loath to throw good money after bad. The IMF then steps in, offering to give its approval to credit markets so that the country may get loans on condition that governments make specific structural adjustments. They must shrink budget deficits, adopt monetarist policies, and open trade, but mostly governments must shift the locus of economic decision making from themselves to markets (just as the ANC does through GEAR). In exchange for surrendering much of their authority over economic policy, governments get the loans they need. But they also get unwanted political problems. Their hands are tied by the IMF, just at the time when governments are forced to cope with publics angered by the loss of jobs, subsidies, and social spending. This is what makes the ANC's choice to adopt neoliberalism so striking. It volunteered willingly for the kind of policies that usually are imposed on unwilling governments.

In 1985, international creditors, recoiling from the combination of economic stagnation and political crisis, quit rolling over loans to the apartheid state. As a result, the foreign debt that greeted the ANC was manageable; the IMF's help was not necessary. The apartheid state had incurred substantial debt to domestic lenders in its waning days in a forlorn effort to buy black support, but that did not install the IMF in position to dictate economic policy to the democratic government. If neoliberal policies benefit capital, which is mostly white, and inflict immediate pain on the poor and working classes, which are core ANC constituencies; if the medium- and long-term consequences of structural adjustments on economic growth, which are supposed to make the pain worthwhile, are suspect;[74] if economic growth, even in the event it occurs, turns out to benefit mostly the affluent minority of the population; and if collusive, cross-owned businesses suppress job creation, why did the ANC choose the kinds of policies urged by the IMF, which took the form of GEAR, over the RDP?

The ANC's leadership, especially Mandela, Mbeki, and their senior economic ministers, adopted GEAR mostly for economic reasons. They accepted the principles of neoliberal economics, which maintain that public debt jeopardizes economic growth, that poverty is solved by growth and growth results from giving capital incentives to invest, and that the country was better off instituting neoliberal policies at the time and in a manner of its own choosing. The leadership also appreciated that the antiapartheid movement had given capital reason for the alarm; that the new government was on probation as far as much of world business was concerned; that the ANC's denunciation of capitalism and a string of failed economies in Africa raised doubts about the ANC's reliability; and that adopting GEAR, even if it did not work as promised, allayed doubts about the ANC's orientation towards business. The ANC soothed national and international capital through GEAR. Plus, the ANC appreciated the value of having international institutions—the IMF, the World

Bank—available as scapegoats for disappointed expectations. It could blame international markets and world financial institutions for the slow pace of change. Besides, the ANC had not implemented the RDP fully in the first place. It spoke the language of Keynesianism, but even as it was speaking of growth through redistribution, it was adjusting its economic thinking to neoliberal orthodoxies.[75]

In embracing neoliberal economics in the early 1990s, the ANC repudiated positions it had staked out during the struggle against apartheid. Although its positions had been ambiguous, they certainly had not been neoliberal. The ANC had called for the nationalization of key industries, had sided with the Soviet bloc in Cold War conflicts, and had denounced American power faithfully (and not unreasonably, in view of international alliance structures in southern Africa), and most of its senior leaders during the underground period from the 1960s into the early 1990s also were Communists. But Communist leaders and militant sensibilities had not made for a socialist program. As Thabo Mbeki had noted in 1984, when he was a rising star in both the SACP and the ANC, "the ANC is not a socialist party. It has never pretended to be one, it has never said it was, and it is not trying to be."[76] The ANC's tone, in other words, was more radical than its program. Not only were Mandela and Tambo, the ANC's most prominent leaders, democratic nationalists; the SACP also had compelling reasons of its own for preferring that the ANC not declare itself a socialist organization.

The SACP distinguished between what it considered the national democratic and the socialist revolutions, after the fashion of the Soviet understanding of the Russian Revolution. The SACP assigned the ANC the task of accomplishing the first revolution, of creating a unified republic that would abolish racial distinctions, promulgate equal citizenship, unify the nation, and lay "the basis for the transition to socialism,"[77] and the SACP reserved for itself the honor of achieving actual socialism. If the ANC had become socialist, it would have intruded into the domain, and undermined the purpose, of the SACP. The very alliance that ostensibly demonstrated the ANC's socialism, in other words, really confused the matter.

South African business paid little heed to the dialectics of Communist ideology, of course, but it did recognize opportunities when it saw them. Having been compromised by its association with white supremacy, business needed to quell the rambunctious organs of civil society; to depoliticize the political economy, particularizing and institutionalizing the grievances that white supremacy had generalized into indictments of the capitalist order as a whole; and to detach wealth from its association with whiteness. Inasmuch as only the ANC was in position to sell what business was buying, yet inasmuch as the ANC's intentions were clouded by its alliance with the SACP and its traditional suspicions of business, the politics of the negotiation favored the ANC. But the economics favored business. The economy, on the verge of becoming the ANC's responsibility, desperately required an infusion of capital investment; currency reserves covered only three weeks of imports.[78] Consequently, the ANC had strong incentives for reaching a rapprochement with capital and even for adopting GEAR. But given that neoliberal economic policies were informing the ANC even during the RDP period, because in practice the RDP accepted and worked within the framework of neoliberal economic principles, it is not clear why the RDP had to be disbanded or why it was not allowed to coexist with GEAR, albeit subordinated.

Thabo Mbeki advocated neoliberal economic policies most effectively. The son of a senior figure in the SACP and ANC, Mbeki had risen through the ranks of the ANC in Zambia, ultimately becoming Oliver Tambo's deputy. When the ANC returned to South Africa in 1990, Mbeki emerged as one of the most influential advocates of the returning exiles, who had sustained party organizations from the time of the ANC's banning in 1960 until its unbanning in 1990. Yet the very prospect of the ANC's victory had the paradoxical effect of exposing the weakness of the exiles' position. The exiles had become dispensable, in part because they already had served their historical function of preserving the ANC in the dark years and in part because they did not control what had become the critical levers of power, the organs of civil society and of the township rebellion that had forced the state and capital to abandon apartheid. Nevertheless, the exiles prevailed. Having retained Mandela's loyalty and having mastered the arts of political survival and bureaucratic infighting in Zambia, they remained entrenched in the ANC's central apparatuses. It was from there a short step to enter the highest echelons of the state, the cabinet, the bureaucracies, and so forth once the ANC was elected to govern.

The exiles, therefore, had compelling *political* reasons for seeking alternatives to the RDP. In calling for the participation of trade unions, community associations, women's and religious groups, and civic associations, that is, for civil society, the RDP was seeking to empower the very organizations that the exiles had eclipsed in establishing control over the party and state. As the point was put in the government *White Paper* on the RDP,

> With respect to mass-based organisations of civil society—especially the labour movement and the civics—their role in the establishment of political democracy was central. They have also won very substantial improvements in the social and economic lives of their constituents. A vibrant and independent civil society is essential to the democratisation of our society which is envisaged by the RDP. Mass-based organisations will exercise essential checks and balances on the power of the Government to ensure that Government does not act unilaterally, without transparency, corruptly, or inefficiently. . . . The Government must therefore provide resources in an open and transparent manner, and in compliance with clear and explicit criteria to mass organisations to ensure that they are able to develop or maintain the ability to participate effectively as negotiating partners of the Government. The social partnership envisaged by the RDP does not, however, imply that mass organisations do not retain the right to their own interpretation of and their own goals for the RDP. It does imply that there is agreement to find solutions to constraints, which will emerge in the RDP's implementation. . . . Thus a series of agreements or accords will be negotiated to facilitate the full participation of civil society, together with the Government, in order to find ways to take down the barriers which emerge during the course of the RDP.[79]

States, even those headed by returning exiles, crave order, routine, and autonomy; the RDP was committed to undermining all these things. The RDP talked of partnership between the mass organizations of civil society and the state, which had the effect of curbing the prerogatives of office; compounded the offense by inviting the organizations of civil society to develop and pursue their own agendas; and then committed the state to pay for the independence of civil society. The RDP, in checking the autonomy of the state, making the state accountable to civil society, and enhancing the very activists whom the exiles were in the process of displacing, threatened the interests of the state and the exiles.

GEAR, however, served the interests of the exiles, and not only in shifting the initiative from COSATU and civil society. Precisely because GEAR was anathema to core ANC constituencies, it had to be imposed summarily and pre-emptively, as Mandela and Mbeki had done. And because it could not be sustained consensually and democratically, it accentuated the style of politics practiced by the exiles. Civil society had to be kept at bay; unresponsive party apparatuses had to be safeguarded. Paradoxically, popular dissatisfaction with GEAR favors more centralization and less accountability.

South Africa under ANC government has achieved economic and development successes. The ANC is proud that it has shrunk the annual deficit, which exceeded 9 percent of the GDP just before the transition, to a mere 1 percent; that exports have grown substantially; that it has increased the amounts of social transfer payments—pensions, subsidies for children, disability support, and the like—by about 350 percent; that it has increased recipients from 2.6 million to 6.8 million;[80] and that it now allocates most grants on the basis of need, thus de-racializing them. In 1990, 70 percent of transfer payments went to Africans, increasing to 79 percent in 1995 and 84 percent in 2000.[81] "The poorest 20% of households receive the largest amount from grants, not just as a proportion of income, but also in absolute terms. Fully two-thirds of the income for the poorest quintile [of South Africans] is attributable to state transfers."[82] Social spending, which is being concentrated on the poor, has increased as a proportion of the state budget (from 46 percent in fiscal year 1995–96 to 49 percent in fiscal year 2002–3). Meanwhile, interest payments have decreased from 19 percent to 15 percent of the budget.[83] In effect, the ANC is paying for increases in social spending with savings on interest,[84] and it is magnifying the impact for beneficiaries by shifting spending from richer to poorer, that is, from whites to Africans.

As a result, South Africa is faring reasonably well on some indicators of development. Health care, immunization, and nutrition programs have expanded, and more households have access to clean water.[85] From 1995 to 2000, the proportion of households living in formal dwellings increased by 7 percent,[86] and the proportion receiving clean water increased by 4 percent, even as the number of households was growing.[87] Most impressively, 94 percent of children between seven and fifteen now attend school,[88] girls are attending school at "one of the highest [rates] on the continent,"[89] and the student-teacher ratio is improving too.[90] Nevertheless, the development record of the democratic government is hugely disappointing, partly because the quality of black schools remains spotty and because "in per capita terms, on average, government real non-interest expenditure declined by 1.6 per cent annually between 1995 and 2002,"[91] but mainly because of the HIV/AIDS crisis and the government's ineffectual response to it.

In 1995, life expectancy was 58 years; in 2002, it was 46 years and dropping. In 1995, South Africa scored 0.735 on the United Nations' Human Development Index and ranked below approximately sixty countries. By 2002, the other twenty-seven countries that had registered similar scores (between 0.70 and 0.77) in 1995 still were ranked mostly in the 60s, 70s, and 80s (although three were in the 90s, and Guyana is 104th) on the index.[92] But South Africa fared 119th in the world in 2002 and ranked above only two countries (Gabon and Botswana) that have higher per capita GDPs. Its HDI score trailed behind forty-four countries with lower per capita GDPs.[93] "For South Africa, the gap between its per capita ranking and its HDI ranking has grown from –10 to –64 in 2001, indicating, relative to other countries, the rising gap between the country's per capita performance compared to its progress in human development."[94] A similar statistic, the Human Poverty Index (HPI), "reflects the distribution of progress and measures the backlog of deprivation that still exists."[95] With low numbers being better than high ones, South Africa's HPI was 16.4 in 1995 and 22.3 in 2001.[96]

The ANC's economic performance likewise is controversial, but for opposite reasons. Whereas the ANC's response to HIV/AIDS rejected the consensus of medical research, its response to economic challenges embraces the Washington consensus. Unfortunately, its economic policies are not succeeding in their stated tasks either. Economic inequalities between racial groups, which had narrowed from the mid-1970s until the early 1990s, steadied about the time when the transition was commencing. The per capita income of Africans as percentage of the per capita income of whites, for example, has remained constant since 1990 (12 percent in 1990, 12 percent in 1995, and either 12 percent or 13 percent, depending on whether "optimistic" or "pessimistic" assumptions are made, in 2000).[97] Meanwhile, economic inequalities among Africans, which had increased from the mid-1970s until the early 1990s, likewise leveled in the mid-1990s.[98] In 1993, the lower half of the African population garnered 13 percent of the total income (including wages, transfers, and returns on property) of Africans; by 2000, it got 12 percent. That is, the per capita income of Africans as a percentage of the per capita income of whites and the share of income going to the poorer half of Africans have not grown since the advent of democracy, and, moreover, would have *shrunk* if not for infusions of social spending. The economy is generating inequality and poverty, but more democratic state spending is blunting these developments.

Studies disagree about the extent of poverty—always difficult to define and measure—and its trajectory, whether the proportions of poor South Africans is growing, shrinking, or staying the same. Optimistic interpretations maintain the portion of the population that is poor is slightly lower than when the ANC entered the government, depending on how data are interpreted.[99] By this account, the problem is not that jobs are not being created—that is, the problem is not neoliberalism—but that population growth is exceeding job growth. Pessimistic interpretations, however, warn "the poorest groups of households may be earning proportionately slightly less in 2000 than in 1995."[100] Either way, transfer payments are offsetting the worst costs of poverty and are compensating for the failure to reduce the rate of unemployment.

The number of jobs increased between 1995 and 2000. But the number of people looking for jobs also increased (even with the AIDS pandemic), and "[n]ew job creation in both the formal and informal sectors is not keeping pace with the demand for work."[101] Poverty is growing, in other words, because unemployment is growing. As a result, real per capita incomes declined by 3 percent and the real individual median income by 17 percent between 1995 and 2000.[102] That is, individuals in the middle of the population were 17 percent poorer in 2000 than they had been in 1995, including transfer payments. Put another way, 28 percent of households in 2000 met the income criteria set for the lowest 20 percent in 1995 and 52 percent of households in 2000 met the criteria for the lowest 40 percent in 1995.[103] In 2002, 10.5 percent of the population lived on less than $1 a day and 24 percent on less than $2.[104]

Households headed by Africans in 2000 earned 19 percent less and spent 28 percent less than in 1995.[105] In 1995, 29 percent were in the lowest quintile of income and 53 percent were in the lowest two quintiles; five years later, 33 percent were in the lowest quintile and 60 percent in the lowest two. The results for African households headed by women, predictably, are worse; in 2000, 41 percent were in lowest quintile versus 27 percent for households headed by men.[106] Meanwhile, the incomes of households headed by whites and Coloureds increased in real terms by 15 percent and 19 percent, respectively. The problem, however, is not so much that inequality is worsening as that it is not diminishing anymore. It narrowed in the run-up to democracy, then leveled once democracy was achieved (the gini coefficients for the society as a whole was 0.61 in

1992, 0.56 in 1995, and 0.57 in 2000).[107] But as overall inequalities were declining, inequalities among Africans were rising from 0.49 in 1975 to 0.57 in 1995 and 0.59 in 2000.[108] With inequalities in the society having narrowed and inequality among Africans still widening, inequality among Africans now resembles, even exceeds, that within the society at large.

The macroeconomic data under the democratic government, and especially under GEAR, tell a similar story. The share of total national income going to workers as compensation fell from 50 percent in 1995 to 45 percent in 2002 and going to profits increased from 27 percent to 30 percent.[109] The economy imported capital, but exported almost as much.[110] GEAR was meant to provide incentives for capital to invest, yet "net investment (gross investment minus the consumption of fixed capital) as a percentage of GDP declined sharply from an average of 14.6 per cent during the 1970s to 7.7 per cent during the 1980s. During the 1990s and between 2000 and 2002, it was only 2.8 per cent and 2.3 per cent respectively."[111] The ANC has dispensed with deficit financing; it was 4.2 percent of the GDP in 1995 and merely 0.2 percent in 2002.[112] But unemployment has worsened.

According to the *South Africa Human Development Report*, "Using the extended definition of unemployment, which includes discouraged job seekers, the . . . unemployment rate increases to 42.1 percent. . . . The high and growing rate of unemployment reflects the increasing vulnerability of South African workers and their families. . . . 87 per cent of the bottom 40 per cent of South African households had no or one working family member and relied heavily for their livelihoods on pensions or remittances in 2001.[113]

The data are not precise in all details, but the contours are clear. The poor might or might not be getting poorer, but it is clear that there are more of them; that they still suffer despairing poverty for a middle-income country; that economic inequality among Africans now rivals that among South Africans as a whole; and that transfer payments, not job creation, are what prevent matters from worsening. The compromise for the ANC government is that the arguments it makes in defense of its record effectively belie its fundamental economic strategy. In claiming that transfer payments compensate for shortcomings in the creation of jobs, it implicitly is confessing that supply-side strategies that were to create jobs are not doing what they were supposed to do.

The ANC government has held up its end of the bargain. It defends property rights, slashes state deficits, and curbs inflation. But business, neoliberalism notwithstanding, has not done what was anticipated of it. Growth has not met predictions and the growth that has occurred has not kept pace with increases in job seekers. Consider, on this score, South Africa's economic record divided into three periods: the four years of the transition (1990–1993); the three years of ANC-led governments with the RDP combining with neoliberal polices but without the formal constraints of GEAR (1994–1996); and the four years of GEAR (1997–2000). (See the table below. Technically, GEAR's time has passed, but the policies continue more or less unabated.)

In the first four years of GEAR, economic growth slowed, interest rates increased, and capital formation stalled. (Unemployment probably increased too, but unemployment statistics are unreliable.) Meanwhile, the net inflow of foreign direct investment did not improve much (0 percent in 1994, 1 percent in 1995 and 1996, 3 percent in 1997, 0 percent in 1998, 1 percent in 1999 and 2000).[114] Of course, it does not follow that GEAR necessarily caused these problems—the GEAR years coincide with rapid flows of "hot money" into and out of emerging markets throughout the world—or, even if growth did diminish and unemployment did rise in response to GEAR, that these are not merely temporary dips on the way to sustained growth in the medium and long terms. And the growth rate did improve and interest rates did diminish substantially from the

Key economic indicators before, during, and after transition to democracy

Variables	Four years before democracy (1990–1993)	Three years of democracy and RDP (1994–1996)	Six years since GEAR (1997–2002)
GDP growth (annual %)	Averages −0.56% per year	Averages +3.55% per year	Averages +2.53% per year
GDP growth % per capita per year	Averages −2.60% per year	Averages +1.32% per year	Averages +0.41% per year
Gross fixed capital formation (annual % growth)	Averages −7.44% per year	Averages +11.03% per year	Averages +1.66% per year
Real interest rates	Averages +3.8% per year	Averages +7.66% per year	Averages +8.92% per year

Source: Table developed from World Development Indicators, November 2005.

early years of GEAR to the years after it ended formally. But whatever the cause and whatever the eventual outcome of neoliberal policies, the failure of neo-liberal economic policies to stimulate increases in the living standards of the ANC's core constituencies put the ANC in need of more than neoliberalism. Capitalism is supposed to break down parochial identities and inscribe universalistic standards, but the effect of collusive illiberal capitalism in South Africa is to reproduce and reward racialism.

The black middle classes originated more or less in spite of the state, as shown by their growth in the 1970s through the early 1990s. Apartheid, in keeping with the imperatives of segregation, required a black middle class to serve the needs of blacks (as teachers, nurses, and bureaucrats in the homeland administrations). But rapid economic growth in the 1960s corroded the confines of the black middle classes, as the economy created demand for administrators, supervisors, and professionals that whites could not fill alone. Faced with the conflicting imperatives of segregation and capitalism, the state responded ambivalently and incoherently. It increased the numbers of black students at the primary, secondary, and university levels, but consigned them to dismal schools; it acquiesced to and eventually encouraged the economic gains of middle-class blacks, but insulted them through petty apartheid; and it depended on the labor of middle-class blacks, but denied them freedom, equality, and membership.

Under apartheid, the black middle classes generally refused to sacrifice their politics at the altar of personal economic advancement. Sensitive (like most rising middle classes) to status and prestige, they were unreceptive to feelers put out by reform apartheid, became bulwarks of the UDF, and have come to compose the backbone of the ANC. Growing rapidly, the black middle classes now want economic growth, affirmative action, and access to schools and universities for themselves and their children. They benefit from democracy in South Africa and value their feelings of belonging and membership. But the black middle classes, while treasuring their new-found political influence, do not owe their existence to it. Political influence helps them, but they do not require it. The black middle classes benefit from state patronage, but they depend on their productivity in the modern economy for their existence.

The black middle classes are important politically and economically, but they cannot turn the trick of insulating capitalism from racialist challenges. Legitimating capitalism requires a class of black capitalists, and black capitalists, unlike the black middle classes, are not evolving in response to essentially economic needs. Thus, the black bourgeoisie must be constructed deliberately through political means. To that end, the ANC government pressures companies to promote blacks to senior positions, awards state contracts on the basis of affirmative action, reminds business of the value of political connections, encourages white-owned conglomerates to sell units to Africans, and mandates that specified percentages of shares in mining companies be owned by consortia of black investors. These policies, which pass under the banner of "black economic empowerment" (BEE), persuade conglomerates to sell some of their holdings to the nascent black—and especially African—bourgeoisie, but BEE benefits business too.[115] BEE alters the political import of racial nationalism.

The argument in favor of BEE begins with the vast economic inequalities between whites and blacks. As Mbeki argues, albeit with some exaggeration,

> South Africa is a country of two nations. One of these nations is white, relatively prosperous, regardless of gender or geographic dispersal. It has ready access to a developed economic, physical, educational, communication and other infrastructure. . . . The second and larger nation of South Africa is black and poor, with the worst affected being women in the rural areas, the black rural population in general and the disabled. This nation lives under conditions of a grossly underdeveloped economic, physical, educational, communication and other infrastructure. It has virtually no possibility to exercise what in reality amounts to a theoretical right to equal opportunity, with that right being equal within this black nation only to the extent that it is equally incapable of realisation. This reality of two nations, underwritten by the perpetuation of the racial, gender and spatial disparities born of a very long period of colonial and apartheid white minority domination, constitutes the material base which reinforces the notion that, indeed, we are not one nation, but two nations.[116]

Note that Mbeki, in keeping with the traditions of black resistance to apartheid, locates the origins of South Africa's two nations in the inequalities of the political economy. The "reality of two nations" is "born of . . . domination" and is expressed in the material disparities, not the cultural differences, between blacks and whites. Mbeki does not reject the existence of the two nations; rather, as he put it later, he wants to distribute "wealth and economic power in line with the demographics of our country."[117] That is, race is accepted as a principle for distributing wealth and power; the goal is to raise blacks as a group to become equal with whites as a group.

Mbeki's equation of prosperity with whiteness and poverty with blackness no longer holds true,[118] but it is true that the correlation between class and race remains strong, that most of the upper classes are white and most Africans are poor, and that, therefore, both government and business have reason for worrying about the combustibility of overlapping economic and racial cleavages. As long as capital remains overwhelmingly white, the political economy is prone to polarizing between white haves and black have-nots, to poor blacks mobilizing racial solidarities in support of economic grievances. Previously, "racial domination had the unintended consequence of consolidating and legitimating subordinated racial identity into a potential basis for resistance."[119] Now, racial stratification has the predicted effect of preventing the poor from enlisting racial solidarities in their behalf, of reshuffling the relationship between race and class, and of extending the appeal of the language of racial redress beyond the poor to the upwardly mobile.

Capitalism, by the logic of BEE, becomes legitimate because blacks—and specifically Africans—are becoming capitalists.[120] Economic elites are becoming *multiracial* both in the sense that they are coming to include blacks and whites and in the sense that black elites legitimate the capitalist order. As Mbeki put the point, "As part of our continuing struggle to wipe out the legacy of racism, we must work to ensure that there emerges a black bourgeoisie, whose presence within our economy and society will be part of the process of the deracialisation of the economy and society."[121] The black bourgeoisie, because it is black, stops racial solidarities from being turned against capital (and, therefore, makes African economic elites partners with, not threats to, established elites) and dissociates business from the legacy of white supremacy (which is why the head of Anglo American had called for something along these lines in the mid-1980s). Plus, BEE furnishes these services at a moderate price.

The conglomerates do not give assets away. They sell subsidiaries to consortia of black investors, sometimes at a discount, and frequently finance transactions via banks they own or influence. Through the deals, black consortia attain formal control of a few subsidiaries, but the conglomerates retain influence in the "new" businesses. Senior management changes, but nothing prevents the new BEE company from remaining integrated into the conglomerate, from still supplying and serving as a market for it. And for their troubles, the conglomerates pick up not only politically connected friends, but politically connected friends who share specific interests with them. "Black-empowerment deals," as *The Economist* noted, "have done little to establish genuine businesses."[122] "New" businesses, like the old businesses, recoil from competition, and competition threatens leveraged—that is, African-owned—businesses most of all, inviting collusive businesses to hide their anticompetitive interests behind the fig leaf of racial empowerment.

The record of BEE has been uneven. In 1994, no black-owned companies were listed on the Johannesburg Stock Exchange (JSE); in 1998, black empowerment consortia owned (with borrowed funds) about 7 percent of the value on the JSE, although some companies may have fronted for white interests. By 2002, the market capitalization of black economic empowerment consortia had shriveled to 2.2 percent.[123] Mismanagement, overbidding for shares in the early wave of BEE, and sinking stock prices, especially in the mining industry, typically are blamed for most failures in the first wave of BEEs. But GEAR also contributed to the failure.

GEAR attacked inflation in standard neoliberal fashion, through raising interest rates, thus pitting the *economic* logic of neoliberalism against its *political* counterpart, black economic empowerment.[124] High interest rates raise the costs of sustaining debt loads, causing failures to BEE consortia that borrowed heavily and, in a telling irony, profiting established conglomerates. Most famously, a very prominent BEE consortia (JCI), bought two gold mines from Anglo American. When the price of its shares dropped, JCI sold the mines back to Anglo American, and Anglo American "made a handsome profit on a sale it had originally declared would be a magnanimous gesture towards wealth-sharing."[125]

Business is cooperating actively in building the black bourgeoisie, as was exemplified by its reaction to legislation passed in 2002 that required 15 percent of mining assets to be owned by blacks within five years and 26 percent within ten years. Controversy was stirred by some details of the legislation, but the Chamber of Mines, the organ of the mining houses, insisted from the beginning of consultations that it objected only to the bill's defects, not to its objectives.[126] In due time, the mining houses endorsed the legislation because, as the point was put by the president of the Chamber of Mines, "We don't want to happen here what happened in Zimbabwe. We need urgently to develop a more inclusive economy in

South Africa."[127] Specifically, he argues, "More people in this country have to feel that they are part of the system, that they are benefiting from the system, that the system is working with them and for them, and not excluding them. I don't think there's any doubt that government and industry are in total agreement on that issue."[128]

Whereas conglomerates consider the construction of the African bourgeoisie to be good business, a useful means to the end of secure profits, the ANC is following the time-honored nationalist custom of building a bourgeoisie of its own kind for the good of the people. Some of the means the NP used to build the Afrikaner bourgeoisie were notorious, of course, but it also boosted Afrikaner-owned businesses through parastatals and pressure on English-speaking capital to sell subsidiaries to Afrikaners. For similar reasons, the ANC is building an African bourgeoisie.

The ANC mobilizes the nationalist claim—that the "who" determines the value and meaning of the "what"—to insinuate that the black bourgeoisie behaves differently and better than the white bourgeoisie. Its interests "coincide" with the "immediate interests of [the] majority,"[129] and not only because the black bourgeoisie and the black majority both oppose white racism. The black bourgeoisie should promote "job creation, the fostering of skills development, the empowerment of women, the strengthening of the popular organs of civil society, and active involvement in the fight to end poverty."[130] By the logic of culturalism, the African people, including the poor, prosper because some Africans are being enriched. To quote Mbeki, "As part of the realisation of the aim to eradicate racism in our country, we must strive to create and strengthen a black capitalist class. . . . I would like to urge, very strongly, that we abandon our embarrassment about the possibility of the emergence of successful and therefore prosperous black owners of productive property and think and act in a manner consistent with a realistic response to the real world."[131] The African people, including the poor, are obligated to back the black bourgeoisie as part of the struggle against racism.

But what is good for the goose is not good for the gander. The logic of racialist legitimation has the African poor sublimating their particular interests as poor people to the general interests of the African people, as it is coming to be embodied in the African bourgeoisie. Racialist legitimation does not, however, have African elites sublimating their class interests. They affirm their people by affirming themselves, by becoming prosperous, which counts as a decisive victory over racism. In their economic capacity, African-owned businesses follow economistic incentives, acting to maximize their profits; in their political capacity, they appeal to racial solidarities to convince the poor to go along with policies helpful to them, as owners of businesses.[132]

The ANC also benefits directly and indirectly from the development of the African bourgeoisie. Conceiving of itself as the political expression of the nation, the ANC believes that what strengthens the nation strengthens the party. The new African bourgeoisie puts more resources at the disposal of Africans and puts the Africans with the resources in debt to the ANC for steering state contracts their way, legislating affirmative action requirements, and pressuring white capital. As the African bourgeoisie honors its debt, the ANC's power is augmented. Pallo Jordan, a prominent figure on the *left* wing of the ANC, boasted, "Whereas in the past there were no captains of industry in the leading organs of the ANC; today an NEC [National Executive Committee] member heads one of the largest conglomerates trading on the Johannesburg Stock Exchange. This corporation, moreover, employs thousands of other ANC members as well as ANC supporters!"[133]

African embourgeoisement is particularly helpful to neoliberal tendencies in the ANC. The RDP, remember, had declared poverty and economic inequality as the economic problems and redistribution and development as the solutions, and black embourgeoisement does not address either. Narrowing economic inequality for the RDP was a good thing, preserving and widening it were bad things, and it did not matter much whether the beneficiaries of inequality were white or black. The problems of economic inequality were independent of the racial complexion of the winners and losers. Racial nationalists disagree and congregate around a politics of racial nationalist empowerment. Where the RDP implied skepticism toward business, BEE prefers cooperation; where the RDP pursued economic equality as its objective, BEE values racial empowerment; and where the RDP took economic interests as axes of organization, BEE deploys racial identities for the purpose of stabilizing capitalism. By the logic of BEE, the bourgeoisie legitimates itself as a class through its African fraction.

BEE, in other words, is concerned with the position of groups as groups, independently of the position of most of their members. Establishing equality among groups becomes, on the basis of culturalist assumptions, a value distinct from establishing equality among people outside and without regard for their groups. That is, pursuing economic equality between whites as a group and blacks as a group is different from pursuing economic equality between whites and blacks as individual South Africans (or blacks and blacks for that matter). A rising ceiling does not lift all boats. Means can rise while medians sink, although so far, the medians are sinking without the means rising. The African rich are getting richer, the poor more numerous, and culturalism finds the silver lining.

The point is not that the ANC does not care about the poor or that the gains by the black middle classes are not significant, but that the ANC is being turned toward culturalism—toward black embourgeoisement—by entrenched economic power, and that culturalism is invoked to make a virtue of necessity. The economy is developing a black middle class, which reflects the economy's demand for labor and the black middle class's initiative, and the state is cultivating a black bourgeoisie, yet the share of national wealth going to blacks, including Africans, is not changing much.[134] Meanwhile, poverty and inequality are continuing more or less unabated. The virtue of culturalism (or racialism: the two are the same in South Africa) is that it exaggerates the good of burgeoning elites, provides ways of dealing with the ensuing political and ideological challenges, and serves the ANC's purposes. African economic elites cement the partnership with business; prove the reality of social transformation; benefit the African people; fortify some ideological tendencies in the ANC at the expense of others; "wipe out the legacy of racism";[135] enhance the power of its representative, the ANC; and, in affirming racial empowerment as a value, compensate for ongoing poverty and inequality.

Mbeki's ANC is responding to the power of collusive business structures, extensive economic inequality, and a history of racialism with a politics that centers on implementing neoliberal economic policies, making transfer payments to the poor, encouraging the growth of the black middle classes, and constructing African elites. By Africanizing elites, the ANC broadens the racial coalition that benefits from collusive business organization, depoliticizes economic inequality (by detaching it from the "two nations"), and manipulates racialism. The new African bourgeoisie, because it shares racial identities with the bulk of the poor and class interests with white economic elites, is in position to mediate the reinforcing cleavages between rich whites and poor blacks without having to make more radical changes (and to offer role models to the black middle classes). Cutting in the African bourgeoisie enlists new elites in collusive businesses, but does not expose old ones to new competition; reforms the racial character of economic inequality, but does not narrow it much;

and rewards racialist political strategies of legitimation and stabilization, but does not furnish the African poor with effective institutional recourse. BEE changes the beneficiaries of and the justifications for the political economy, but not its logic.

It frequently is remarked that socioeconomic divisions have supplanted racial divisions.[136] In the new South Africa, "insiders"—the 30–60 percent, depending on the estimate, of the population that is doing reasonably well in the formal economy—participate in the benefits of South Africa's prosperity. "Outsiders"—the 40–70 percent or so of the population that is poor, unemployed, and disproportionately rural, young, and female—suffer crushing poverty and disease and barely taste the national wealth. The ANC has made important strides for the "outs" by building housing, delivering water, and shifting state spending to the poor, but business has not reciprocated by increasing investment, generating growth and jobs, and narrowing economic inequality.

Nevertheless, those who are being left behind have little recourse through the ANC, due to centralization, or through elections, due to racial voting. Some of the poor, therefore, are reviving militant civil society, which had been eclipsed by the process of democratization. Where white supremacy had aligned most of civil society behind the general demand for full and equal citizenship, democracy particularizes and unbundles grievances, routinizes governance, and supersedes civil society. But the ANC's neoliberal economic policies are geared for the long term, having failed to redress poverty and inequality much in the short term. Civil society is stepping into the breach, in effect becoming the opposition to a government that, although not meeting popular hopes for prosperity and redistribution, remains invincible electorally. Intent on organizing those without influence in the state and economy, the poor and sick mostly, the more ideological elements in civil society are challenging "the South African government and the dominant global economic ideology"[137] and blaming the ANC for what Patrick Bond calls the ANC's "moral surrender" to "global apartheid."[138] Committed to reversing the effects of poverty, championing ideals of economic transformation and popular empowerment, and reviving the tradition of popular struggle and direct action, radical civil society harkens back to the heroism of the struggle of apartheid, celebrates direct democracy, mass participation, and redistribution, and challenges the routines of democratic capitalism.

In challenging the government, in connecting particular grievances to the ANC's acquiescence in globalization,[139] and in exposing the underside of dividing society between "ins" and "outs," radicals encounter two problems. First, organizing the poor is hard. The poor, precisely because they and their leaders are caught in the daily struggle for survival, are especially susceptible to patronage. The ANC can offer jobs (in the legislative and executive branches of government at the municipal, provincial, and national levels), and talented leaders, lacking resources and alternatives, can be brought into the ANC. Thus, when radicals in civil society are challenging the government, they also are identifying, developing, and recruiting political talent for the ANC.[140]

Second, civil society presses demands and wins particular victories, but radicals want more; they want to challenge neoliberalism and global capitalism. They attribute "global apartheid" to the ANC's opportunism. But the ANC's accommodation with business originates in the power of capital and uses racial nationalism to win democratic sanction. In combination, democracy and racial nationalism complicate and demobilize; they mutate racial identities from a source of resistance into a pillar of governance, mobilize voters, and frustrate opponents. Apartheid could not legitimate itself; "global apartheid," by contrast, is legitimated democratically, making the struggle against "global apartheid" vastly different from the struggle against apartheid.

8

The Who, Not the What

I prefer a country run like hell by Filipinos to a country run like heaven by Americans.

—MANUEL QUEZON, FILIPINO NATIONALIST AND FORMER PRESIDENT OF THE PHILIPPINES

It is a truism of politics that states seek control over territory and people. It also is a truism, an unpleasant one, that states generally originate in violence, coercion, and repression, a point made by theorists of a realist wont.[1] But violence, although necessary to defeat rivals to the state's sovereignty, also is expensive, costing money, time, energy, attention, and goodwill. If, however, states can secure control through persuasion and consent, they can spare themselves the trouble of having to exact obedience from recalcitrant subjects. Consequently, states are in the market for ways of convincing their members to accept their integrity, for strategies of legitimation.

The point was made elegantly by Jean-Jacques Rousseau. "The strongest," he noted, "is never strong enough to be master forever unless he transforms his force into right and obedience into duty."[2] The more citizens identify with "their" states, the fewer resources states must expend on convincing citizens to accept their legitimacy, which is why states are interested in associating citizenship with national identities, and in promoting the idea that people of like identities belong together in states that express their likeness. If organizing on the basis of common national identities makes states stronger,[3] states develop powerful incentives for seeking nationalist legitimation.

Democracies usually are thought to produce legitimacy, but the reverse holds too. Democracies not only produce legitimate states; legitimate states also favor democratic government. If states do not have to deal with questions of membership and boundaries, do not have to resolve who may participate and where their writ runs, states avoid disputes that are difficult to decide through discussion (and not only because the disputants argue about who may participate in the discussions). National identities identify who is and is not to be enfranchised as citizens in states, who belongs together and who belongs apart, and which state should control what territory. The more citizens think they belong together, the more democratically their states can behave. The sense of common nationhood not only helps resolve central political issues—who belongs, what unites members, where institutions extend—but helps settle them without violence, peacefully and democratically. If citizens agree that they belong together in the state because the state expresses them as a people, consent, discussion, and compromise within institutions can come to the forefront, and coercion, repression, and violence can recede into the background.

Common national identities not only favor democratic government; they also answer a question raised by the idea of democratic legitimacy. Democracies rarely are thought to need legitimation, being considered to be self-legitimating. Democracies operate through consent and consent produces legitimacy; democracies, therefore, are inherently legitimate. But buried beneath the democratic syllogism is an unstated premise. If consent from the people is what produces legitimacy, if the state is justified because "the people" choose it, something must account for whose consent produces the legitimacy, for what makes the choice of some people relevant and the choice of others irrelevant. By the logic of consent, the people choosing the state must be chosen *before* they can choose the state. States, after all, do not require consent from all people, only from those people whose consent is deemed to matter. Some principle of selection, therefore, logically precedes the offering of democratic consent, again bringing nations into the picture. Nations identify who makes up the people, who belongs in a state, and whose consent matters. As John Stuart Mill put the point, "Where the sentiment of nationality exists in any force, there is a prima facie case for uniting all the members of the nationality under the same government, and a government to themselves apart. This is merely saying that the question of government ought to be decided by the governed."[4] By the logic of democratic legitimation, nations are prior logically to democracy. States derive from consent and consent derives from identity.

By corollary, national identities solve a related problem for democracies. Democracies must justify who does and does not qualify for the bounty of citizenship. They proclaim equality and invoke universalistic ideals, but admitting all comers as citizens would flood and overpopulate democracies, and it also would deprive them of control over their membership and identity. Torn between impulses to universality and responsibilities of government, democracies must restrict membership without compromising ideals. "National" identities, by furnishing principled criteria for citizenship, identify who belongs and curb unrealistic stirrings toward universality.

National identities perform much different services too. Democracy has come to be defined largely as a way of making decisions, of arbitrating public disputes. It is conceived as a set of procedures, as a *method* of governing, and one that respects individual rights and clears space for the equality of all citizens. "Democracy's guiding principle," as Guillermo O'Donnell and Philippe Schmitter write, "is that of *citizenship*. This involves both the right to be treated by fellow human beings as equal with respect to the making of collective choices and the obligations of those implementing such choices to be equally accountable and accessible to all members of the polity."[5] John Rawls maintains a similar balance between citizenship and procedure: "Each person has an equal claim to a fully adequate scheme of equal basic rights and liberties, which scheme is compatible with the same scheme for all; and in this scheme the equal political liberties, and only those liberties, are to be guaranteed their fair value."[6]

Rawls and O'Donnell and Schmitter conceive of democracy largely in terms of procedural equality within the state. But Rawls draws an additional corollary from the guarantee of equality in citizenship. If citizens are to be truly equal, they must hold citizenship that is equal—citizenship, that is, that does not elevate some of them over others. Consequently, Rawls's democracies may not adopt positions on controversies about values; they may not take positions that endorse the substantive values of some of their citizens to the detriment of others.[7] Citizenship may not be invidious. For example, democracies may not implement distinctly Christian policies lest they diminish Christian citizens who believe in the separation of church and state, not to mention citizens who are not Christian in the first place. Rawls makes the public sphere into the sphere of procedural rights and the private sphere into the sphere of substantive morality. It follows that Rawls's democracies do not provide public purposes and that consensus on fairness, reasonableness, mutual respect, and toleration as public values must be enough to sustain them.

But the proceduralism of much democratic theory hides a problem. Democratic theory builds on a syllogism, by which democracies are legitimate because they respect procedures and procedures are legitimate because citizens value them. The syllogism works, however, only on condition that procedural rights and toleration are valued in the first place.

In societies in which procedural values and mutual respect have not been internalized, respecting them does not buy the state much legitimacy. It is preaching to the converted. To compensate—to furnish the public meanings that bind citizens without compromising liberal equality by prescribing public ends—procedural democracies quietly ground themselves in communities that are supposed to be older than and to exist prior to procedural democracies. The nation—conceived as given culturally—fills the existential void procedural democracies leave. Nations furnish a foundation of unexamined purposes, of pre-political meanings, and infuse democracies with passion and solidarity, with the goals—advancing "the people"—that are to be pursued procedurally. Democratic government can become about means because national identities take care of ends.

If national identities ground democratic states, identify who deserves citizenship, convince citizens that the borders grouping them together are fair, imply consent, facilitate democratic methods, and put proceduralism in the services of public purposes, a lot rides on how they are conceived. Conceived politically, nations are open to all citizens; conceived ethnoculturally, they orbit around exclusive nuclei. In opposition, the ANC promised that a common citizenship would produce a common nation; as citizenship expanded, the nation would expand commensurately. South Africans would become one people, would become *South African*, because they were to share common citizenship. But most democracies incline toward culturalist conceptions of nations, treating nations as if they precede states.

It is common for democratic governments in multiracial societies to make accommodations with racialism. They declare it as a private affair, *culturalizing* it, and point out that they cannot abolish racial solidarities and identities and that, indeed, they do not have the power or the right. But conceiving of races as cultures is not merely the default option; it also does a lot of work for democracies, allowing them to withhold formal status from races without challenging the importance of race in informal, or private, associations. Conceiving of races as cultures comes at the expense, however, of conceptual and empirical complications, especially in South Africa. Conceptually, cultural practices can be adopted, assimilated into and switched out of, and combined. Individuals may be born into and reared in one culture, but they can change their allegiances and even can combine cultural practices. Races, though, are conceived differently. By virtue of their pseudoscientific connotations, they are taken to be fixed genetically. Skin color, hair texture, and outward manifestations of "race" cannot be changed, and internal ones cannot be changed either. A white cannot become black, nor can a black become white.

If races cannot be opted out of and if races are entwined with cultures, it follows that cultural identities are unalterable too. Culturalists refrain from making the inference explicitly, for obvious reasons. But in practice they do treat cultural identities as if they are bestowed by race. White liberals take for granted, for example, that the ANC is an "African" party, an assessment that discounts its Westernizing, modernist proclivities. Even though the ANC is proclaiming liberal democratic values, is upholding capitalism and instituting neoliberal economic policies, and is elevating English into the language of government, culturalists regard the ANC as "African" for a clear reason. The ANC's culture—and, therefore, its politics—is determined by its race, and race is indelible.

Black culturalists make similar assumptions, as shown by the terms they used for denouncing blacks who worked with apartheid. Apartheid's blacks were denounced as "collaborators" and were accused of "betraying" their race, charges that presume the premises of culturalist politics. Referring to blacks as "collaborators" implied, in the first instance, that they were not the real enemy. They served the enemy, as stooges and dupes; but they could not *become* the enemy, and not only because apartheid's racism relegated them to a subordinate status. For calling them "collaborators" implied, in the second instance, that blacks could not escape the political obligations implicit in their race. Collaborators are traitors who betray something—their *race*—that remains *theirs* to betray and that can not be unmade by choice. Race, it has been said, does not wash off.

If the conceptual problem with equating races and cultures is that cultures are rendered as fixed, the empirical problem is that races and cultures are made coterminous. If ethnic and cultural groups are equivalent, and if cultural and racial groups also are equivalent, then ethnic and racial groups must be equivalent too. But racial and ethno-cultural groups are not and never have been interchangeable in South Africa, something the ANC recognized when it conceived of races as clearing houses for the political affairs of tribes and the white state recognized when it defined both Afrikaners and English-speakers as "whites." Races, unlike ethnic groups, are not based on perceived kinship and are not based on shared cultural practices either (which is why South Africa's new African elites can adopt Western lifestyles while remaining African). Culturalists, in other words, can ground *both* race and ethnicity in culture only by erasing the distinction between the two categories, something they are loath to do.

Confusion about what race means is reflected in the double meaning of the word "black." In the 1970s and 1980s, the antiapartheid movement used "black" in a Bikoist sense, highlighting the political determinates of race. Race, it implied, derives from sides forged through political conflicts, allowing "Coloureds" and "Asians" as well as "Africans" to become "black." In practice the politicism of the antiapartheid struggle may have been permeated by culturalism, which is why blacks working with apartheid were scorned as "collaborators." But it was politicist conceptions of race that endangered the ideological foundations of apartheid by attacking the notion that identities are given, unchangeable, conflicting, and best kept apart in separate polities.

Reflexively, the apartheid state countered by affirming culture as the source of political identities. It reserved the word "black" for Africans only, highlighting the cultural determinates of identity and differentiating apartheid's "blacks" from Biko's "blacks," and prescribed that political participation be organized communally. Apartheid's blacks, because culturally distinct from Coloureds and Asians (and often from each other too), had to be kept politically distinct as well. Thus, the apartheid state, when forced to acquiesce to popular pressure in the early 1980s, responded with "tri-cameralism." Whites retained political control, Coloureds and Asians received separate and subordinate "representation" in the central government, and Africans were denied an assembly of their own in the central government (because they had been denationalized by separate development) but were accorded a voice in underfunded and essentially powerless municipal governments. Apartheid, in other words, manipulated "cultural" identities on behalf and in concealment of political interests.

Apartheid exploited ambiguities in the meaning of "black," but it did not have to invent them. Ambiguities were there to be exploited already, generated by the rival conceptions of race. To the extent race is conceived politically, blacks were forged from those injured by white conquest, white appropriation of land and wealth, and white racism. But to the extent race is conceived culturally, Africans were a community, incipiently if not consciously, waiting to be "awakened" even before their encounter with white power. What is changing in the democratic era, tellingly, are not the conceptions of race, but the advocates of the rival conceptions. During the heyday of the antiapartheid struggle, culturalist conceptions of race were the preserve of the state. They remain embedded in the state, even though the post-apartheid state is democratic and is governed by the ANC. Culturalism is coming to serve the ANC's needs.

The culturalist nation grounds democracy. It identifies members, furnishes purposes, and avoids the politicist circularity of having nations being produced by democracies and democracies presuming nations. Avoiding politicist dialectics, culturalists propagate myths of pre-political nations. They tell members of one culture that they are one politically because they are one culturally; that boundaries between members and nonmembers, citizens and noncitizens, are set by culture; that what benefits the nation benefits its members; and that nations precede states. Culturalists may have their history wrong in insinuating nations as integral, but their shibboleths can work political magic anyway. Imagining nations as cultures has the effect of grounding the nation in the culture (and the state in the nation), and escapes the tautology of having the people who are presumed to have called for the state actually turning out to have grown from the state.

Culturalists contend that governors and governed are likely to bond if they hail from similar backgrounds. Joseph Raz was thinking about personal relationships when he spoke about the intimacy that is possible only within one's group, but he could have been talking about government too. Culturalists claim that the ANC, because of its insight into and identification with the African majority, governs differently than whites, and they back their claim with some evidence. The ANC government has improved access to water and electricity for millions of blacks;[8] has implemented affirmative action; has cut military spending; has appointed new judges and officeholders; has introduced "transformation" to blacken the leadership of public and private institutions; and has dropped the insults, the condescension, the racism, the violence, and the late-night pass raids that the racial state had directed against the majority of the people. But changing government priorities does not necessarily prove culturalist points for two reasons.

First, culturalists attribute changes in policies, priorities, and preferences to the identity of the governors. As Africans, they understand and care more deeply about the people. But the ANC's accomplishments also are attributable to democracy and its interest in responding to the electorate. Second, culturalists claim not only that Africans govern differently than whites, but also that identities matter in their own right, independently of what governors do. Of course, citizens identifying with the government for reasons of racial solidarities expect rewards for their loyalty and grumble if rewards are not forthcoming. But culturalist legitimation does not derive from the receipt of benefits and does not depend on delivering goods and services. It revolves around identification, not exchange, around *who* governors *are*. The culturalist credo is that the subject in the sentence matters regardless of the predicate; the person who does something matters independently of what it is that he or she does. The "who" matters not just instrumentally, not just because the who influences the what, but it also matters expressively. The point for culturalists is that "we" are acting for "ourselves," in "our" own name.

Culturalist legitimation superficially resembles democratic legitimation. Both have "the people" doing the legitimating and both have governors representing the people. But the two modes diverge on one pivotal score. What matters to culturalists (and nationalists and racialists) is that the people are represented, in the sense of being *made present,* in government when governors act on the basis of identities they share with the governed. Governors may be distinguished from the governed by an array of differences (class, power, office), but they are united through cultural identification. What matters to democrats, however, is that representatives are accountable to people and that accountability is assured through impartial procedures (such as free elections). For democrats, the "how" and "what" count for more than the "who."

The South African state is explicitly non-racial and the ANC's traditions are largely politicist. But the general nature of democracy and the particular configuration of South Africa's political economy are pushing the ANC toward culturalism. With the economy failing to meet the expectations of many Africans, whose living standards are stagnating or declining, with inequalities widening among Africans, and with collusive capitalism interfering with the plans for creating jobs, the ANC is under pressure to recast the nation. It wants to win elections and the power of business has checked its egalitarian impulses, encouraging it to seek a *cause* above transfer payments to justify itself. Sometimes it is visibly reluctant to endorse culturalist definitions of the people, to endorse conceptions that privilege *the* people over actual people. But culturalism tempts with one overriding attraction. In positing an integral people and making group identities the fulcrum of politics, it provides the ANC with a realistic, more achievable agenda than economic redistribution.

South African democracy is facilitating, managing, and legitimating capitalism in the manner of other capitalist democracies. But democracy in

South Africa bears the additional burden of having to save capitalism from the consequences of its association with white supremacy, from the overlap of race and class, and from extreme economic inequality. The value of democratic government dawned gradually on business leaders from the mid-1980s onward, as they struggled to disassociate themselves from what had become the permanent crises in apartheid. Consider, for example, the views of Harry Oppenheimer, a former chair of Anglo American Corporation and head of the family that controlled it. "I am of the opinion," he said in an interview in 1987, "that you have to have one-man, one-vote."[9] Around the same time, Cyril Ramaphosa, then the Secretary-General of the National Union of Mineworkers and later the chief architect of the constitution, said, "We obviously see a country where the wealth of the country is going to be fairly and equally shared amongst all, where the main sources of revenue are going to be owned by the people of this country, and not to be owned by the capitalists, as is the case now. We see a country where socialist principles are adhered to which will ensure that the wealth of the country is *shared equally by everybody*."[10] (Ramaphosa went on to head one of the most important black empowerment corporations.)

Business, in other words, was coming to need democracy almost as much as democracy would come to need it. Faced with the prospect of ungovernability and compromised by past involvement with white supremacy, business needed to be cleansed of the original sin of racial capitalism and to be baptized as multiracial by a government with the democratic credentials to rein in and supersede popular movements. This is why the ANC government was especially attractive to business: having been legitimated by nationalism, the ANC could provide stable democratic government, and democratic government could legitimate capitalism.

The apartheid state had incurred large budgetary deficits, subsidized employment, and bred inflation. Lacking legitimacy, the apartheid state subordinated monetary and fiscal policy to the imperatives of political survival and to the detriment of business. The reluctance of business to invest made the point clearly: it lost confidence in apartheid. The democratic state, however, can get away with instituting the economic policies business seeks. As one democratic theorist put the point,

> We have now seen a number of examples where countries in Latin America, Eastern Europe and East Asia have voted out of office governments they associated with the pain of globalization reforms. The

> new governments that came in made some adjustments but kept more or less the same globalizing, marketizing policies. How did they get away with that? Because the democratic process gave the public in these countries a sense of ownership over the painful process of economic policy reform. It was no longer something completely alien that was being done to them. They were being consulted on it and given a choice about at least the speed of the process, if not the direction. Moreover, as a result of the opportunity to participate in the process and throw out people who they felt had moved too harshly and abruptly, or too corruptly or insensitively, the whole process had much greater political legitimacy, and thus more sustainability.[11]

Democratic governments not only guarantee property rights; they also can respond to the unpalatable implications of the fact that economies suffering low investment need investments from business. Democratic states respect the rule of law, militate against arbitrary rule, differentiate between areas where it is appropriate and inappropriate to exercise political power, and adhere to rules themselves, going only where they are authorized to go and behaving themselves while there. But democratic states also, because they are legitimate, can enact less populist economic policies than authoritarian governments. Where apartheid compiled debts in a futile attempt to court popularity, the ANC cuts public debts.

Liberal democracies also draw political disputes into institutions, where they are contained, normalized, and resolved. In establishing institutions for redressing grievances, democracies shift challenges from whatever settings are at hand—shop floors, schools, streets—into institutions. And when they are brought into institutions, disputes are addressed, limited, and regulated according to norms. Labor disputes, for example, are taken to labor courts, where they are to be adjudicated on the basis of the terms of the case and the provisions of the law. Disputes are localized, particularized, insulated: particular grievances do not metastasize into general indictments of the whole social order.

Apartheid politicized and generalized grievances by rooting them in political statuses, forcing blacks to achieve the standing to press for reforms as the precondition of seeking reform and making radical transformation the condition of moderate reforms. Democracy, though, narrows and muffles grievances, reconciles and depoliticizes them. It relegates some disputes to the "private" realm, where they are deemed to be beyond the scope of political redress, and addresses others through political institutions. Apartheid made revolution into the precondition of reform; democracy advances reform as an alternative to revolution.

Democratic states, having furnished favorable policies and conducive institutions, provide a final service to business. They promise, as Rawls and O'Donnell and Schmitter note, the equality of citizens *as citizens:* citizens are equal in the state and under the law. Of course, democracies often fall short of their promises in practice, but by definition they affirm the principle of political equality and the ideal of freedom. The practice of freedom inevitably produces economic inequalities, as some people succeed and others fail in their freedom. But democracies have an answer: unequal results prove the reality of freedom. Thus, democracies pit the principles of freedom and equality against each other. Both are necessary and honored; democracies balance—they do not eliminate—the conflicting imperatives of freedom and equality.

Something passes unsaid when democratic theorists debate the relationship of freedom and equality, however. They regard conflicts between political equality and economic inequality as irresolvable within the framework of democracy. But the relationship of freedom and equality also is dialectical, with the two elements—equality in the state promised by citizenship and inequality in society that results from freedom—constituting and reproducing each other. Equality in citizenship and under the law is bounded inside the state. Citizens are equal in the state, but not necessarily outside the state. They may be unequal in their other capacities, outside citizenship.[12]

Thus the subtext of political equality: democracies must treat citizens as equal in principle, but they must allow and protect (some of the) inequalities that develop outside the state, in the realm of society. Inequality, to the extent it does not originate in or define citizenship, is legitimated precisely by the ideal of political equality. Equal citizenship implies equal opportunity, and equal opportunity constitutes proof that winners deserve the fruits of their victories. They have earned them. Economic inequality is legitimate on the grounds that citizens, because equal under the law, hold (more or less) equal chances of determining their own fates. "Public" equality blesses "private" inequalities, a priceless benefit to capital in South Africa.

Democracies expect growth and prosperity in return for their contribution to capitalism, but business has not held up its end in South Africa. In funneling its bounty to a minority of the people and in making no dent in the numbers of unemployed and poor, business effectively prevents the democratic government from delivering general prosperity. In compensation, the government uses the economic advances of the black upper and middle classes to mediate between ideals of public equality and realities of private inequality.

Racialism lubricates democratic capitalism. It insinuates pre-democratic bonds among the people; deepens and personalizes identification with the democratic state, relieving pressure on the government to satisfy actors with its performance; and attaches people to the state's decisions because they identify racially with the decision makers, adding intimacy to the relationship between citizen and leader, between electorate and elected. Thus, racialism facilitates democracy and democracy normalizes capitalism, removing it as a topic of political controversy (no small gift in the context of South Africa). In turn, business constructs an African bourgeoisie, reinforcing the nationalism that validates the democracy that confirms capitalism. But black economic elites legitimate economic inequality only if the African poor accept that the race of business matters independently of outcomes, that is, that racialism justifies.

South Africa's formula for capitalist democracy declares equality in citizenship; relegates race to the "private" realm; rewards parties for appealing to private interests and identities to win elections; encourages the rising black middle classes; and empowers black economic elites. The formula legitimates the capitalist economy and the democratic government, strengthens the governing party, and complicates the relationship between race and class. It also goes along with the economic flow, to the detriment of the substance of non-racialism and the needs of the poor.

The ANC had inherited a dicey situation. Capital controls—it *is*—the scarce resource and can come and go in pursuit of lower risks and higher profits. The ANC's early plans for redistribution, for narrowing economic inequalities and eradicating poverty, were dashed by capital (whose power and prerogatives, as O'Donnell and Schmitter had warned, had to be respected as inviolable if democracy was to be achieved). Perhaps the ANC might have negotiated a better deal, but capital was committed to preserving its particular forms—collusive, uncompetitive, oligopical, and illiberal—and it had the upper hand. Thus prevented by the terms of the transition from delivering on redistribution, the ANC concentrates on its constituencies in the black middle and (aspiring) upper classes. It does what it can.

Upwardly mobile blacks have grievances and ambitions of their own and want to make the higher rungs of society more "representative" for reasons of both justice and self-interest. They maintain, not unreasonably, that it is not right that whites continue to receive dividends from white supremacy, and it is not good politics either. The ANC, accordingly, is making *representativeness*—the idea that the racial composition of middle and upper classes should reflect the demographics of the country—a high priority, both because blacks deserve better chances and because changes reflect well on the ANC. Although the demands for representativeness and affirmative action are criticized by the ANC's parliamentary opposition (the Democratic Alliance), the problem is not using state power to offset the effects of accumulated injustices. The problem is that racializing representativeness in the context of illiberal capitalism has the effect of deferring poor Africans.

The underside of culturalism is that, in measuring democracy by the representation of identities, economic priorities that are disconnected from identities become less urgent. Respecting identities is one thing, but emphasizing them amid spreading poverty and unabating economic inequalities is another. It not only lowers the priority of poverty, but spurs a conservative racial logic. The less the pressure exerted for economic equality, the less equalization will be achieved; and the less the economic equality, the more important become the improvements that have occurred, the broadening of the racial composition of elites. The ANC is responding to demands from upwardly mobile blacks for more upward mobility by pressuring institutions to become blacker, to become more "representative." That is good and just; but enduring poverty and economic inequality mean that representativeness and black economic empowerment are not components of a larger transformation of the political economy. They are the transformation.

The ANC assumed responsibility for a vastly unequal economy through a deal with capital. In exchange for the acquiescence of state and capital to democracy, the ANC agreed to respect the "market" and implement neoliberal, supply-side policies, limiting what it could do about poverty. Unable to make much progress on reducing inequality and poverty because its hands are tied, but able to make progress in promoting blacks into the middle and upper classes, the ANC is pushed toward culturalism by the political economy. But the concession carries costs.

The term "non-racialism," whatever its technical meanings, is understood by South Africa's minorities to mean that people are weaned from concern with race. Minorities take to heart connotations of full belonging and inclusion. "Non-racialism" for them means what it seems to mean: negating, or striving to negate, the social meaning of race. Smuggling racial content into non-racial forms might seem like rough justice for whites, but it contrasts a racial "us" to a "them," and the "them" is made up of South African citizens.

Whites still derive benefits from the economic and social capital they amassed under apartheid, and under the circumstances it is fair to offset advantages still accruing to whites. And the ANC chooses its words carefully when discussing racial redress; it speaks about what is due "blacks," not "Africans," a more exclusivist term. It speaks of "*black* economic empowerment." But the tones and atmospherics—plus calls for the ANC to wage "a continuing battle to assert African hegemony in the context of a multi-cultural and non-racial society"[13]—raise suspicions that the ANC is exploiting ambiguities in the word "black" to insinuate culturalist appeals, hinting that it means "African" when it says "black." To the extent "black" refers to "African," the ANC marginalizes Asians and Coloureds, repudiates the principles of non-racialism, and abandons the construction of a non-racial people. According to the position the ANC advanced during the struggle against apartheid, the South African people are not given by nature or culture. It is the state's mission to manufacture non-racial South Africans through full citizenship in the universal state. If, therefore, the state's non-racialism is merely formal, it follows that the non-racial people remain merely formal too.

Minorities suffer from racialism, and so do many Africans. Racialism assumes identities of interest on the basis of identities of identity, flattening class and power disparities between insiders and outsiders. African interests, in this logic, are represented—in the sense of being made present—because their *representatives* are African, regardless of differences in their particular interests. The fallacy, of course, is that African representatives may represent Africans as *Africans* without necessarily representing them in their other capacities (as workers, squatters, the unemployed, women, children, the ill, and the elderly, for instance). The culturalist claim is persuasive up to a point. As African economic elites are African, they can be counted on to combat white racism; but as economic elites, they cannot be counted on to combat poverty and inequality with the same fervor. The culturalist logic, through sleight of hand, disappears the particular interests of the black poor into the general interests of Africans.

Racialism shares the credo of cultural nationalism that who does something matters more than what is done. That is the secret of its appeal. In enshrining the "who" as the principle governing political representation, racialism diminishes what representatives actually do, the actions they take and the policies they enact, and it gets capital off the hook cheaply. Racialism invites black elites to mobilize group solidarities on behalf of *their* sectional demands and business to go along with demands for representative elites. Governing in the name of "their" people, the elites start by saying they sublimate their interests to the greater good of their people as a whole. Then they reverse the equation, equating their particular interests with general interests. Originally, what benefits the people benefits the elites; now, what benefits elites benefits the people (since elites do, after all, represent the people). The particular interests of the poor are subordinated to group interests, and then the interests of upwardly mobile blacks are substituted for the interests the group.

Under apartheid, races marked communities of shared interests and experiences that grew out of white domination. Under democracy, those interests and experiences are changing. If racial solidarities nonetheless are to be drawn upon for purposes of legitimation and representation, solidarities based on races per se must supplant solidarities expressed through race. Races, in other words, must be reified; they must be lifted above the experiences of life they once indicated. The indicator of race supersedes the experiences it previously indicated. Operating on a seductive logic, racialism maintains that helping some members of a group helps the group, and helping the group helps all of its members. Elites serve their people by serving themselves.

African elites, therefore, are in a delicate position. Material benefits flow to them as "representatives" of Africans, but many of those they "represent" are not benefiting materially from the representation. That, of course, is much of the appeal of culturalist representation. Breaking down the overlap of economic and racial grievances, it makes them manageable. But the strategy of creating prosperous blacks to mediate between white capital and poor blacks complicates the maintenance of African unity, the condition for empowering black economic elites in the first place. Racialism bestows both instrumental and intrinsic values on elites, but it must be its own reward for poor Africans. The African poor, whose votes do ground African political power, must accept that racialism is *intrinsically* valuable, that it matters independently of instrumental considerations if the legitimating formula of democratic capitalism is to succeed, which is where culturalist claims come in. Cultural communities are heterogeneous, conflicted, and layered, yet culturists bestow unifying and surpassing purposes onto them. If, by the logic of culturalism, blacks were made into a group by cultural similarities, they will not be unmade as a group by hugely dissimilar experiences of democratic capitalism.

There are compelling reasons for using state power to force Africans into hitherto white citadels of power. Unless Africans assume positions of responsibility, talk of non-racial transformation is delusional. Whites remain subjects and blacks objects, just as before. But it is one thing to identify elites as a field, a particularly strategic field, of de-racialization, and it is another to equate the interests of African elites with the interests of those whose living standards are stagnating or deteriorating. In conflating the interests of the poor with the group and the group with its representatives, the poor are dealt to the margins of the group by a fast shuffle. The interests of the group are separated from the interests of those who actually compose the group, which is why culturalism reifies, why it raises the group above and deems the group prior to its members.

The main victims of the emphasis on symbolic representation, contra white liberals, are not those who do not see themselves in the persons of the elites, but those diverted by the razzle-dazzle of culturalist representation, those locked by the "ethnic census" into voting for parties that have little incentive to court them with substantive appeals. The political economy defines the poor out of prosperity; culturalism eases them out of representation.

Conclusion

While Bill talked about social change, I embodied it.
—HILLARY CLINTON

The argument of this book is that what made whites "white," what organized them into a community and differentiated the community of whites from "blacks," was citizenship. Whites were citizens, blacks were noncitizens, and the white state infused the discrepancy between whiteness and blackness with economic substance, elevated whites over blacks in society, and defined whites and blacks relationally and politically. Citizenship defined color, in the sense of helping to shape what color meant, and color identified citizens, in the sense of selecting who would and would not be citizens. Whites were citizens and citizens were white, and blacks were noncitizens and noncitizens were black.

The state, made up of whites, and national capital, owned by whites but devoted to profits, agreed on the framework of racial capitalism. The bargain between citizenship and capital prescribed that each would honor the essential needs of the other. Capital respected the prerogatives of citizenship (or whiteness) and got cheap labor, monopoly or oligopical control, and a pliant state in return. Citizenship respected capital and got protections from the market and a cut of the surplus generated by noncitizens in return. But racial capitalism required that black labor remain disenfranchised, and eventually the combination of economically essential yet politically disenfranchised blacks proved unsustainable. Blacks demanded political rights; the demand could not be met within the framework of white supremacy yet could not be suppressed within the framework of capitalist stability; and disorder ensued, portending chaos. Forced to choose between preserving racism and saving capitalism, conservatives in business and the state opted to negotiate a new constitution with the ANC. By reorganizing state power, making it democratic and "nonracial," capitalism was regrounded and sustained. But the political economy was not de-racialized; it was *multi*racialized.

The transition from apartheid to democracy occurred through a deal. In its broadest sweep, whites traded the racial state, which expressed and favored their identity and interests, for assurances about civil liberties, property, and economic policy. The disenfranchised majority received democratic political institutions, empowering them to elect black leaders, but on condition that property rights were respected and orthodox economic policies were adopted. The ANC, as representative of the disenfranchised, superseded radicals in civil society, and business and the state recognized the legitimacy of the new political framework, non-racial democracy.

Non-racialism is an altruistic ideal, reflecting the best of the liberal tradition. It affirms human dignity, democratic rights, and freedom, and it prohibits the state from seeing the race of citizens (with important exceptions for the purpose of redressing past injustices). But non-racialism, as a liberal ideal, does not foreclose a politics centered informally on racial interests and identities. It implies one. In denying the *official* status of race, non-racialism acknowledges the *unofficial* role of race, outside the state. The ideal of non-racialism intimates the practice of racialism, belying its sincere hopes for a truly universal state and society. Citizens are free of race formally and ideally, not actually and practically. Racial communities, in other words, may act and express themselves through democratic institutions, which is what solves the legitimation and political crises that had beset white supremacy.

Racial groups legitimate democratic government; democratic government affirms equality under the law, which eventually justifies economic inequality as the result of the free play of capitalism; and state and capital confirm and materialize the importance of racial groups by applauding the black middle classes and nurturing black economic elites. The grounding of capitalism in democracy and democracy in racial nationalism contributes to one of the most striking features of post-apartheid South African politics. The political economy remains stable and the ANC remains invincible, even though economic elites remain predominately white and Africans remain mostly poor. Multiracialism, in the form of African economic elites that are promoted because of their race, counters the danger that racial identities and economic interests will reinforce and embitter each other and that society will be polarized between rich whites and poor Africans. The new African economic elites, in assuming the economic interests of established economic elites while retaining the racial identities they share with poor Africans, make cleavages crosscutting, offsetting the tendency toward polarization. Under white supremacy, racialism polarized; under non-racial democracy, multiracialism mediates. But in both cases, racialism accommodates the imperatives of capital.

The strategy of building political stability through black economic empowerment entails a specific conception of racial groups. In the struggle against apartheid, the ANC and the Black Consciousness movement gravitated toward politicist conceptions of the nation. Rather than seeing the nation as originating in culture and then expressing itself in politics, both traditions understood the nation to originate in response to common oppression. By that logic, however, the nation may be unmade by disparate experiences of power, for example, by the embourgeoisement of a small minority of Africans. Consequently, the ANC is in the market for conceptions that present the nation as given, as prior to and independent of disparate experiences of power. Nations, to the extent that they are understood culturally, can encompass vast economic and political disparities. Accordingly, the ANC is resuscitating culturalist conceptions of politics. Culturalism, in combining identity and interest to the advantage of new black elites, avails itself of the great lesson of twentieth-century politics: who does something counts for more than what it is that is done.

The political economy of identity in South Africa raises difficult questions for reigning theories of democracy and difference. These theories celebrate democracy, value difference, and count South Africa as an illustrious success (except for the government's policies on AIDS). They admire the heroic struggle for democracy and against racial domination, and they thrill in the new constitution, which heeds their advice about how to combine democracy and difference. South Africa's constitution accepts the "democratic standard of civic equality, broadly understood to include equal freedom and opportunity for all individuals";[1] promises social protections for the poor and vulnerable; and recognizes the "civic equality, equal freedom, and basic opportunity"[2] of identity groups. The constitution sings the song of democracy and difference.

South Africa's constitution guarantees "every citizen is equally protected by law,"[3] "the rule of law,"[4] and "the right to equal protection and benefit of the law."[5] It assures universal adult suffrage, "non-racialism and non-sexism,"[6] common and equal citizenship, and promises freedom of conscience, association, and expression. South Africans hold fundamental political rights to assembly and a free press, "to make political choices,"[7] and to form and campaign for political parties of their choice. By virtue of their citizenship, they are entitled to vote in "free, fair and regular elections,"[8] are entitled to travel freely throughout the country, and cannot have their citizenship stripped from them. The constitution prohibits unfair discrimination and provides the right "to make decisions concerning reproduction" too.[9]

The democratic constitution, in addition to proclaiming standard democratic rights, also promulgates "pink" ones. Under the constitution, South Africans have the social rights to form and join trade unions, to environmental protection, to have "access to adequate housing,"[10] "to health care services . . . sufficient food and water, and social security."[11] Even children are guaranteed explicit rights "to basic nutrition, shelter, basic health care services, and social services,"[12] and "to be protected from maltreatment, neglect, abuse or degradation."[13]

The constitution also declares cultural rights. It recognizes eleven official languages and obligates the state to "take practical and positive measures to elevate the status and advance the use of [the eleven] languages."[14] It permits "legislative and other measures designed to protect or advance persons or categories of persons" who have been "disadvantaged by unfair discrimination,"[15] affirms the dignity of all South Africans, and prohibits "advocacy of hatred that is based on race, ethnicity, gender or religion and that constitutes incitement to cause harm."[16] It recognizes the "institution, status and role of traditional leadership, according to customary law,"[17] and allows for the recognition of marriages "concluded under any tradition," subject to other commitments in the constitution.[18]

The democratic constitution, in other words, opens the political system to universal rights, free activity, and total participation; overcomes a nasty history of exclusion with a politics of non-racialism; replaces white supremacy with democratic respect for differences; and affirms the universal and accommodates the different, just as democracy and difference theories counsel. These theories call for broad democratic participation partly because it is rewarding, as it is an intrinsically valuable experience, and partly because broad democratic participation improves the quality of public decisions, as it is instrumentally useful in advancing the public good. The greater the number of different voices participating in public deliberations, the more democratic and the more just are the outcomes produced by the deliberations. The airing of differences benefits minorities, of course, because minorities are heard. But it also improves the quality of decisions and reconciles different identities to each other, to the benefit of the society as a whole. Thus, where the ethnic census thesis has democracy registering and confirming differences, democracy and difference theories conceive of democracy more hopefully. They present democracy as transformative, as developing more comprehensive and less self-interested publics because of the process of accommodating, recognizing, and valuing different identities.

Democracy and difference theorists agree about the moral imperative of recognizing the identities of all groups of citizens, but they disagree about whether the particular identities that are to be recognized must defer to universal principles of justice (the position of liberals) or whether "universal" principles of justice really are highfalutin names—misrepresentations really—for the values of the strongest culture (the position of pure multiculturalists). For pure multiculturalists, "A constitution can seek to impose one cultural practice, one way of rule following, or it can recognise a diversity of cultural ways of being a citizen, but it cannot eliminate, overcome or transcend this cultural dimension of politics."[19] That is, "culture is an irreducible and constituent aspect of politics"[20]; many—perhaps most—political conflicts at root are cultural conflicts; and neutrality among conflicting cultures is impossible, because all standpoints are steeped in and inflected by cultures. With politics being inextricable from culture, the meaningful political question for pure multiculturalists is whether states recognize all cultures equally or whether they favor some unequally.

Pure multiculturalists make a normative demand. They want "recognition of cultural diversity."[21] That is, their point of departure is the claim that diverse cultures deserve political recognition, that, by inference, cultures are there to be recognized, that cultures precede and provide the stuff of politics. Cultural actors make demands; politics registers and reacts to them, recognizing or denying the status of cultures or doing something in-between. For multiculturalists, politics plays a reactive, not a constituting, role in *making* cultural actors. Cultures exist more or less independently of what states and politics do.

Charles Taylor comes closer than most democracy and difference theorists to escaping culturalism: "Our identity is partly shaped by recognition or its absence, often by the *mis*recognition of others, and so a person or group of people can suffer real damage, real distortion, if the people or society around them mirror back to them a confining or demeaning or contemptible picture of themselves."[22] Taylor has groups—or their members—being affected by interactions with other groups. But note

Taylor's construction. Recognizing or misrecognizing cultures influences how members of cultures feel about themselves individually and collectively. So far, so good. But members for Taylor are united by culture before they are affected by interaction; they feel the impacts of recognition or misrecognition precisely because culture already has organized them as members of a group. Politics does not much influence who does the feeling, who is in the group, how the group is made, how recruitment into it operates. Politics influences how members of groups feel about themselves, the "group's sense of collective worth."[23] But political interactions do not constitute groups themselves.

Culturalism, therefore, fits nicely into a classically liberal logic. Liberals usually have governments responding to concerns that arise in the private realm (the economy, society, culture). Culturalism, by taking groups as integral, makes assumptions that liberals prefer: it posits the existence of collective selves prior to politics, as the subjects that are to be represented. If, contrarily, identities were to be seen as substantially political in origin or content (à la Biko), liberals would approach representing them differently. The state would be representing its own constructions, something more troubling for liberals than representing private interests and identities. Better, therefore, that groups are decreed to originate outside and prior to politics, in culture, that groups be taken as pre-political formations that are demanding public equality for themselves, and that groups be treated as units in a world of their own making, not as actors *doing* things to reproduce systems. Groups do not act in larger contexts for pure multiculturalists: they create the contexts.

Multiculturalists favor recognizing all identities, while acknowledging that real recognition can involve treating different identities differently. As Iris Marion Young argues, "The politics of difference sometimes implies overriding a principle of equal treatment with the principle that group differences should be acknowledged in public policies . . . in order to reduce actual or potential oppression."[24] Democracy and difference theories, in other words, do not necessarily "tolerate" differences in the old-fashioned liberal sense. They are not saying that differences should be accepted without penalty. They are requiring that differences be welcomed, given voice, endorsed as equally legitimate, and, in the process, are smuggling in another assumption: that identities are compatible, are capable of mutual recognition. Although democracy and difference theorists often have identities identifying themselves on the basis of difference, of differentiation, they do not dwell on the possibility that some identities deny the legitimacy of other identities as a condition of asserting their own legitimacy. Multiculturalists, in other words, assume a safe world: they can assume all identities can be represented equally only on the shoulders of the prior, unstated assumption that representing some identities does not carry entailments for representing other identities.

Liberal theories of democracy and difference disagree with pure multiculturalist theories on one important score. They expect minority identities to respect universal principles as part of the process that recognizes them. Seyla Benhabib, for example, maintains that including different identities in deliberations abets the pursuit of universal justice. When minorities make reasoned arguments in public places—parliaments, social movements, voluntary associations, public debates—on behalf of their preferences, they contribute to making decisions on the basis of rational persuasion, the source of justice. The process of deliberation—putting forth ideas, listening to rival ideas, subjecting both to the scrutiny of rationality—broadens outlooks, harmonizes voices, and produces integrated policies. Not only does reason prevail, but also democracy is enriched by the expression of difference in public spaces.[25]

Democracy and difference theorists do not claim democracies actually work as they say. In the deliberative versions, they are making normative arguments, claiming that particular societies are democratic insofar as they resemble the specifications of democratic theorists. "The deliberative conception of democracy is organized around an ideal of political justification. According to this ideal, justification of the exercise of collective political power is to proceed on the basis of a free public reasoning among equals. A deliberative democracy institutionalizes this ideal."[26] Decisions, by this logic, are democratic when they are made in a zone that is free from power, when participants—of all races, ethno-cultures, genders, and sexual orientations—participate equally and defer only to the imperatives of reason and rationality. Banishing power from public decisions and rising above interests permits participants to surpass their particular subjective viewpoints and "to take a more objective or general view of political issues" and "creates a public."[27] Young notes, "Democratic processes are oriented around discussing [the] common good rather than competing for the promotion of the private good of each."[28] Much debate about democracy and differences consists, therefore, of figuring out how to create equality—that is, how to eliminate inequalities in power—in deliberations that occur amid differences.

Deliberative democracy and difference theories imagine public spaces where the expression of all voices makes for more just public policy. Policies are adopted because of the "force of the better argument,"[29] not because of power in the public space. "A primary virtue of a deliberative model of democracy . . . is that it promotes a conception of reason over power in politics."[30] But disagreements about the status of difference and universality notwithstanding, liberal and pure multicultural theories of democracy and difference concur on the points that matter for South Africa: they agree in deeming public spaces as power-free zones; agree in valuing expressive, not instrumental, politics; agree in locating identities in cultures; and (apart from the stray comment) agree in assuming that cultures evolve without relationality to each other.

Democracy and difference theorists, especially in deliberative versions, idealize democracy, advocate more rights, and extol diversity, just like South Africa's constitution. Yet their goal of removing power from political deliberations, of conceiving of politics as something that happens sans power, blinds them to obstacles to building democracy in South Africa. "The deliberative ideal" may want to "eliminate the influence of economic and political power,"[31] but power—precisely because it gets its way[32]—cannot be banished from political considerations. Power situates interactions between interests and identities, bending groups to the imperatives of the political economy, and frustrates hopes for economic equality in spite of democratic political institutions. Deliberative democracy and difference theories do not mean to turn ideals against realities; they do not say that democracies should be judged as if the constraints of power are irrelevant. But in proclaiming a politics without power, they deprive themselves of the terms that are necessary to make sense of democracy—its accomplishments and its shortcomings—in South Africa. They also drain the lifeblood from politics.

In conceiving of democracy without power, deliberative democracy and difference theories in effect are conceiving of democracy without capitalism (even as they assume the bounties of capitalist development). "Participants in an ideal process of deliberative democracy must be equal in the sense that none of them is in a position to coerce or threaten others into accepting certain proposals or outcomes."[33] Because capital creates inequalities and coerces choices, exerting pressure for certain economic policies as a condition of investment, democracy and difference theorists effectively prohibit capital from participating in institutions (because it has power). But pretending capital does not—or should not—exert influence in deliberation does not help either in understanding or in judging South African—or any other—democracy.

Tellingly, South Africa's constitution (which capital helped write) gets the point. The democracy and difference sensibility honors the constitution for expanding rights and recognizing difference. But the constitution ultimately pays the piper. Rather than avoiding the fact of political and economic power inside the state, it recognizes explicitly the power of capital in the form of the Reserve Bank. In a microcosm of the compromise between democracy and capital at the heart of the transition, the constitution guarantees the independence of the Reserve Bank.

> (1) The primary object of the South African Reserve Bank is to protect the value of the currency in the interest of balanced and sustainable economic growth in the Republic.
> (2) The South African Reserve Bank, in pursuit of its primary object, must perform its functions independently and without fear, favour or prejudice.[34]

The Reserve Bank, by the terms of the constitution, must consult with the government; but after consulting, it still must preserve the value of money (by fighting inflation, raising interest rates, and lowering budget deficits), even at the expense of losing jobs and reducing access to housing, health care, and the like. The constitution, in other words, subordinates social rights to capitalist power. As it says in a phrase used three times, the "state must take reasonable legislative and other measures, *within its available resources.*"[35]

Theories of democracy and difference miss the point of democracy in societies like South Africa, and not only because they ignore the structural import of democracy, the legitimating purposes it serves, and the roles actually played by identities in the political economy. Democracy is a great achievement, both for what it abolishes and what it accomplishes. It awards priceless benefits to South Africans—civil liberties, dignity, political freedom—and solves political and legitimation crises. But democracy must grapple with the power of capital, with far-reaching ramifications for how it evolves. Democracy bridges the identities of the majority of South Africans with the realities of economic power, partly through political procedures (such as elections) that represent popular power and partly through symbolic identification of the poor with economic elites.

South Africa has elections and private enterprise, but both government and business favor a cozy partnership (not for the first time in South Africa's history) and blunt the competition that invigorates full-fledged capitalist democracies. Political competition is limited by the dialectics of identity politics, by racial voting and racialist organizing, and economic competition is muffled by colluding, cross-owned conglomerates. But these shortcomings originate in the power politics of the situation, not in the moral corruption of South Africans. The majority, acting mostly through the ANC, has developed a more humane, orderly, and democratic political system and has reached accommodations with capital. The ANC might have promoted a better, more competitive form of capitalism. But criticism must acknowledge the fact that capital has a strong hand, that capital is mobile and scarce whereas labor is stationary and plentiful, and that the power of the democratic state is narrowed by the terms of transition and confined by the imperatives of the global economy.

"Politics," wrote Max Weber, "is a strong and slow boring of hard boards. It takes both passion and perspective. Certainly all historical experience confirms the truth—that man would not have attained the possible unless time and again he had reached out for the impossible."[36] The pursuit of the impossible in South Africa is the pursuit of systematic and thorough democracy, the extension of the principle of equality to the whole political economy. The representation of identities, which throughout South African history has organized political power and cloaked economic power, is not what extends the realm of the possible. The history of white supremacy, the paragon of identity politics, screams the danger of cramming life and political participation into the unchosen, assigned cages that reproduce power. The impossible is unlocking cages of ascribed identities and freeing people to define themselves.

Notes

Bibliography

Index

Notes

Introduction

1. A note on terminology: The words "African" and "black" are used to refer to different people. Africans are those who were classified as "Native," "Bantu," or "black" under apartheid. "Black," on the other hand, is used to refer inclusively to those who were classified as "Coloured" and "Asian" as well as Africans. Occasionally, the term "black" is used to mean "African," usually because a source is being quoted directly. Such cases should be clear from the context.

1. The Logic of White Supremacy

1. George M. Fredrickson, *White Supremacy: A Comparative Study in American and South African History* (New York: Oxford University Press, 1981), 139–198.
2. This discussion of segregation and apartheid speaks in terms of ideal types. Segregation and apartheid are complex phenomena, encompass long periods of time in varied parts of South Africa, never were implemented fully and completely, and were resisted in practice by countless South Africans, as was documented meticulously in Charles van Onselen, *The Seed Is Mine: The Life of Kas Maine, a South African Sharecropper, 1894–1985* (New York: Hill and Wang, 1996). Differences within the models of segregation and apartheid are real and important, but so are the similarities. Using ideal types highlights them.
3. R. F. Alfred Hoernlé, *South African Native Policy and the Liberal Spirit* (New York: Negro Universities Press, 1969). Hoernlé's analysis of segregation is reminiscent of Frantz Fanon's discussion of relations between settlers and natives in colonialism in Frantz Fanon, *The Wretched of the Earth* (New York: Grove Press, 1968), 35–53. The similarities between Hoernlé and Fanon are no coincidence. Each, having been influenced by Hegel, conceived of their interactions along the lines of Hegel's discussions of masters and slaves.
4. Hoernlé, *South African Native Policy,* 26–28.

5. J. C. Smuts, *Africa and Some World Problems* (Oxford: Clarendon Press, 1930), 75.
6. Ibid., 47.
7. Ibid., 76.
8. Ibid., 78.
9. Ibid., 90.
10. Ibid., 93.
11. Mahmood Mamdani, *Citizen and Subject: Contemporary Africa and the Legacy of Late Colonialism* (Princeton, NJ: Princeton University Press, 1996), 62–108 offers a comprehensive discussion of the evolution of "indirect rule" in South Africa, that is, the use of customary authorities to extend and reproduce the colonial state. Mamdani stresses the continuities between segregation and apartheid, which is not inconsistent with the point made here. Mamdani focuses on ethnicity and the multiple faces of state power in rural areas. The point here focuses on ideology and the role of race in extending and reproducing state power.
12. Roberta Balstad Miller shows that H. F. Verwoerd, who was a lecturer in psychology before becoming the architect of apartheid, had rejected several tenets of racist thinking while lecturing at Stellenbosch University. In particular, he denied that there "were any biological differences between the big race groups" and maintained that "there was no demonstrable difference in the intelligence of whites and blacks." He did, however, believe that groups have specific personality traits. Roberta Balstad Miller, "Science and Society in the Early Career of H. F. Verwoerd," *Journal of Southern African Studies* 19, no. 4 (December 1993): 648, 650–651.
13. Hermann Giliomee, "The Growth of Afrikaner Identity," in Heribert Adam and Hermann Giliomee, *Ethnic Power Mobilized: Can South Africa Change?* (New Haven, CT: Yale University Press, 1979), 118–119.
14. The ethno-cultural mission of the National Party (NP) served to obscure from Afrikaners the racist thrust of apartheid. The NP could be understood as an ethno-cultural party advancing the cause of Afrikaners, not as a racist party oppressing blacks. The belief of Afrikaners that they were seeking liberation from a history of oppression is one reason why their political leaders were loath to apologize for apartheid during and after the transition to liberal democracy. They insisted that the purpose of apartheid was to promote Afrikaners against English-speakers, a just cause as far as Afrikaners were concerned. And if their hearts were pure, their deeds, in good Protestant fashion, were moral. F. W. de Klerk, for example, writes, "The people depicted in the murals were the heroes of whose deeds I learned at my mother's knee. The dream that they had dreamt of being a free and separate people, with their own right to national self-determination in their own national state in southern Africa, had been the dream that had motivated the ancestors who stared sternly at me from our old family photographs. It had been the central goal of my own father, who had been cabinet minister during

the 1950s and 60s." F. W. de Klerk, *The Last Trek—a New Beginning: The Autobiography* (London: Macmillan, 1998), xviii.

15. Jason Myers, "The Spontaneous Ideology of Tradition in Post-Apartheid South Africa," *Politikon* 26, no. 1 (1999). Jason Myers, "Fancy Dress: Concealment and Ideology in South Africa," *Transformation* 30 (1996).

2. The Mother of Identity Politics

1. Saul Dubow, "The Elaboration of Segregationist Ideology," in *Segregation and Apartheid in Twentieth-Century South Africa,* ed. William Beinart and Saul Dubow (London: Routledge, 1995), 145–175. For a full examination of the issue of scientific racism in South Africa, see Saul Dubow, *Scientific Racism in Modern South Africa* (Cambridge: Cambridge University Press, 1995).
2. Anthony D. Smith, *The Ethnic Origins of Nations* (Oxford: Blackwell, 1986), 17.
3. Ibid., 212.
4. Ibid., 156.
5. Ibid., 24.
6. Ibid., 32.
7. Ibid., 22.
8. Donald L. Horowitz, *Ethnic Groups in Conflict* (Berkeley: University of California Press, 1985), 41.
9. Ibid., 78.
10. Ibid., 57.
11. Ibid., 41–42.
12. Ibid., 50.
13. Ibid., 187.
14. Ibid., 82.
15. Ibid., 53.
16. Ibid., 42–44.
17. Ibid., 52.
18. Joseph Raz, *Ethics in the Public Domain: Essays in the Morality of Law and Politics* (Oxford: Clarendon Press, 1994), 178.
19. Ibid., 174.
20. Will Kymlicka, *Multicultural Citizenship: A Liberal Theory of Minority Rights* (Oxford: Clarendon Press, 1995), 105.
21. Ibid., 52.
22. Yael Tamir, *Liberal Nationalism* (Princeton, NJ: Princeton University Press, 1993), 8.
23. Raz, *Ethics in the Public Domain,* 177.
24. Ibid., 177–178.
25. Tamir, *Liberal Nationalism,* xxix.
26. Ibid., xiii.

27. Ibid., xxix.
28. Kymlicka, *Multicultural Citizenship,* 189.
29. Ibid., 51–52.
30. Tamir, *Liberal Nationalism,* 54.
31. Charles Taylor, *Multiculturalism and "The Politics of Recognition"* (Princeton, NJ: Princeton University Press, 1992), 60–61.
32. Kymlicka, *Multicultural Citizenship,* 152.
33. Leo Marquard, *The Peoples and Policies of South Africa* (London: Oxford University Press, 1952), 245.
34. Edward Hallett Carr, *The Twenty Years' Crisis, 1919–1939* (New York: Harper Torchbook, Harper & Row, 1964), 41–62.
35. Marquard, *The Peoples and Policies of South Africa,* 32. Italics added.
36. See, for example, Hermann Giliomee, "Presidential Address: Liberal and Populist Democracy in South Africa: Challenges, New Threats to Liberalism" (Johannesburg: South African Institute of Race Relations, 1996), 15–24.
37. F. van Zyl Slabbert and David Welsh, *South Africa's Options: Strategies for Sharing Power* (Cape Town: David Philip, 1981), 14.
38. Ibid., 30.
39. Ibid., 133.
40. Ibid., 153.
41. Michael MacDonald, "The Siren's Song: The Political Logic of Power-Sharing in South Africa," *Journal of Southern African Studies* 18, no. 4 (December 1992): 709–725.
42. Slabbert and Welsh, *South Africa's Options,* 167.
43. Max Weber, *Economy and Society: An Outline of Interpretive Sociology,* ed. Guenther Roth and Claus Wittich (Berkeley: University of California Press, 1978), vol. 1, 389.
44. Ibid., vol. 1, 395.
45. Ibid.
46. Ibid., vol. 1, 394.
47. Ibid., vol. 1, 395.
48. Ibid., vol. 1, 389.
49. Ibid., vol. 1, 393.
50. Ibid., vol. 1, 397–398.
51. Charles Tilly, "Reflections on the History of European State-Making," and Samuel E. Einer, "State- and Nation-Building in Europe: The Role of the Military," in Charles Tilly, ed., *The Formation of National States in Western Europe* (Princeton, NJ: Princeton University Press, 1975), 78–80 and 87–90.
52. Weber, *Economy and Society,* vol. 1, 389.
53. Ibid., vol. 2, 921.
54. Ibid., vol. 2, 922. Italics in original.
55. Ibid., vol. 1, 398.

56. Smith is a good example of this. See, for example, Anthony D. Smith, *National Identity* (Reno: University of Nevada Press, 1991), 43–70.
57. Smith, for example, plays down the importance of outsiders in constituting common ethnicity (Smith, *National Identity,* 27). Some multiculturalists, however, do sense the problem confronting them. In particular, Taylor suggests that identities develop "dialogically," through conversations with the "other," and multiculturalists routinely stress the importance of difference (Taylor, *Multiculturalism,* 25–37). But the weight of Taylor's argument implies that interactions affect how people *feel* about themselves and their group, that groups exist prior to and independently of interactions. When groups encounter the other, they identify themselves in terms of particular attributes, of "difference." But the group already is a group before the interaction because it formed around nuclei (culture or language). Groups may seem to form on the basis of differences, but really they form around attributes. The function of difference, à la Smith, is to identify the group that is assumed from the beginning. Power and powerlessness become properties—not sources—of groups.
58. Weber, *Economy and Society,* vol. 1, 385. First italics added.
59. For a nice example of this, see Mandela's autobiography, where he gives a brief history of the Xhosa people and notes in passing that "each Xhosa belongs to a clan that traces its descent back to a specific forefather." Nelson Mandela, *Long Walk to Freedom: The Autobiography of Nelson Mandela* (Boston: Little, Brown, 1994), 4.

3. The White Man's Burden

1. David Miller, ed., *The Blackwell Encyclopedia of Political Thought* (New York: Basil Blackwell, 1987), 413–414. For fuller treatments of this question, see George M. Fredrickson, *Racism: A Short History* (Princeton, NJ: Princeton University Press, 2002) and Ivan Hannaford, *Race: The History of an Idea in the West* (Washington, DC and Baltimore: Woodrow Wilson Center Press and The Johns Hopkins University Press, 1996). Fredrickson takes exception to dating the beginnings of racism this late, locating its origins in the fourteenth and fifteenth centuries. Hannaford, however, sees the idea of race developing more recently, from 1684 onward.
2. George M. Fredrickson, *White Supremacy: A Comparative Study in American and South African History* (New York: Oxford University Press, 1981), 70.
3. There is some debate over the extent of manumission. Fredrickson's point, and much of his argument, is criticized by Timothy Keegan. But Keegan also confirms many of Fredrickson's particular and general points. Although Keegan suggests little correlation between baptism and manumission, he also notes that slave owners preferred Muslim slaves and that Muslim slaves outnumbered Christian slaves by a three-to-one margin in 1820 and suggests,

"there seems to have been from early on a certain aversion to slave baptism, based on a perceived fear that Christian slaves might have some vague claim to rights that non-Christians did not have." Timothy Keegan, *Colonial South Africa and the Origins of the Racial Order* (Charlottesville: University Press of Virginia, 1996), 17.

4. Fredrickson, *White Supremacy,* 88.
5. Ibid., xi.
6. "During the eighteenth century the commando became the single most important symbol of the cultural and social cohesion of the frontier burghers, and the chief instrument of their common interest in dispossessing and subjugating indigenous peoples." Keegan, *Colonial South Africa,* 30.
7. Interestingly, Fredrickson's critics make a similar point more directly. "Although in general there was little discrimination in law against free people of colour, at least until the late eighteenth century, the social order was never colour-blind." Ibid., 20.
8. Ibid., 14.
9. Fredrickson, *White Supremacy,* 147.
10. Keegan, *Colonial South Africa*, 25. Keegan speaks of a militia that was formed in 1787 from those born out of wedlock. Membership soon expanded and included "all those whose parents, even if married, had not been born in a state of freedom. The implication was that one had to be of putatively European ancestry to be fully accepted within the ranks of the dominant, respectable free burgher population" (23–24). Keegan's point is well put. What became a racial order was evolving in practice, but race had not yet been elevated into a principle of political organization. It was implicit; it was not explicit.
11. André du Toit and Hermann Giliomee, *Afrikaner Political Thought: Analysis and Documents,* vol. 1, *1780–1850* (Cape Town: David Philip, 1983), 17.
12. Fredrickson, *White Supremacy*, 169.
13. Du Toit and Giliomee, *Afrikaner Political Thought,* 34.
14. Fredrickson, *White Supremacy,* 162–163.
15. Ibid., 166.
16. Hermann Giliomee, *The Afrikaners: Biography of a People* (Charlottesville: University of Virginia Press, 2003), 90.
17. Ibid., 6.
18. Ibid., 59.
19. Ibid., 56, 117.
20. Ibid., 36.
21. Ibid., 88.
22. Ibid., 14, 18.
23. Ibid., 115.
24. Ibid., 144.
25. Ibid., 147.
26. Ibid., 150.

27. The Xhosa sometimes referred to whites as "Christians" and whites sometimes referred to themselves as "Christians." Ibid., 71, 75.
28. M. Hannay, *Van Dale: Handwoordenboek, Nederlands-Engels,* 3rd ed. (Utrecht: Van Dale Lexicografie, 1996), 112. Paul Simon, a former student at Williams College, helped immeasurably with the etymologies of the Dutch.
29. Leonard Thompson, "Great Britain and the Afrikaner Republics, 1870–1899," in *The Oxford History of South Africa,* vol. 2: *South Africa 1870–1966*, ed. Monica Wilson and Leonard Thompson (New York: Oxford University Press, 1971), 310.
30. C. W. De Kiewiet, *A History of South Africa: Social and Economic* (New York: Oxford University Press, 1957), 131.
31. Thompson, "Great Britain and the Afrikaner Republics," 309.
32. Hermann Giliomee, "The Beginnings of Afrikaner Ethnic Consciousness, 1850–1915," in *The Creation of Tribalism in Southern Africa,* ed. Leroy Vail (London: James Curry, 1989), 35.
33. Leonard Thompson, "The Subjection of the African Chiefdoms, 1870–1898," in *The Oxford History of South Africa,* 246.
34. Christopher Saunders, "Political Processes in the Southern African Frontier Zones" and Hermann Giliomee, "Processes in Development of the Southern African Frontier," in *The Frontier in History: North America and Southern Africa Compared,* ed. Howard Lamar and Leonard Thompson (New Haven, CT: Yale University Press, 1981), 162.
35. Saunders, "Political Processes," 151.
36. J. B. Peires, *The House of Phalo: A History of the Xhosa People in the Days of Their Independence* (Berkeley: University of California Press, 1982), 79.
37. Saunders, "Political Processes," 150.
38. Quoted in Leonard Thompson, "The Compromise of Union," in *The Oxford History of South Africa,* 330. Italics in original.
39. Quoted in ibid., 331.
40. Ibid., 353–354.
41. Actually, the qualifications were lifted for white males and preserved for Africans in Natal too. In Natal, Africans technically were eligible to vote; they just failed to qualify. As one historian put the point, "In Natal the franchise was theoretically open to the native [the African]. But the road to qualification was beset by conditions so onerous that the chances of gaining the franchise were, not figuratively but literally, one in several million. In 1936 Natal contained a single native voter!" De Kiewiet, *A History of South Africa,* 238–239.
42. Rogers Brubaker, *Citizenship and Nationhood in France and Germany* (Cambridge, MA: Harvard University Press, 1992), 40–41.
43. Hermann Giliomee, "The Afrikaner Economic Advance," in Heribert Adam and Hermann Giliomee, *Ethnic Power Mobilized: Can South Africa Change?* (New Haven, CT: Yale University Press, 1979), 145–176.

4. The Politics of the Political Economy

1. Heribert Adam, *Modernizing Racial Domination: The Dynamics of South African Politics* (Berkeley: University of California Press, 1971), 8.
2. George M. Fredrickson, *Racism: A Short History* (Princeton, NJ: Princeton University Press, 2002), as quoted on 134.
3. Karl Marx, "On the Jewish Question," in *Karl Marx: Early Writings*, ed. T. B. Bottomore (New York: McGraw-Hill, 1964).
4. Milton Friedman, *Capitalism and Freedom* (Chicago: University of Chicago Press, 1962), 108–118.
5. Merle Lipton, *Capitalism and Apartheid: South Africa, 1910–84* (Totowa, NJ: Rowman & Allanheld, 1985), 43.
6. Ibid., 6.
7. Ibid., 7.
8. Ibid., 6.
9. Frederick A. Johnstone, *Class, Race and Gold: A Study of Class Relations and Racial Discrimination in South Africa* (London: Routledge and Kegan Paul, 1976), 14, 17.
10. Ibid., 16, 27–28, 36, 38, 43.
11. The point was made by Harold Wolpe, "Capitalism and Cheap Labour Power in South Africa: From Segregation to Apartheid," in *Segregation and Apartheid in Twentieth-Century South Africa,* ed. William Beinart and Saul Dubow (London: Routledge, 1995). Interestingly, Wolpe is describing how South African capital circumvented one of the upward pressures on wages that Karl Marx had described. Marx thought that employers were forced to pay wages that would allow workers to reproduce labor, to raise the children that would serve as workers in the future. Wolpe, however, understood South African capital to have shifted this expense to the "traditional" sectors of the economy.
12. Colin Bundy, *The Rise and Fall of the South African Peasantry* (Berkeley: University of California Press, 1979), 115.
13. Ibid., 116.
14. Diana Wylie, *Starving on a Full Stomach: Hunger and the Triumph of Cultural Racism in Modern South Africa* (Charlottesville: University of Virginia Press, 2001), 205.
15. Bundy, *The Rise and Fall of the South African Peasantry,* 116.
16. Stanley B. Greenberg, *Race and State in Capitalist Development* (New Haven, CT: Yale University Press, 1980), 90.
17. Johnstone, *Class, Race and Gold,* 25.
18. Ibid., 14.
19. Greenberg, *Race and State,* 26.
20. No Sizwe (Neville Alexander), *One Azania, One Nation: The National Question in South Africa* (London: Zed Press, 1979) and Neville Alexander, *Sow the Wind: Contemporary Speeches* (Johannesburg: Skotaville Publishers, 1987).

21. Greenberg, *Race and State,* 26.
22. Wolpe, "Capitalism and Cheap Labour Power," 67–68.
23. Social historians are uncomfortable with the stark structuralism of Marxist political economy. Taking the spread of capitalism as the point of departure, they pay particular attention to the struggles of rural Africans. See, for example, William Beinhart, *Twentieth Century South Africa* (Cape Town: Oxford University Press, 1994); William Beinart, *The Political Economy of Pondoland, 1860 to 1930* (Johannesburg: Ravan Press, 1982); Shula Marks and Anthony Atmore, eds., *Economy and Society in Pre-Industrial South Africa* (London: Longman, 1980); William Beinart and Colin Bundy, *Hidden Struggles in Rural South Africa: Politics and Popular Movements in the Transkei and Eastern Cape* (London: James Currey, 1987); Shula Marks, *The Ambiguities of Dependence in South Africa* (Johannesburg: Ravan Press, 1986); Charles van Onselen, *The Seed Is Mine: The Life of Kas Maine, a South African Sharecropper, 1894–1985* (New York: Hill and Wang, 1986); Shula Marks and Richard Rathbone, eds., *Industrialisation and Social Change in South Africa* (New York: Longman, 1982); Shula Marks and Stanley Trapido, eds., *The Politics of Race, Class, and Nationalism in Twentieth Century South Africa* (London: Longman, 1987).
24. Friedman, *Capitalism and Freedom,* 34 and Robert W. Cox, *Production, Power, and World Order: Social Forces in the Making of History* (New York: Columbia University Press, 1987), 129–143 discuss from, respectively, liberal and Marxist perspectives the chores the state must perform in capitalist society.
25. Dan O'Meara, *Volkskapitalisme: Class, Capital and Ideology in the Development of Afrikaner Nationalism, 1934–1948* (Johannesburg: Ravan Press, 1983), 57–178.
26. The role of the state as the patron of the Afrikaner bourgeoisie has not been subjected to much sustained research. The predominant sense is that the NP used state contracts, old boyism, loans, jawboning, and various forms of pressure to promote the Afrikaner bourgeoisie. This view is plausible. The NP was interested in promoting the Afrikaner people, patronage is common practice for ethnic parties, and English-speakers held a stranglehold on business. Besides, the NP did worse things than help Afrikaner capital at the expense of English-speaking capital, the state was secretive, English-speaking businesses complained about favoritism toward Afrikaners, large parastatals did promote Afrikaners to senior positions, the National Party government did exert pressure on Anglo American to sell an important subsidiary to Afrikaner interests, and the Afrikaner bourgeoisie did grow rapidly under the NP. Yet for all the reasons to suspect systematic favoritism for Afrikaner businesses from the NP, not much evidence actually has been advanced.

    Hermann Giliomee, who recently examined the issue, confirms the role of government pressure in inducing Anglo American to sell an important subsidiary (General Mining, which became Gencor) to Afrikaner interests and the importance of Afrikaners in the large state corporations, a large and growing component of the economy. "The state corporations at their senior level were almost exclusively manned by Afrikaners. They provided a training school outside the private sector where Afrikaner entrepreneurs, managers and scientists could acquire technical skills and managerial ability. Between 1948 and 1976 the public sector's share of the economy nearly doubled. Annual expenditure of the public sector as a percentage of gross domestic fixed investment increased from 36.5 per cent in 1973 to 53 per cent in 1976" (60). But otherwise Giliomee does not find much evidence of systematic government support for Afrikaner business. He suggests the government did not play favorites lest it antagonize English-speaking business, divide Afrikaner businesses between the beneficiaries and victims of favoritism, and jeopardize white supremacy by compromising white unity. "[I]n general there were no procurement policies or empowerment schemes that could assist budding Afrikaner entrepreneurs" (7). Hermann Giliomee, "Afrikaner Entrepreneurship and the Afrikaner Economic advance, 1900–2000: A Tale with a Puzzle and Some Twists," paper presented to the Centre for Development and Enterprise, Johannesburg, November 22, 1999.

27. Charles van Onselen, *Studies in the Social and Economic History of Witwatersrand, 1886–1914*, vol. 2 (Harlow, Essex: Longman, 1982), 112.
28. Ibid.
29. Ibid., vol. 2, 161.
30. Ibid., vol. 2, 160.
31. George M. Fredrickson, *Black Liberation: A Comparative History of Black Ideologies in the United States and South Africa* (New York: Oxford University Press, 1995), 20 makes reference to the "badge of honor" conferred by the franchise.
32. Leonard Thompson, "Great Britain and the Afrikaner Republics, 1870–1899," in *The Oxford History of South Africa*, vol. 2: *South Africa 1870–1966*, ed. Monica Wilson and Leonard Thompson (New York: Oxford University Press, 1971), 309.
33. Leonard Thompson, "The Compromise of Union," in *The Oxford History of South Africa,* 353–354.
34. David Yudelman, *The Emergence of Modern South Africa: State, Capital and the Incorporation of Organized Labor on the South African Gold Fields, 1902–1939* (Westport, CT: Greenwood Press, 1983), 19.
35. Deborah Posel, "The Meaning of Apartheid before 1948: Conflicting Interests and Forces within the Afrikaner Nationalist Alliance," in *Segregation and Apartheid in Twentieth-Century South Africa,* 218.
36. Anthony W. Marx, *Making Race and Nation: A Comparison of South Africa, the United States, and Brazil* (Cambridge: Cambridge University Press, 1998), 12.

5. The Power Politics of the Transition to Democracy

1. Nelson Mandela, *Long Walk to Freedom: The Autobiography of Nelson Mandela* (Boston: Little, Brown, 1994). Pages 63–92 provide a nice portrait of how Africans from various tribal backgrounds blended into one people and developed political consciousness in Johannesburg in the 1940s.
2. Hermann Giliomee, "The Growth of Afrikaner Identity," in Heribert Adam and Hermann Giliomee, *Ethnic Power Mobilized: Can South Africa Change?* (New Haven, CT: Yale University Press, 1979), 115–127.
3. For a list of apartheid legislation see Brian Bunting, *The Rise of the South African Reich* (Harmondsworth, Middlesex: Penguin Books, 1964), 142–159.
4. The argument here stresses the *principles* of organization the state decreed. But the principles were not always enforced in practice, as is shown brilliantly by Charles van Onselen, *The Seed Is Mine: The Life of Kas Maine, a South African Sharecropper, 1894–1985* (New York: Hill and Wang, 1996).
5. Mahmood Mamdani, *Citizen and Subject: Contemporary Africa and the Legacy of Late Colonialism* (Princeton, NJ: Princeton University Press, 1996), 62–108.
6. One of the most prescient exceptions to the sense that apartheid was entrenched and immutable was Heribert Adam, who understood racial domination pragmatically and expected it to shift, and eventually to fall, in response to changing interests. Heribert Adam, *Modernizing Racial Domination: The Dynamics of South African Politics* (Berkeley: University of California Press, 1971).
7. Ibid., 8.
8. International Monetary Fund, *International Financial Statistics Yearbook, 2000* (Washington, DC: International Monetary Fund, 2000), 888–889, lines 62a and 62b. Interestingly, stock values climbed dramatically in the 1990s in the face of considerable political uncertainty as it became clear that apartheid was doomed.
9. International Monetary Fund, *International Financial Statistics Yearbook, 1991* (Washington, DC: International Monetary Fund, 1991). The percentage was calculated from the table on 668–669. The value of the rand was especially strong in 1980, in large part due to the spike in the price of gold.
10. International Monetary Fund, 1991. The percentage was calculated from the table on 668–669. Of course, apartheid was not the only problem with the currency's value, as proved by the steady decline in the rand until 2002–3.
11. *Report of the Commission of Inquiry into the Riots at Soweto and Elsewhere from the 16th of June 1976 to the 28th of February, 1977* (Cillie Commission Report) (Pretoria: Government Printing Office, 1980), 104.
12. Ibid., 555.

13. Ibid., 602.
14. Ibid., 640.
15. Hermann Giliomee and Lawrence Schlemmer, *From Apartheid to Nation-Building* (Cape Town: Oxford University Press, 1989), 114–149.
16. For a good study of South African foreign policy at this time, see Joseph Hanlon, *Beggar Your Neighbours: Apartheid Power in Southern Africa* (Bloomington: Indiana University Press, 1986).
17. Stanley B. Greenberg, *Legitimating the Illegitimate: State, Markets, and Resistance in South Africa* (Berkeley: University of California Press, 1987), 76–84.
18. Merle Lipton, *Capitalism and Apartheid: South Africa, 1910–84* (Totowa, NJ: Rowman & Allanheld, 1985). Pages 5–13 discuss the reasons why capital became dissatisfied with apartheid, stressing the "increasing need for skilled [black] labour" (7).
19. As quoted in Allister Sparks, *The Mind of South Africa: The Story of the Rise and Fall of Apartheid* (London: Mandarin Paperbacks, 1991), 359.
20. Robert M. Price, *The Apartheid State in Crisis: Political Transformation in South Africa, 1975–1990* (New York: Oxford University Press, 1991), 106.
21. Jack D. Glen and Mariusz A. Sumlinski, "Trends in Private Investment in Developing Countries 1995, Statistics for 1980–93," Discussion Paper Number 25 (Washington, DC: International Finance Corporation, The World Bank, 1995). The percentages were calculated from pp. 13–14.
22. Stephen R. Lewis Jr., *The Economics of Apartheid* (New York: Council of Foreign Relations Press, 1990), 63, 71. Lewis provides useful figures on page 178 on the new inflow of capital as percentages of GDP and domestic investment from 1946 to 1987.
23. For a good discussion of the principal role of political unrest in the investment calculations of business, see Elisabeth Jean Wood, *Forging Democracy from Below: Insurgent Transitions in South Africa and El Salvador* (Cambridge: Cambridge University Press, 2000), 152–158.
24. Stephen Gelb, "South Africa's Economic Crisis," in *South Africa's Economic Crisis: An Overview*, ed. Stephen Gelb (Cape Town: David Philip, 1991), 1–32, and Hein Marais, *South Africa: Limits to Change: The Political Economy of Transition* (Cape Town: University of Cape Town Press, 1998) discuss the exhaustion of the import substitution model of economic development and the ensuing political crises.
25. V. I. Lenin, *What Is to Be Done? Burning Questions of Our Movement* (New York: International Publishers, 1972), 169.
26. Samuel P. Huntington, *Political Order in Changing Societies* (New Haven, CT: Yale University Press, 1968), 4–5.
27. Josette Cole provides a good illustration of what Huntington fears, albeit from a much different political perspective. In a study of Crossroads, the large squatter camp outside Cape Town, Cole describes how the migrant labor system exacerbated gender conflict (15); how the state's contradictory

efforts to disband and control squatter camps and "reform" and repress them provoked factionalism and violence (47); how conflict in squatter camps sowed divisions between men and women (65–66); how the state exploited resentment of comrades to divide opposition (120); and how pervasive disorder and insecurity provided the background for personal ambitions. Eventually, power struggles became "endemic" (158), the camp was razed, and the opposition was disorganized. Josette Cole, *Crossroads: The Politics of Reform and Repression, 1976–1986* (Johannesburg: Ravan Press, 1987).

28. Edmund Burke, *Reflections on the Revolution in France* (Harmondsworth, Middlesex: Penguin Books, 1973), 135.
29. Mamphela Ramphele, *A Bed Called Home: Life in the Migrant Labour Hostels of Cape Town* (Cape Town: David Philip, 1993), 78.
30. Mark Mathabane, *Kaffir Boy: The True Story of a Black Youth Coming of Age in Apartheid South Africa* (New York: New American Library, 1986), 36.
31. Ibid., 37–38.
32. Ibid., 43.
33. Ibid.
34. Ibid., 54–57.
35. Ibid., 68.
36. Shula Marks and Neil Andersson, "The Epidemiology and Culture of Violence," in *Political Violence and the Struggle in South Africa,* ed. N. Chabani Manganyi and André du Toit (Halfway House, South Africa: Southern Book Publishers, 1990), 37.
37. Dale T. McKinley, *The ANC and the Liberation Struggle: A Critical Political Biography* (London: Pluto Press, 1997), 63–65.
38. Sparks, *The Mind of South Africa,* 330.
39. Mark Swilling, "The United Democratic Front and Township Revolt," in *Popular Struggles in South Africa,* ed. William Cobbett and Robin Cohen (London: James Currey, 1988), 90.
40. Jeremy Seekings, "The Origins of Political Mobilisation in PMV Townships, 1980–84," in *Popular Struggles in South Africa,* 70.
41. Jeremy Seekings, *The UDF: A History of the United Democratic Front in South Africa, 1983–1991* (Oxford: James Currey, 2000), 2.
42. Ibid., 61.
43. Ibid., 120.
44. Ibid., 18.
45. Ibid., 120.
46. Ibid., 3.
47. Swilling, "Township Revolt," 90.
48. Seekings, *The UDF,* 23.
49. Ibid., 91, 40, 199.
50. Ibid., 292.
51. "Political Report and Communiqué of the Second National Conference of the African National Congress," July 1985, excerpts reprinted in *Mandela,*

Tambo and the African National Congress: The Struggle Against Apartheid, 1948–1990: A Documentary Survey, ed Sheridan Johns and R. Hunt Davis, Jr. (New York: Oxford University Press, 1991), 289, 292.

52. William Finnegan, *Crossing the Line: A Year in the Land of Apartheid* (New York: Harper and Row, 1986), 196.
53. Price, *The Apartheid State in Crisis,* 190–191.
54. Sparks, *The Mind of South Africa,* 340.
55. Seekings, *The UDF,* 162.
56. Ibid., 173.
57. Ibid., 227.
58. Price, *The Apartheid State in Crisis,* 193.
59. The fear of political collapse and social disintegration was widespread in the 1980s. Among other examples, it was the point of departure for Nadine Gordimer, *July's People* (New York: Penguin, 1982), and was one of two "plausible" futures envisioned in "Degenerative Collapse," *The Economist,* August 17, 1985.
60. Gavin Relly, "The Costs of Disinvestment," *Foreign Policy* 63 (Summer 1986): 137.
61. Ibid., 141.
62. Ibid., 142.
63. Stephen Ellis and Tsepo Sechaba, *Comrades against Apartheid: The ANC and the South African Communist Party in Exile* (London: James Currey, 1992), 58.
64. Ibid., 174.
65. Anthony W. Marx, *Lessons of Struggle: South African Internal Opposition, 1960–1990* (New York: Oxford University Press, 1992), 189–234.
66. Mandela, *Long Walk to Freedom,* 547.
67. Guillermo O'Donnell and Philippe C. Schmitter, *Transitions from Authoritarian Rule: Tentative Conclusions about Uncertain Democracies* (Baltimore: The Johns Hopkins University Press, 1991), 7.
68. Ibid., 8.
69. Ibid., 4.
70. Ibid., 4–5.
71. Ibid., 69.
72. Ibid., 37.
73. Ibid., 38. The term "democracy on the installment plan" is quoted from Dankwart Rustow.
74. Ibid., 54.
75. Ibid., 55–56.
76. Ibid., 56.
77. Ibid., 72.
78. One of the critical moments in the transition occurred in April 1993, when Chris Hani was assassinated. Hani, a senior figure in MK and the SACP as well as the ANC, was murdered by several white right-wingers. The assas-

sination was committed at a time when negotiations seemed to be deadlocked on the question of power-sharing and minority vetoes. "The tragic death of Chris Hani plunged South Africa into a perilous crisis; anger and frustration, especially among township youth, had long been building over the protracted pace of talks. Every expectation was that the townships would explode, spiraling out of control and plunging South Africa into anarchy. Mandela, as if to underscore that power was shifting slowly away from the white minority government, appeared presidential in an unprecedented national address on state television, appealing for calm and restraint." At that point, Mandela showed that the ANC—and not the NP—could perform the critical responsibility of government, securing public order, and from then on negotiations went the ANC's way. Timothy D. Sisk, *Democratization in South Africa: The Elusive Social Contract* (Princeton, NJ: Princeton University Press, 1995), 228.

79. O'Donnell and Schmitter, *Transitions from Authoritarian Rule,* 24.
80. See Michael MacDonald, "The Siren's Song: The Political Logic of Power-Sharing in South Africa," *Journal of Southern African Studies* 18, no. 4 (1992): 709–725 for an analysis of the powers that would have resided with the NP in a power-sharing government.
81. For a scholarly treatment of the process of negotiations in South Africa, with a particular emphasis on the challenges posed by ethnic and racial divisions, see Sisk, *Democratization in South Africa*. For a well-informed journalistic account, see Allister Sparks, *Tomorrow Is Another Country: The Inside Story of South Africa's Road to Change* (Chicago: University of Chicago Press, 1996).
82. Tom Lodge, Bill Nasson, Steven Mufson, Khehla Shubane, and Nokwanda Sithole, *All, Here, and Now: Black Politics in South Africa in the 1980s* (Cape Town: Ford Foundation, David Philip, 1991), 35. Lodge is describing the politics of mostly young activists who allied with the United Democratic Front and recognized the leadership of the ANC. He does not claim the ANC fully supported these objectives.
83. Victor Khupiso, "Comrades Kill Grandson over Woman's 20R Bill," *Sunday Times* (Johannesburg), May 8, 1994, 8.
84. Nelson Mandela, "Address by President of the Republic," Republic of South Africa, *Joint Sittings of Both Houses of Parliament (Hansard),* Second Session-First Parliament, 17 February to 1 March 1995 (Cape Town: The Government Printer) 1–19. This argument is developed more fully in Michael MacDonald, "Power Politics in the New South Africa," *Journal of Southern African Studies* 22, no. 2 (June 1996).

6. Non-Racialism as an Ideology

1. Republic of South Africa, *Constitution of the Republic of South Africa* (Pretoria: Government Printer, 1996), §1, 1 (b).

2. This chapter deals with the construction of the meaning of non-racialism by organized political actors. For a different approach and a different interpretation, see Rupert Taylor, including Rupert Taylor and Mark Orkin, "The Racialisation of Social Scientific Research on South Africa," in *The Politics of Social Science Research: "Race," Ethnicity and Social Change,* ed. Peter Ratcliffe (New York: Palgrave, 2001), 61–84; Rupert Taylor and Don Foster, "Advancing Non-Racialism in Post-Apartheid South Africa," in *National Identity and Democracy in Africa,* ed. Mai Palmberg (Belville, South Africa: Mayibuye Centre of the University of the Western Cape, Nordic Africa Institute, 1999), 328–341; and Rupert Taylor, "South Africa: From 'Race' to 'Non-Racialism,' " in *Race, Ethnicity and Nation: International Perspectives on Social Conflict,* ed. Peter Ratcliffe (London: UCL Press, 1994), 91–107.
3. A note on terminology: The Communist Party changed its name from the Communist Party of South Africa (CPSA) to the South African Communist Party (SACP) in the early 1950s. The CPSA was banned and reorganized itself as an underground party, with the same program and leadership, in the name of the SACP.
4. Neville Alexander, *Sow the Wind: Contemporary Speeches* (Johannesburg: Skotaville Publishers, 1985), 141–142.
5. Ibid., 151–152.
6. Ibid., 53.
7. Sheridan Johns III, ed., *Protest and Hope, 1882–1934*, vol. 1, *From Protest to Challenge: A Documentary History of African Politics in South Africa, 1882–1964,* ed. Thomas Karis and Gwendolen M. Carter (Stanford, CA: Hoover Institution Press, 1987), 3.
8. The ANC's uncertainties about the term are apparent in the way it was used. For example, a leader of the Cape Province National Congress observed in 1921 that "the English and the loyal Dutch . . . agreed to . . . sink racial differences and join hands in the formation of a new party on non-racial lines." "The Exclusion of the Bantu," Address by the Rev. Z. R. Muhabane, President of the Cape Province National Congress, 1921. Ibid., 291.
9. One example: In 1927, the government was proposing to eliminate the Cape franchise. As part of the process, it consulted with tribal leaders. In one consultation, members of the Transkeian Native General Council observed, "Your committee wishes to stress the point that their claim to the retention of the franchise are in no way coupled with the claims to social equality." "Testimony of Charles Sakwe, Elijah Qamata, and William Mlandu of the Transkeian Native General Council, before the Select Committee on Subject of Native Bills, May 6, 1927 [Extracts]," in *Protest and Hope,* 198.
10. One important African political figure, who was not a member of the ANC, D. D. T. Jabavu, argued that for the Native "to become civilized he begins by renouncing barbarism and develops political aspirations that are harmonious with progress and modern culture. Barbarism, as an inferior stage of ethnic development, can always be subjugated by civilization." "Testimony

of Professor D. D. T. Jabavu, Walter Rubusana, and the Rev. Abner Mtimkulu of the Cape Native Voters' Convention and Meshach Pelem of the Bantu Union, before the Select Committee on Subject of Native Bills, May 30, 1927, in *Protest and Hope,* 205.

11. Ibid., 207–208.
12. "Proceedings and Resolutions of the National European-Bantu Conference, July 1933," in *Protest and Hope,* 250.
13. "Proceedings and Resolutions of the Governor-General's Native Conference, 1926," in *Protest and Hope,* 183.
14. Ibid., 181.
15. "Constitution of the South African Native National Congress, September 1919," in *Protest and Hope,* 77.
16. Pixley Ka Isaka Seme, "Native Union," in *Protest and Hope,* 72.
17. The idea that nationalism invents nations was advanced by Ernest Gellner, *Nations and Nationalism* (Ithaca, NY: Cornell University Press, 1983), 48–49 and was developed by E. J. Hobsbawm, *Nations and Nationalism since 1780: Programme, Myth, Reality* (Cambridge: Cambridge University Press, 1990).
18. Chief A. J. Lutuli, "The Road to Freedom Is Via the Cross," in *Hope and Challenge, 1935–1952,* ed. Thomas Karis, vol. 2, *From Protest to Challenge: A Documentary History of African Politics in South Africa, 1882–1964,* ed. Thomas Karis and Gwendolen M. Carter (Stanford, CA: Hoover Institution Press, 1987), 487.
19. A. M. Lembede, "Policy of the Congress Youth League," in *Hope and Challenge,* 317.
20. "Letter from the ANC Youth League (Transvaal) to the Secretary of the Progressive Youth Council," in *Hope and Challenge,* 316.
21. For a full treatment of the role of chiefs, see Peter Walshe, *The Rise of African Nationalism in South Africa: The African National Congress, 1912–1952* (Berkeley: University of California Press, 1971).
22. Provisional Committee of the Congress Youth League, "Congress Youth League Manifesto," in *Hope and Challenge,* 301.
23. National Executive Committee of the ANC Youth League, "Basic Policy of Congress Youth League," in *Hope and Challenge,* 329.
24. A. M. Lembede, "Policy of the Congress Youth League," in *Hope and Challenge,* 317–318.
25. National Executive Committee of the ANC Youth League, "Basic Policy of Congress Youth League," in *Hope and Challenge,* 329.
26. Report of the National Executive Committee of the ANC, submitted to the Annual Conference, December 12–13, 1959, in *Challenge and Violence, 1953–1964,* ed. Thomas Karis and Gail M. Gerhardt, vol. 3, *From Protest to Challenge: A Documentary History of African Politics in South Africa, 1882–1964,* ed. Thomas Karis and Gwendolen M. Carter (Stanford, CA: Hoover Institution Press, 1987), 488.
27. "Address by Professor Z. K. Matthews," in *Challenge and Violence*, 221.

28. Chief A. J. Lutuli, "Special Presidential Message," in *Challenge and Violence*, 213–214.
29. Nelson Mandela, "Statements in Court," October 22 and November 7, 1962, in *Challenge and Violence*, 728–735.
30. Chief A. J. Lutuli, "Letter on the Current Situation and Suggesting a Multi-Racial Convention from Chief A. J. Lutuli to Prime Minister Strijdom," in *Challenge and Violence,* 400.
31. Chief A. J. Lutuli, "Freedom Is the Apex," in *Challenge and Violence,* 456.
32. E. S. Reddy, ed., *Luthuli: Speeches of Chief Albert John Luthuli* (Durban: Madiba Publishers, 1991), 102–103. This edition of Lutuli's speeches spells the chief's name differently.
33. Ibid., 103.
34. Joe Matthews, " 'Africanism' under the Microscope," in *Challenge and Violence,* 541.
35. Govan Mbeki, *The Struggle for Liberation in South Africa: A Short History* (Cape Town: David Philip, 1992), 26.
36. Mandela, "Statements in Court," 739.
37. Reddy, *Luthuli,* 128.
38. Nelson Mandela, "Statement during the Rivonia Trial," in *Challenge and Violence,* 796.
39. Reddy, *Luthuli,* 127.
40. See Edward Roux, *S. P. Bunting: A Political Biography* (Bellville, South Africa: Mayibuye Books, 1993), 100–140 and Sheridan Johns, *Raising the Red Flag: The International Socialist League and the Communist Party of South Africa, 1914–1932* (Bellville, South Africa: Mayibuye Books, 1995) for useful discussions of the politics and debates in the Communist Party of South Africa during the 1920s and 1930s.
41. V. I. Lenin, *Imperialism: The Highest Stage of Capitalism* (New York: International Publishers, 1972).
42. Shlomo Avineri, *The Making of Modern Zionism: The Intellectual Origins of the Jewish State* (New York: Basic Books, 1981), especially 3–13.
43. Steve Biko, "The Righteousness of Our Strength," in *I Write What I Like,* ed. Aelred Stubbs (London: C. R. Heinemann, 1987), 123.
44. Anthony W. Marx, *Lessons of Struggle: South African Internal Opposition, 1960–1990* (New York: Oxford University Press, 1992), 42.
45. Biko, "The Definition of Black Consciousness," in *I Write What I Like,* 50.
46. Biko, "What Is Black Consciousness?" in *I Write What I Like,* 100.
47. Biko, "White Racism and Black Consciousness," in *I Write What I Like,* 66.
48. Ibid., 62.
49. Biko, "Black Souls in White Skins?" in *I Write What I Like,* 20.
50. Biko, "The Definition of Black Consciousness," 48–49.
51. Biko, "We Blacks," in *I Write What I Like,* 28–29.
52. Biko, "The Definition of Black Consciousness," 50.
53. Biko, "White Racism and Black Consciousness," 66.

54. Ibid., 64. Italics in original.
55. Biko, "Black Souls in White Skins?" 23.
56. Biko, "The Quest for a True Humanity," in *I Write What I Like,* 97.
57. Biko, "White Racism and Black Consciousness," 68.
58. Marx, *Lessons,* 51.
59. Ibid., 93.
60. Biko, "White Racism and Black Consciousness," 68.

7. The Poltical Economy of Identity Politics

1. Nelson Mandela challenged the right of white courts to try him, arguing that it violated the principle of equality under the law and equating equality under the law with democratic rights. "In its proper meaning, equality before the law means the right to participate in the making of the laws by which one is governed. It means a constitution which guarantees democratic rights to all sections of the population, the right to approach the court for protection or relief in the case of the violation of the rights guaranteed in the constitution, and the right to take part in the administration of justice as judges, magistrates, attorney general, prosecutors, law advisers, and similar positions. In the absence of these safeguards the phrase 'equality under the law' insofar as it is intended to apply to us, is meaningless and misleading." Nelson Mandela, "Black Man in a White Man's Court," in *Mandela, Tambo, and the African National Congress: The Struggle Against Apartheid, 1948–1990: A Documentary Survey,* ed. Sheridan Johns and R. Hunt Davis, Jr. (New York: Oxford University Press, 1991), 112.
2. F. A. Hayek, *The Road to Serfdom* (Chicago: University of Chicago Press, 1972), 79–80.
3. ANC discussion document, "The State and Social Transformation," 5.20, November 1996, www.anc.org.za/ancdocs/policy/s&st.html.
4. Ibid., 5.24.
5. Pluralists are especially interested in the representation of private interests in the state. Robert Dahl, one of the foremost pluralists, sees pluralism as stressing "the role played in political life by associations, organizations, and groups that [are] relatively independent of the state and one another." Robert A. Dahl, "Pluralism," in *Toward Democracy: A Journey,* vol. 1, *Reflections, 1940–1997* (Berkeley: Institute of Governmental Studies Press, University of California, 1997), 283.
6. See on this point John Gaventa, *Power and Powerlessness: Quiescence and Rebellion in an Appalachian Valley* (Urbana: University of Illinois Press, 1980); Giuseppe Fiori, *Antonio Gramsci: Life of a Revolutionary* (New York: Schocken Books, 1970), 238; and Ralph Miliband, *The State in Capitalist Society: The Analysis of the Western System of Power* (London: Quartet Books, 1976), 67–69.
7. Mandela, "I Am Prepared to Die: Excerpted from Courtroom Statement,

Rivonia Trial, October 20, 1964," in *Mandela, Tambo, and the African National Congress*, 126.

8. Allister Sparks, *Beyond the Miracle: Inside the New South Africa* (Johannesburg: Jonathan Ball Publishers, 2003), 16.
9. Hein Marais, "The Logic of Expediency: Post-Apartheid Shifts in Macroeconomic Policy," in *Thabo Mbeki's World: The Politics and Ideology of the South African President*, ed. Sean Jacobs and Richard Calland (London: Zed Books, 2002), 92.
10. Hein Marais, *South Africa: Limits to Change: The Political Economy of Transition* (Cape Town: University of Cape Town Press, 1998), 160.
11. White liberals are not a monolithic tradition. Culturalists, who set much of the tone for liberals under apartheid and who advance a distinct interpretation of South African society, stress groups. Individualists, who have become more prominent among liberals since the advent of democracy, resemble European liberals, emphasizing individualism and property rights.
12. It is for this reason that culturalist political scientists have been especially interested in two political scientists writing in the United States: Donald Horowitz and Arend Lijphart. See Donald L. Horowitz, *A Democratic South Africa? Constitutional Engineering in a Divided Society* (Berkeley: University of California Press, 1991) and Arend Lijphart, *Power-Sharing in South Africa* (Berkeley: Institute of International Studies, University of California, 1985). Although Lijphart and Horowitz offered rival proposals for South Africa's post-apartheid constitution, they agreed on the point of departure, that individualism was a fiction in South Africa.
13. Note, in this context, the discussions of white liberals by two prominent liberals, David Welsh and R. W. Johnson. Each insists that not all liberals are white, yet use the term "white liberal" to characterize their tradition. See David Welsh, "Introduction: The Liberal Inheritance," and R. W. Johnson, "The Best of Enemies? Black Intellectuals and White Liberals," in *Ironic Victory: Liberalism in Post-Liberation South Africa,* ed. R. W. Johnson and David Welsh (Cape Town: Oxford University Press, 1998).
14. Donald L. Horowitz, *Ethnic Groups in Conflict* (Berkeley: University of California Press, 1985), 86.
15. For an incisive critique of the ethnic census thesis in South Africa, see Robert Mattes and Jessica Piombo, "Opposition Parties and the Voters in South Africa's 1999 Election," *Democratization* 8, no. 13 (Autumn 2001): 101–128. It is worth noting that Mattes and Piombo do not deny the relationship between race and voting; they seek to explain it. "[T]here is no denying the clear relationship between race, ethnicity, and voting patterns in South Africa's first two national elections. It remains by far the most salient line of political cleavage in the country. But what is important is how we interpret these relations, for as is well known, correlation does not equal causation" (102).

16. R. W. Johnson, "The 1994 Election: Outcome and Analysis," in *Launching Democracy in South Africa: The First Open Election, April 1994,* ed. R. W. Johnson and Lawrence Schlemmer (New Haven, CT: Yale University Press, 1996), 319.
17. Nelson Mandela, "Report by the President of the ANC to the 50th National Conference of the African National Congress," 1997. www.anc.org.za/ancdocs/history/conf/conference50/presaddress.html.
18. Donald L. Horowitz, *A Democratic South Africa?* 91–100.
19. Hermann Giliomee, "Presidential Address: Liberal and Populist Democracy in South Africa: Challenges, New Threats to Liberalism" (Johannesburg: South African Institute of Race Relations, 1996), 16.
20. Heribert Adam, Frederick Van Zyl Slabbert, and Kogila Moodley, *Comrades in Business: Post-Liberation Politics in South Africa* (Cape Town: Tafelberg, 1997), 87. For a discussion of the efforts of national leaders to control provinces, see Tom Lodge, *South African Politics since 1994* (Cape Town: David Philip Publishers, 1999), 20–23.
21. Robert Mattes, "South Africa: Democracy Without the People?" *Journal of Democracy* 13, no. 1 (2002): 26. See also Roger Southall, "The State of Party Politics: Struggles within the Tripartite Alliance and the Decline of Opposition," in *State of the Nation: South Africa 2003–2004*, ed. John Daniel, Adam Habib, and Roger Southall (Cape Town: HSRC, 2003), 57–61.
22. For a full treatment of the relations between provincial parties and the central party, see Geoffrey Hawker, "Political Leadership in the ANC: The South African Provinces 1994–99," *Journal of Modern African Studies* 38, no. 4 (2000). Hawker notes on page 631 that Thabo Mbeki had three of the ANC's seven provincial premiers removed just weeks before the campaign began for national elections in 1999.
23. Farouk Chothia and Sean Jacobs, "Remaking the Presidency: The Tension between Co-ordination and Centralisation," in *Thabo Mbeki's World,* 151.
24. Raymond Suttner, " 'It Is Your Mother Who Is the Enemy Now!' An Account of the Imprint of African National Congress Underground Activity in the 'Lull' after Rivonia" (paper presented to the International Political Science Association Conference, Durban, July 2003), 3. For rival accounts of the influence of the SACP on the ANC, see Vladimir Shubin, *ANC: A View from Moscow* (Bellville: Mayibuye Books, University of the Western Cape, 1999) and Stephen Ellis and Tsepo Sechaba, *Comrades against Apartheid: The ANC and the South African Communist Party in Exile* (London: James Currey, 1992).
25. According to Allister Sparks, the Democrats accused the Mandela government of requiring "employers to draft a plan showing how they intended to advance blacks in their work force and then submit annual progress reports to the government. In a crude bit of overstatement the DP claimed this effectively reintroduced a system of race classification and criminalized 'colour-blindness', and warned that 'racial legislation is a very slippery slope:

apartheid, American segregation and Nazi Germany all had small beginnings'." Sparks, *Beyond the Miracle,* 12.

26. Mahmood Mamdani makes a point relevant here about the strategies of the defenders of racial privilege. "Racial privilege not only receded into . . . society, but defended itself in the language of civil rights, of individual rights and institutional autonomy. To victims of racism the vocabulary of rights rang hollow, a lullaby for perpetuating racial privilege. Their demands were formulated in the language of nationalism and social justice. The result was a breach between the discourse on rights and the one on justice, with the language of rights appearing as a fig leaf over privilege and power appearing as the guarantor of social justice and redress." Mahmood Mamdani, *Citizen and Subject: Contemporary Africa and the Legacy of Late Colonialism* (Princeton, NJ: Princeton University Press, 1996), 20–21.
27. The argument was made most fully by an American, Donald Horowitz, but was adopted by South African culturalists. See Horowitz, *A Democratic South Africa?* 91–100.
28. The World Bank, *Social Indicators of Development* (Baltimore: The Johns Hopkins University Press, 1995), x–xi.
29. The World Bank, "Key Indicators of Poverty in South Africa," analysis prepared for the Office of Reconstruction and Development Programme (Pretoria: South African Communication Service, 1995), 3.
30. The World Bank, *Social Indicators of Development*, 316.
31. The World Bank, "Key Indicators of Poverty," 7, table 2.
32. Ibid., 3.
33. Central Statistics Service, *Statistics in Brief* (Pretoria: Central Statistics Service, 1997), 5.3. The statistics were compiled in October 1995.
34. Ros Hirschowitz, "Earning and Spending in South Africa: Selected Findings of the 1995 Income and Expenditure Survey" (Pretoria: Central Statistics Service, 1997), 50, table 11.
35. Ibid., 44.
36. Ibid., 48.
37. Ibid., 46, figure 18.
38. Ibid. The numbers may seem wrong, but an explanation is possible. Because Africans make up much larger households than whites, the number of people in a quintile made up of households can exceed 20 percent.
39. The World Bank, "Key Indicators of Poverty," 12. The World Bank defines the two bottom quintiles as poor (8).
40. Julian May, I. Woolard, and S. Klasen, "Input Paper: Poverty and Inequality Report—The Measurement and Nature of Poverty and Inequality," August 1997, 1, www.info.gov.za/otherdocs/1998/poverty/nature.pdf, accessed September 12, 2005.
41. United Nations Development Programme, *South Africa Human Development Report: The Challenge of Sustainable Development: Unlocking People's Creativity,*

2003, 3, Human Development Report Office, undp.org.za/NHDR2003 .htm, 43, accessed September 13, 2005.

42. The World Bank, *Poverty and Inequality,* 23, table 3.
43. Hirschowitz, "Earning and Spending" (1997), 50.
44. Murray V. Leibbrandt, Christopher D. Woolard, and Ingrid D. Woolard, "The Contribution of Income Components to Income Inequality in South Africa: A Decomposable Gini Analysis" (Living Standards Measurement Study, Working Paper No. 125) (Washington, DC: World Bank, 1996), 1.
45. Andrew Whiteford and Dirk Ernst van Seventer, "Winners and Losers: South Africa's Changing Income Distribution in the 1990s" (Johannesburg: Wharton Economic Forecasting Associates, 1999); summarized by Howard Barrell, "Democracy: Black Elite Benefit Most," *Weekly Mail and Guardian,* January 28 to February 3, 2000, 5. Quotes from *Weekly Mail* story.
46. P. J. Mohr et al., *The Practical Guide to South African Economic Indicators* (Johannesburg: Lexicon Publishers, 1995), 76.
47. The African National Congress, *The Reconstruction and Development Programme: A Policy Framework* (Johannesburg: Umanyano Publications, 1994), 4.
48. Republic of South Africa, *White Paper on Reconstruction and Development: Government's Strategy for Fundamental Transformation* (Cape Town: Office of the Presidency, November 1994), www.info.gov.za/documents/whitepapers/index.html, 23.
49. The African National Congress, *The Reconstruction and Development Programme,* 6.
50. Ibid.
51. Republic of South Africa, *White Paper on Reconstruction and Development,* 20.
52. Ibid., 39.
53. The African National Congress, *The Reconstruction and Development Programme,* 7.
54. Desmond Lachman et al., eds., "Economic Policies for a New South Africa," occasional paper 91 (Washington, DC: International Monetary Fund, 1992), 2.
55. Robert Corker and Tamim Bayoumi, "Apartheid, Growth and Income Distribution in South Africa: Past History and Future Prospects," IMF working paper (Washington, DC: International Monetary Fund, 1991), 1–2.
56. Lachman et al., "Economic Policies," 13.
57. Republic of South Africa, Department of Finance, "Growth, Employment and Redistribution: A Macroeconomic Strategy (GEAR)" (Pretoria: Department of Finance, 1996), 1–2, www.gov.za/govdocs/policy/growth .html, accessed September 12, 2005.
58. GEAR, 2.
59. Ibid., 6.

60. Joseph E. Stiglitz, *Globalization and Its Discontents* (New York: W. W. Norton, 2002), xiv, 15–18, 72, 188, 209.
61. Frederick A. Johnstone, *Class, Race and Gold: A Study of Class Relations and Racial Discrimination in South Africa* (London: Routledge and Kegan Paul, 1976), 14.
62. Avril Joffe, David Kaplan, Raphael Kaplinsky, and David Lewis, *Improving Manufacturing Performance in South Africa: The Report of the Industrial Strategy Project,* International Development Research Centre (Rondebosch: University of Cape Town Press, 1995), 149.
63. *McGregor's Who Owns Whom in South Africa,* 21st ed. (Westgate, South Africa: PSG Online, 2001), xix. The difference in the ten years is accountable mainly to the rise of ownership groups with significant black influence, which accounted for 5.6 percent of market capitalization in 2000 and a negligible amount in 1990, and institutional holders, which increased from 4.9 percent in 1990 to 11.6 percent in 2000.
64. Joffe et al., *Improving Manufacturing Performance,* 153.
65. *McGregor's Who Owns Whom in South Africa*, 21st ed., 46 and 156.
66. *McGregor's Who Owns Whom in South Africa, 2002,* 22nd ed. (Westgate, South Africa: Carla Soares Publisher, 2002), 482, 586, 600, 460, and 105. For an important history of the concentration of South African business, especially in the hands of Anglo American, see Duncan Innes, *Anglo American and the Rise of Modern South Africa* (London: Heinemann, 1984), esp. 188–228.
67. William J. Baumol and Alan S. Blinder, *Economics: Principles and Policy,* 6th ed. (Fort Worth, TX: The Dryden Press, Harcourt Brace & Company, 1994), 277. The economic logic of monopolies and the importance of monopolies to the South African economy were impressed on me by Michael Samson of the Economic Policy Research Institute in Cape Town and Williams College.
68. Stephen R. Lewis, Jr., *The Economics of Apartheid* (New York: Council of Foreign Relations Press, 1990), 63–64.
69. Joffe et al., *Improving Manufacturing Performance,* 69.
70. Lewis, *Economics of Apartheid,* 63–64.
71. Joffe et al., *Improving Manufacturing Performance,* 141–45.
72. Ibid., 138.
73. As quoted in "The Evolution of Policy in SA: Proposed Guidelines for Competition Policy: A Framework for Competition, Competitiveness and Development" (Pretoria: Department of Trade and Industry, November 27, 1997), 1.3.2.1.
74. Stiglitz, *Globalization and Its Discontents,* 15–22.
75. Marais, "The Logic of Expediency," 83–104.
76. As quoted in John S. Saul, "Cry for the Beloved Country: The Post-Apartheid Denouement," in *Thabo Mbeki's World,* 43.
77. South African Communist Party, "The Path to Power: Programme of the

South African Communist Party" (Johannesburg: South African Communist Party, 1990), 37. The ANC modified its two-stage conception of revolution in 1995. See Vishwas Satgar, "Thabo Mbeki and the South African Communist Party," in *Thabo Mbebiki's World,* 171.

78. Sparks, *Beyond the Miracle, 16.*
79. Republic of South Africa, *White Paper on Reconstruction and Development,* 41.
80. Policy Co-ordinating and Advisory Services, The Presidency, *Towards a Ten Year Review: Synthesis Report on Implementation of Government Programmes, Discussion Document,* October 2003, 17, www.gcis.gov.za/docs/publica tions/10years.htm. The document provides a spirited defense of the ANC's successes and record.
81. Servaas van der Berg and Megan Louw, "Changing Patterns of South African Income Distribution: Towards Time Series Estimates of Distribution and Poverty," *South African Journal of Economics* 72, no. 8 (September 2004), Special Conference Issue, 14, developed from table 1.
82. Policy Co-ordinating and Advisory Services, *Synthesis Report,* 18.
83. Stephen Gelb, "Inequality in South Africa: Nature, Causes and Responses," African Development and Poverty Reduction: The Macro-Micro Linkage, Forum Paper, Development Policy Research Institute, 2004, 12, table 13.
84. Thabo Mbeki, "Address of the President, Thabo Mbeki, at the Opening of the 51st National Conference of the African National Congress," Stellenbosch, December 16, 2002, www.anc.org.za/ancdocs/history/mbeki/2002/tm1216.html, accessed September 20, 2005.
85. Policy Co-ordinating and Advisory Services, *Synthesis Report,* 21, 24.
86. Ros Hirschowitz, "Earning and Spending in South Africa: Selected Findings and Comparisons from the Income and Expenditure Surveys of October 1995 and October 2000" (Pretoria: Statistics South Africa, 2002), 2.
87. Ibid., 3.
88. Ibid., 2.
89. United Nations Development Programme, *South Africa Human Development Report,* 24.
90. Policy Co-ordinating and Advisory Services, *Synthesis Report,* 19.
91. United Nations Development Programme, *South Africa Human Development Report,* 16.
92. The comparisons are based on "2 Human Development Index Trends," HDR 2004, Human Development Reports, http://hdr.undp.org/statistics/data/indic_16_1_1.html.
93. The comparisons are based on "13 Economic Performance," HDR 2004, Human Development Reports, http://hdr.undp.org/statistics/data/indic _123_1_1.html.
94. United Nations Development Programme, *South Africa Human Development Report,* 44–45.
95. Ibid., 45.

96. Ibid.
97. Van der Berg and Louw, "Changing Patterns of South African Income Distribution," 14, developed from table 1.
98. Ibid., 18, developed from table 3.
99. Ibid., 22, developed from table 5.
100. Hirschowitz, "Earning and Spending" (2002), 46.
101. Ibid., 2.
102. Ibid., 4.
103. Ibid., 28, table 3.1.
104. United Nations Development Programme, *South Africa Human Development Report,* 41, table 2.20.
105. Hirschowitz, "Earning and Spending" (2002), 33.
106. Ibid., 42, figure 4.7.
107. Ibid., 48.
108. Van der Berg and Louw, "Changing Patterns of South African Income Distribution," 18, from table 3. The same pattern was reflected in a study that calculates inequality differently. According to Statistics South Africa, the gini coefficients for the country were .56 in 1995 and .57 in 2000 and for Africans were .50 in 1995 and .49 in 2000. Hirschowitz, "Earning and Spending" (2002), 48.
109. United Nations Development Programme, *South Africa Human Development Report,* 12, figure 2.1.
110. Ibid., 14, table 2.1.
111. Ibid., 13.
112. Ibid., 17, table 2.3.
113. Ibid., 20–21.
114. World Bank Group, *World Development Indicators* (Washington, DC: World Bank Group, August 2005). The table was calculated from the country data for South Africa, the time series data, and the data for the specific variables.
115. For a thorough and informative discussion of BEE, see Okechukwu C. Iheduru, "Black Economic Power and Nation-Building in Post-Apartheid South Africa," *Journal of Modern African Studies* 42, no. 1 (2004).
116. "Statement of Deputy President Thabo Mbeki at the Opening of the Debate in the National Assembly, on 'Reconciliation and Nation Building,' National Assembly, Cape Town, 29 May 1998," www.dfa.gov.za/docs/speeches/1998/mbek0529.htm.
117. "State of the Nation Address by the President of South Africa, Thabo Mbeki, to the Joint Sitting of the Houses of Parliament, Cape Town, 8 February 2002," www.info.gov.za/speeches/2002/0202281146a1001.htm.
118. For a critique, see Nicoli Nattrass and Jeremy Seekings, " 'Two Nations'? Race and Economic Inequality in South Africa Today," *Daedalus—Journal of the American Academy of Arts and Sciences,* 130, no. 1 (Winter 2001): 45–70.
119. Anthony W. Marx, *Making Race and Nation: A Comparison of South Africa,*

the United States, and Brazil (Cambridge: Cambridge University Press, 1998), 20.

120. Iheduru notes that the "government and ANC's statements and the implementation of BEE so far . . . indicate a clear preference for the black African population." Iheduru, "Black Economic Power," 3.
121. Thabo Mbeki, "Speech at the Annual National Conference of the Black Management Forum," November 20, 1999, www.anc.org.za/ancdocs/history/mbeki/1999/tm1120.html.
122. "Paper Lions," *The Economist,* April 17, 1999, 65.
123. Rachel L. Swarns, "Rarity of Black-Run Businesses Worries South Africa's Leaders," *New York Times,* November 13, 2002.
124. Iheduru notes that "neo-liberals see privatisation as a strategy to 'shrink' the state. The South African government, in contrast, has used its programme to advance BEE goals by requiring bidders for divested state assets to satisfy minimum 'empowerment' equity ownership/participation in the privatized company." Iheduru, "Black Economic Power," 11.
125. "Cautionary Tale of Black Business: South Africa," *The Economist,* January 10, 1998, 38.
126. Patrick Laurence, "Stage Set for Mining Stoush," *Australian Financial Review,* June 26, 2002.
127. "Mining Man Digging His Company out of a Hole: Interview Barry Davison," *Financial Times,* October 10, 2002.
128. Barry Davison, chair of Anglo American Platinum and president of the Chamber of Mines, as quoted in Swarns, "Rarity of Black-Run Businesses."
129. "ANC Strategy and Tactics as adopted by the 50th National Congress," December 1997, www.anc.org.za/ancdocs/history/conf/conference50/strategy amend.html.
130. Z. Pallo Jordan, "The National Question in Post 1994 South Africa. A discussion paper in preparation for the ANC's 50th National Conference," August 1997, www.anc.org.za/ancdocs/discussion/natquestion.html.
131. Mbeki, "Speech at the Annual National Conference of the Black Management Forum."
132. Adam et al., *Comrades in Business,* 217, writing as the process was just commencing, observed the dual logic of racialist legitimation, noting the possibility that "the greed of the parasitic elite could further reinforce the alienation of the marginalized underclass."
133. Jordan, "The National Question in Post 1994 South Africa."
134. Van der Berg and Louw, "Changing Patterns of South African Income Distribution," 14, table 1, present data that show that the white share of the national income was 50 percent in 1995 and either 50 percent (the pessimistic numbers) or 48 percent (the optimistic numbers) in 2000 and that the African share of national income was 38 percent in 1995 and either 38 percent (the pessimistic numbers) or 41 percent (the optimistic numbers) in 2000.

135. Mbeki, "Speech at the Annual National Conference of the Black Management Forum."
136. Marais, *South Africa: Limits to Change,* 5–6, estimates that only 30 percent are insiders, whereas Adam et al., *Comrades in Business,* 208, speak of 40 percent outsiders.
137. Elke K. Zuern, "Formal Democracy and the Fate of Participatory Governance: Contentious South Africans" (paper presented at the International Political Science Association, Durban, July 2, 2003) 18.
138. The term was coined by Patrick Bond, *Against Global Apartheid: South Africa Meets the World Bank, IMF, and International Finance* (London: Zed Books, 2001). For a novel perspective on the connection between civil society in general and "millennial capitalism," see Jean Comaroff and John L. Comaroff, eds., *Millennial Capitalism and the Culture of Neoliberalism* (Durham, NC: Duke University Press, 2001). For a good discussion of civil society in South Africa since the end of apartheid, see Adam Habib, "State–Civil Society Relations in Post-Apartheid South Africa," in *State of the Nation, 2003–2004,* 236–237. Habib distinguishes between two different types of civil society responses to neoliberal economics. "The first involves the proliferation of informal, survivalist community-based organizations, networks and associations, which enable poor and marginalised communities to simply survive against the daily ravages of neoliberalism" (236). The second are "social movement organizations," which "have a distinct leadership and membership, often supported by a middle class activist base. . . . They are not survivalist agencies, but are more political animals. Indeed, they have been largely established with the explicit political aim of organizing and mobilising the poor and marginalized, and contesting and/or engaging the state and other social actors around the implementation of neoliberal social policies" (257).
139. An excellent example of the linkage of particular grievances with the forces of global capitalism is the conflict over "cost recovery" for the provision of water and electricity. The issue is addressed comprehensively in David A. McDonald and John Pape, eds., *Cost Recovery and the Crisis of Service Delivery in South Africa* (Cape Town: HSRC Publishers, 2002).
140. Zuern, "Formal Democracy and the Fate of Participatory Governance," 15, provides several instances of patronage. Also see Sakhela Buhlungu, "From 'Madiba Magic' to 'Mbeki Logic': Mbeki and the ANC's Trade Union Allies," in *Thabo Mbeki's World,* 189–196, for a discussion of the role of patronage in controlling COSATU.

8. The Who, Not the What

1. The point is made one way or another by Niccolo Machiavelli, Thomas Hobbes, Edmund Burke, Karl Marx, Max Weber, and Charles Tilly.
2. Jean-Jacques Rousseau, "The Right of the Strongest," in *On the Social Con-*

tract, book 1, ed. Roger D. Masters, trans. Judith R. Masters (New York: St. Martin's Press, 1978), 48.

3. Charles Tilly, ed., *The Formation of National States in Western Europe* (Princeton, NJ: Princeton University Press, 1975), 79.
4. John Stuart Mill, *Utilitarianism, Liberty, and Representative Government* (London: J. M. Dent & Sons; New York: E. P. Dutton, 1910), 360–361.
5. Guillermo O'Donnell and Philippe C. Schmitter, *Transitions from Authoritarian Rule: Tentative Conclusions about Uncertain Democracies* (Baltimore: The Johns Hopkins University Press, 1991), 7. Italics in original.
6. John Rawls, *Political Liberalism* (New York: Columbia University Press, 1993), 5.
7. Ibid., 157–158.
8. A controversy is developing over how to pay for water and electricity services, whether they should be subsidized by the government or paid in full by consumers. For a good argument against the idea that poor consumers should pay full costs for water and electricity, see David A. McDonald and John Pape, eds., *Cost Recovery and the Crisis of Service Delivery in South Africa* (Cape Town: HSRC Publishers, 2002).
9. Alan Fischer and Michel Albeldas, eds., *A Question of Survival: Conversations with Key South Africans* (Johannesburg: Johnathan Ball Publishers, 1987), 337.
10. Ibid., 286. Italics added.
11. Larry Diamond, as quoted in Thomas L. Friedman, *The Lexus and the Olive Tree: Understanding Globalization* (New York: Anchor Books, 2000), 450–451.
12. Karl Marx, "On the Jewish Question," in *Karl Marx: Early Writings,* ed. T. B. Bottomore (New York: McGraw-Hill, 1964).
13. "Nation-Formation and Nation Building: The National Question in South Africa," 50th National Conference Documents, December 16–20, 1997, thesis 7, anc.org.za/ancdocs/discussion/nation.html. The quotation is a centerpiece of Democratic Alliance criticism of the ANC. It is interesting, therefore, to note the ambivalence of the document on the issue of black economic empowerment. Four theses earlier, the document acknowledges that "an important part of this is that the NDR [National Democratic Revolution] also entails the building of a black bourgeoisie. . . . The reality is that the bigger and more successful this black bourgeoisie becomes, the more diminished its race consciousness will become, for example in its attitude to workers, and dealing with unions" (thesis 3).

Conclusion

1. Amy Gutmann, *Identity in Democracy* (Princeton, NJ: Princeton University Press, 2003), 26.
2. Ibid., 28.

3. Republic of South Africa, *Constitution of the Republic of South Africa,* preamble (Pretoria: Government Printer, 1996).
4. Ibid., §1, 1, c.
5. Ibid., §2, 9, (1).
6. Ibid., §1, 1, b.
7. Ibid., §2, 19, (1).
8. Ibid., §2, 19, (2).
9. Ibid., §2, 12, (2), a.
10. Ibid., §2, 26, (1).
11. Ibid., §2, 27, (1), a, b, and c.
12. Ibid., §2, 28, (1), c.
13. Ibid., §2, 28, (1), d.
14. Ibid., §1, 6, (2).
15. Ibid., §2, 9, (2).
16. Ibid., §2, 16, (2), c.
17. Ibid., §12, 211 (1).
18. Ibid., §2, 15, (3), a, i.
19. James Tully, *Strange Multiplicity: Constitutionalism in an Age of Diversity* (Cambridge: Cambridge University Press, 1995), 6.
20. Ibid., 5.
21. Ibid., 1. For a provocative and much different discussion of the relationship between cultural diversity and democracy in South Africa, see Jean Comaroff and John Comaroff, "Reflections on Liberalism, Policulturalism, and ID-ology: Citizenship and Difference in South Africa," *Social Identities* 9, no. 4 (2003): 445–473.
22. Charles Taylor, *Multiculturalism and "The Politics of Recognition"* (Princeton, NJ: Princeton University Press, 1992), 25.
23. Seyla Benhabib, *The Claims of Culture: Equality and Diversity in the Global Era* (Princeton, NJ: Princeton University Press, 2002), 51.
24. Iris Marion Young, *Justice and the Politics of Difference* (Princeton, NJ: Princeton University Press, 1990), 11.
25. Seyla Benhabib, "Towards a Deliberative Model of Democratic Legitimacy," in *Democracy and Difference,* ed. Seyla Benhabib (Princeton, NJ: Princeton University Press, 1996), 67–94.
26. Joshua Cohen, "Procedure and Substance in Deliberative Democracy," in *Democracy and Difference,* 99.
27. Iris Marion Young, "Communication and the Other: Beyond Deliberative Democracy," in *Democracy and Difference,* 121.
28. Ibid.
29. Ibid.
30. Ibid., 122.
31. Ibid.
32. " 'Power' is the probability that one actor within a social relationship will be in a position to carry out his own will despite resistance." Max Weber,

Economy and Society: An Outline of Interpretive Sociology vol. 1, ed. Guenther Roth and Claus Wittich (Berkelely: University of California Press, 1978), 53.

33. Iris Marion Young, *Inclusion and Democracy* (New York: Oxford University Press, 2000), 23.
34. *Constitution of the Republic of South Africa,* §13, 224 (1) and (2).
35. Ibid., §2, 25(5); §2, 26 (2); §2, 27 (2). Italics added.
36. Max Weber, "Politics as a Vocation," in *From Max Weber: Essays in Sociology,* ed. H. H. Gerth and C. Wright Mills (New York: Oxford University Press, 1958), 128.

Bibliography

Adam, Heribert. *Modernizing Racial Domination: The Dynamics of South African Politics.* Berkeley: University of California Press, 1971.

———, ed. *South Africa: Sociological Perspectives.* London: Oxford University Press, 1971.

Adam, Heribert, and Hermann Giliomee. *Ethnic Power Mobilized: Can South Africa Change?* New Haven, CT: Yale University Press, 1979.

Adam, Heribert, and Kogila Moodley. *South Africa Without Apartheid: Dismantling Racial Domination.* Berkeley: University of California Press, 1986.

Adam, Heribert, Frederik Van Zyl Slabbert, and Kogila Moodley. *Comrades in Business: Post-Liberation Politics in South Africa.* Utrecht: International Books, 1998.

African National Congress. "ANC Strategy and Tactics as adopted by the 50th National Congress." December 1997. www.anc.org.za/ancdocs/history/conf/conference50/strategyamend.html.

———. Conference Documents, 50th National Conference, Mafikeng, South Africa, December 16–20, 1997. www.anc.org.za/ancdocs/history/conf/conference50/.

———. Conference Documents, 51st National Conference, University of Stellenbosch, December 16–20, 2000. www.anc.org.za/ancdocs/history/conf/conference51/main.html.

———. Discussion document, "The State and Social Transformation." November 1996. www.anc.org.za/ancdocs/policy/s&st.html.

———. "Nation-Formation and Nation Building: The National Question in South Africa." The 50th National Conference of the ANC, Mafikeng, South Africa, December 16–20, 1997. www.anc.org.za/ancdocs/discussion/nation.html.

———. *The Reconstruction and Development Programme: A Policy Framework.* Johannesburg: Umanyano Publisher, 1994.

Aletta, J. Norval. *Deconstructing Apartheid Discourse.* London: Verso, 1996.

Alexander, Neville (No Sizwe). *One Azania, One Nation: The National Question in South Africa.* London: Zed Books, 1979.

———. *An Ordinary Country: Issues in the Transitions from Apartheid to Democracy in South Africa.* Scottsville, South Africa: University of Natal Press, 2002.

———. *Sow the Wind: Contemporary Speeches.* Johannesburg: Skotaville Publishers, 1985.

Anderson, Benedict. *Imagined Communities: Reflections on the Origin and Spread of Nationalism.* 2nd ed. London: Verso, 1991.

Avineri, Shlomo. *The Making of Modern Zionism: The Intellectual Origins of the Jewish State.* New York: Basic Books, 1981.

Ball, Terry, with Dumisa Buhle. *Unfinished Business: South Africa, Apartheid and Truth.* London: Verso, 2003.

Baskin, Jeremy. *Striking Back: A History of COSATU.* Johannesburg: Ravan Press, 1991.

Baumol, William J., and Alan S. Blinder. *Economics: Principles and Policy.* 6th ed. Fort Worth, TX: The Dryden Press, Harcourt Brace & Company, 1994.

Beinart, William. *The Political Economy of Pondoland, 1860–1930.* Cambridge: Cambridge University Press, 1982.

———. *Twentieth Century South Africa.* Cape Town: Oxford University Press, 1994.

Beinart, William, and Colin Bundy. *Hidden Struggles in Rural South Africa: Politics and Popular Movements in the Transkei and Eastern Cape, 1890–1930.* Berkeley: University of California Press, 1987.

Beinart, William, and Saul Dubow, eds. *Segregation and Apartheid in Twentieth-Century South Africa.* London: Routledge, 1995.

Benhabib, Seyla. *The Claims of Culture: Equality and Diversity in the Global Era.* Princeton, NJ: Princeton University Press, 2002.

———, ed. *Democracy and Difference: Contesting the Boundaries of the Political.* Princeton, NJ: Princeton University Press, 1996.

Benson, Mary. *Nelson Mandela: The Man and the Movement.* New York: W. W. Norton, 1986.

Biko, Steve. *I Write What I Like.* Edited by Aelred Stubbs. London: C. R. Heinemann, 1987.

Bond, Patrick. *Against Global Apartheid: South Africa Meets the World Bank, IMF, and International Finance.* London: Zed Books, 2001.

———, ed. *Fanon's Warning: A Civil Society Reader on the New Partnership for Africa's Development.* Trenton, NJ: Africa World Press, 2002.

Bonner, Philip, Peter Delius, and Deborah Posel, eds. *Apartheid's Genesis, 1935–1962.* Braamfontein, South Africa: Ravan Press, 1993.

Bottomore, T. B., ed. *Karl Marx: Early Writings.* New York: McGraw-Hill, 1964.

Breytenbach, Breyten. *The True Confessions of an Albino Terrorist.* New York: McGraw-Hill, 1986.

Brown, Wendy. *States of Injury: Power and Freedom in Late Modernity.* Princeton, NJ: Princeton University Press, 1995.

Brubaker, Rogers. *Citizenship and Nationhood in France and Germany.* Cambridge, MA: Harvard University Press, 1992.

Bundy, Colin. *The Rise and Fall of the South African Peasantry*. Berkeley: University of California Press, 1979.

Bunting, Brian. *The Rise of the South African Reich*. Harmondsworth, Middlesex: Penguin Books, 1964.

Burke, Edmund. *Reflections on the Revolution in France*. Harmondsworth, Middlesex: Penguin Books, 1973.

Butler, Anthony. *Democracy and Apartheid: Political Theory, Comparative Politics and the Modern South African State*. New York: St. Martin's Press, 1998.

Butler, Jeffrey, Richard Elphick, and David Welsh, eds. *Democratic Liberalism in South Africa: Its History and Prospect*. Middletown, CT: Wesleyan University Press, 1987.

Carr, Edward Hallett. *The Twenty Years' Crisis, 1919–1939: An Introduction to the Study of International Relations*. New York: Harper and Row, 1964.

Clingman, Stephen. *Bram Fischer: Afrikaner Revolutionary*. Amherst: University of Massachusetts Press, 1998.

Cobbett, William, and Robin Cohen, eds. *Popular Struggles in South Africa*. London: James Currey, 1988.

Cole, Josette. *Crossroads: The Politics of Reform and Repression, 1976–1986*. Johannesburg: Ravan Press, 1987.

Comaroff, Jean, and John L. Comaroff. *Millennial Capitalism and the Culture of Neoliberalism*. Durham, NC: Duke University Press, 2001.

———. "Reflections on Liberalism, Policulturalism, and ID-ology: Citizenship and Difference in South Africa." *Social Identities* 9, no. 4 (2003): 445–474.

Connor, Walker. *Ethnonationalism: The Quest for Understanding*. Princeton, NJ: Princeton University Press, 1994.

Corker, Robert, and Tamim Bayoumi. "Apartheid, Growth and Income Distribution in South Africa: Past History and Future Prospects." IMF working paper. Washington, DC: International Monetary Fund, 1991.

Cox, Robert W. *Production, Power, and World Order: Social Forces in the Making of History*. New York: Columbia University Press, 1987.

Dahl, Robert. *Democracy and Its Critics*. New Haven, CT: Yale University Press, 1989.

———. *Polyarchy: Participation and Opposition*. New Haven, CT: Yale University Press, 1971.

———. *Toward Democracy: A Journey*. Vol. 1, *Reflections, 1940–1997*. Berkeley: Institute of Governmental Studies Press, University of California, 1997.

Daniel, John, Adam Habib, and Roger Southall, eds. *State of the Nation: South Africa 2003–2004*. Cape Town: HSRC, 2003.

Davenport, T. R. H. *The Birth of a New South Africa*. Toronto: University of Toronto Press, 1998.

———. *South Africa: A Modern History*. 3rd ed. Toronto: University of Toronto Press, 1987.

Davies, Richard, David Kaplan, M. Morris, and Dan O'Meara. "Class Struggle and a Periodisation of the South African State." *Review of African Political Economy* 3, no. 7 (1976).

Davis, Stephen. *Apartheid's Rebels: Inside South Africa's Hidden War.* New Haven, CT: Yale University Press, 1987.

De Kiewiet, C. W. *A History of South Africa: Social and Economic.* New York: Oxford University Press, 1957.

De Klerk, F. W. *The Last Trek—a New Beginning: The Autobiography.* London: Macmillan, 1998.

Dubow, Saul. *The African National Congress.* Phoenix Mill: Sutton Publishing, 2000.

———. *Racial Segregation and the Origins of Apartheid in South Africa, 1919–36.* Houndsmill, England: Palgrave Macmillan, 1989.

———. *Scientific Racism in Modern South Africa.* Cambridge: Cambridge University Press, 1995.

Du Toit, André, and Hermann Giliomee. *Afrikaner Political Thought: Analysis and Documents.* Vol. 1, *1780–1850.* Cape Town: David Philip, 1983.

Ellis, Stephen, and Tsepho Sechaba. *Comrades Against Apartheid: The ANC and the South African Communist Party in Exile.* Bloomington: Indiana University Press, 1992.

Elphick, Richard, and Hermann Giliomee, eds. *The Shaping of South African Society, 1652–1840.* Middletown, CT: Wesleyan University Press, 1989.

Evans, Peter B., Dietrich Rueschemeyer, and Theda Skocpol, eds. *Bringing the State Back In.* New York: Cambridge University Press, 1985.

Fanon, Frantz. *The Wretched of the Earth.* New York: Grove Press, 1968.

Fine, Robert, with Dennis Davis. *Beyond Apartheid: Labour and Liberation in South Africa.* Johannesburg: Ravan Press, 1990.

Finnegan, William. *Crossing the Line: A Year in the Land of Apartheid.* New York: Harper and Row, 1986.

Fiori, Giuseppe. *Antonio Gramsci: Life of a Revolutionary.* New York: Schocken Books, 1970.

Fischer, Alan, and Michel Albeldas, eds. *A Question of Survival: Conversations with Key South Africans.* Johannesburg: Johnathan Ball Publishers, 1987.

Frankel, Philip, Noam Pines, and Mark Swilling, eds. *State, Resistance, and Change in South Africa.* London: Croom Helm, 1988.

Frederikse, Julie. *The Unbreakable Thread: Non-Racialism in South Africa.* Bloomington: Indiana University Press, 1990.

Fredrickson, George M. *Black Liberation: A Comparative History of Black Ideologies in the United States and South Africa.* New York: Oxford University Press, 1995.

———. *Racism: A Short History.* Princeton, NJ: Princeton University Press, 2003.

———. *White Supremacy: A Comparative Study in American and South African History.* New York: Oxford University Press, 1981.

Friedman, Milton. *Capitalism and Freedom.* Chicago: University of Chicago Press, 1962.

Friedman, Steven. *Building Tomorrow Today: African Workers in Trade Unions, 1970–1984*. Johannesburg: Ravan Press, 1987.

———, ed. *The Long Journey: South Africa's Quest for a Negotiated Settlement*. Braamfontein, South Africa: Ravan Press, 1993.

Friedman, Steven, and Doreen Atkinson, eds. *South African Review 7: The Small Miracle*. Randburg, South Africa: Ravan Press, 1994.

Friedman, Thomas L. *The Lexus and the Olive Tree: Understanding Globalization*. New York: Anchor Books, 2000.

Frueh, Jamie. *Political Identity and Social Change: The Remaking of the South African Social Order*. Albany: State University of New York Press, 2003.

Gaventa, John. *Power and Powerlessness: Quiescence and Rebellion in an Appalachian Valley*. Urbana: University of Illinois Press, 1980.

Gelb, Stephen. "Inequality in South Africa: Nature, Causes and Responses." African Development and Poverty Reduction: The Macro-Micro Linkage, forum paper. Johannesburg: Development Policy Research Unit, 2004.

———, ed. *South Africa's Economic Crisis*. Cape Town: David Philip, 1991.

Gellner, Ernest. *Nations and Nationalism*. Ithaca, NY: Cornell University Press, 1983.

Gerhart, Gail. *Black Power in South Africa: The Evolution of an Ideology*. Berkeley: University of California Press, 1978.

Giliomee, Hermann. "Afrikaner Entrepreneurship and the Afrikaner Economic Advance, 1900–2000: A Tale with a Puzzle and Some Twists." Paper presented to the Centre for Development and Enterprise, Johannesburg, November 22, 1999.

———. *The Afrikaners: Biography of a People*. Charlottesville: University of Virginia Press, 2003.

———. "Presidential Address: Liberal and Populist Democracy in South Africa: Challenges, New Threats to Liberalism." Johannesburg: South African Institute of Race Relations, 1996.

Giliomee, Hermann, and Lawrence Schlemmer. *From Apartheid to Nation-Building*. New York: Oxford University Press, 1989.

Giliomee, Hermann, and Charles Simkins, eds. *The Awkward Embrace: One-Party Domination and Democracy*. Cape Town: Tafelberg Publishers, 1999.

Gilroy, Paul. *Against Race: Imagining Political Culture Beyond the Color Line*. Cambridge, MA: Harvard University Press, 2000.

———. *There Ain't No Black in the Union Jack: The Cultural Politics of Race and Nation*. Chicago: University of Chicago Press, 1991.

Glen, Jack D., and Mariusz A. Sumlinski. "Trends in Private Investment in Developing Countries 1995, Statistics for 1980–93." Discussion Paper Number 25. Washington, DC: International Finance Corporation, The World Bank, 1995.

Goldberg, David Theo. *The Racial State*. Malden, MA: Blackwell, 2002.

———, ed. *Multiculturalism: A Critical Reader*. Oxford: Blackwell, 1998.

Gordimer, Nadine. *July's People*. New York: Penguin, 1982.

Greenberg, Stanley B. *Legitimating the Illegitimate: State, Markets, and Resistance in South Africa.* Berkeley: University of California Press, 1987.

———. *Race and State in Capitalist Development: Comparative Perspectives.* New Haven, CT: Yale University Press, 1980.

Gregor, James A. *Contemporary Radical Ideologies: Totalitarian Thought in the Twentieth Century.* New York: Random House, 1968.

Gutmann, Amy. *Identity in Democracy.* Princeton, NJ: Princeton University Press, 2003.

Habib, Adam. "State–Civil Society Relations in Post-Apartheid South Africa." In *State of the Nation 2003–2004*, edited by John Daniels, Adam Habib, and Roger Southall, Cape Town: HSRC Publishers, 2003.

Hadland, Adrian, and Jovial Rantao. *The Life and Times of Thabo Mbeki.* Rivonia, South Africa: Southern Books, 1999.

Halisi, C. R. D. *Black Political Thought in the Making of South African Democracy.* Bloomington: Indiana University Press, 1999.

Hanlon, Joseph. *Beggar Your Neighbours: Apartheid Power in Southern Africa.* Bloomington, Indiana: Indiana University Press, 1986.

Hannaford, Ivan. *Race: The History of an Idea in the West.* Baltimore: The Johns Hopkins University Press, 1996.

Hannay, M. *Van Dale: Handwoordenboek, Nederlands-Engels.* 3rd ed. Utrecht: Van Dale Lexicografie, 1996.

Hawker, Geoffrey. "Political Leadership in the ANC: The South African Provinces 1994–99." *Journal of Modern African Studies* 38, no. 4 (2000): 631–657.

Hayek, F. A. *The Road to Serfdom.* Chicago: University of Chicago Press, 1972.

Hegel, G. W. F. *The Phenomenology of Mind.* New York: Harper Torchbook, 1967.

Hirschowitz, Ros. "Earning and Spending in South Africa: Selected Findings and Comparisons from the Income and Expenditure Surveys of October 1995 and October 2000." Pretoria: Statistics South Africa, 2002.

———. "Earning and Spending in South Africa: Selected Findings of the 1995 Income and Expenditure Survey." Pretoria: Central Statistics Service, 1997.

———. *Measuring Poverty in South Africa.* Pretoria: Statistics South Africa, 2000.

Hobbes, Thomas. *Leviathan.* London: Penguin Books, 1985.

Hobsbawm, E. J. *Nations and Nationalism since 1780: Programme, Myth, Reality.* Cambridge: Cambridge University Press, 1990.

Hoernlé, R. F. Alfred. *South African Native Policy and the Liberal Spirit.* New York: Negro Universities Press, 1969.

Holland, Heidi. *The Struggle: A History of the African National Congress.* London: Grafton Books, 1989.

Horowitz, Donald L. *A Democratic South Africa: Constitutional Engineering in a Divided Society.* Berkeley: University of California Press, 1991.

———. *Ethnic Groups in Conflict.* Berkeley: University of California Press, 1985.

Horwitz, Robert B. *Communication and Democratic Reform in South Africa.* Cambridge: Cambridge University Press, 2001.

Huntington, Samuel P. *Political Order in Changing Societies.* New Haven, CT: Yale University Press, 1968.

Iheduru, Okechukwu G. "Black Economic Power and Nation-Building in Post-Apartheid South Africa." *Journal of Modern African Studies* 42, no. 1 (2004): 1–30.

International Monetary Fund. *International Financial Statistics Yearbook, 2000.* Washington, DC: International Monetary Fund, 2000.

Jacobs, Sean, and Richard Caland, eds. *Thabo Mbeki's World: The Politics and Ideology of the South African President.* Pietermaritzburg: University of Natal Press, 2002.

James, Wilmot G. *Our Precious Metal: African Labour in South Africa's Gold Industry, 1970–1990.* Cape Town: David Philip, 1992.

Joffe, Avril, David Kaplan, Raphael Kaplinsky, and David Lewis. *Improving Manufacturing Performance in South Africa: The Report of the Industrial Strategy Project.* International Development Research Centre. Rondebosch, South Africa: University of Cape Town Press, 1995.

Johns, Sheridan. *Raising the Red Flag: The International Socialist League and the Communist Party of South Africa, 1914–1932.* Bellville, South Africa: Mayibuye Books, 1995.

Johns, Sheridan, and R. Hunt Davis, Jr., eds. *Mandela, Tambo and the African National Congress: The Struggle Against Apartheid, 1948–1990: A Documentary Survey.* New York: Oxford University Press, 1991.

Johnson, R. W., and Lawrence Schlemmer, eds. *Launching Democracy in South Africa: The First Open Election.* New Haven, CT: Yale University Press, 1996.

Johnson, R. W., and David Welsh, eds. *Ironic Victory: Liberalism in Post-Liberation South Africa.* Cape Town: Oxford University Press, 1998.

Johnstone, Frederick A. *Class, Race and Gold: A Study of Class Relations and Racial Discrimination in South Africa.* London: Routledge and Kegan Paul, 1976.

Jordan, Z. Pallo. "The National Question in Post 1994 South Africa. A discussion paper in preparation for the ANC's 50th National Conference." www.anc.org.za/ancdocs/discussion/natquestion.html.

Karis, Thomas, and Gwendolen M. Carter, eds. *From Protest to Challenge: A Documentary History of African Politics in South Africa, 1882–1964.* Vol. 1, *Protest and Hope, 1882–1934.* Edited by Sheridan Johns III. Stanford, CA: Hoover Institution Press, 1987.

———. *From Protest to Challenge: A Documentary History of African Politics in South Africa, 1882–1964.* Vol. 2, *Hope and Challenge, 1935–1952.* Edited by Thomas Karis. Stanford, CA: Hoover Institution Press, 1987.

———. *From Protest to Challenge: A Documentary History of African Politics in South Africa, 1882–1964.* Vol. 3, *Challenge and Violence, 1953–1964.* Edited by Thomas Karis and Gail M. Gerhart. Stanford, CA: Hoover Institution Press, 1987.

Karis, Thomas G., and Gail M. Gerhart. *From Protest to Challenge: A Documentary History of African Politics in South Africa, 1882–1990.* Vol. 5, *Nadir and Resurgence, 1964–1979.* Bloomington: Indiana University Press, 1997.

Keegan, Timothy. *Colonial South Africa and the Origins of the Racial Order*. Charlottesville: University Press of Virginia, 1996.

Klopp, Jacqueline M., and Elke Zuern. "The Politics of Violence in Democratization." Paper prepared for delivery at the European Consortium for Political Research (ECPR) Annual Conference, September 18–21, 2003.

Kymlicka, Will. *Multicultural Citizenship: A Liberal Theory of Minority Rights*. Oxford: Clarendon Press, 1995.

Lachman, Desmond, and Kenneth Bercuson, eds. "Economic Policies for a New South Africa." Occasional Paper 91. Washington, DC: International Monetary Fund, 1992.

Lamar, Howard, and Leonard Thompson, eds. *The Frontier in History: North America and Southern Africa Compared*. New Haven, CT: Yale University Press, 1981.

Legassick, Martin. "South Africa: Capital Accumulation and Violence." *Economy and Society* 3, no. 3 (1974).

Leibbrandt, Murray V., Christopher D. Woolard, and Ingrid D. Woolard. "The Contribution of Income Components to Income Inequality in South Africa: A Decomposable Gini Analysis." Living Standards Measurement Study Working Paper No. 125. Washington, DC: World Bank, 1996.

Lelyveld, Joseph. *Move Your Shadow: South Africa, Black and White*. New York: Penguin Books, 1986.

Lenin, V. I. *Imperialism: The Highest Stage of Capitalism*. New York: International Publishers, 1972.

———. *National Liberation, Socialism, and Imperialism: Selected Writings by V. I. Lenin*. New York: International Publishers, 1970.

———. *What Is to Be Done?* New York: International Publishers, 1972.

Lewis, Stephen R., Jr. *The Economics of Apartheid*. New York: Council of Foreign Relations Press, 1990.

Lijphart, Arend. *Democracy in Plural Societies: A Comparative Exploration*. New Haven, CT: Yale University Press, 1977.

———. *Power-Sharing in South Africa*. Berkeley: Institute of International Studies, University of California, 1985.

Lipton, Merle. *Capitalism and Apartheid: South Africa, 1910–84*. Totowa, NJ: Rowman & Allanheld, 1985.

Lodge, Tom. *Black Politics in South Africa since 1945*. New York: Longman, 1986.

———. *South African Politics since 1994*. Cape Town: David Philip, 1999.

Lodge, Tom, Bill Nasson, Steve Mufson, Khehla Shubane, and Nokwanda Sithole. *All, Here, and Now: Black Politics in South Africa in the 1980s*. Cape Town: Ford Foundation, David Philip, 1991.

Luthuli, Albert. *Let My People Go: An Autobiography*. Johannesburg: Collins, 1962.

MacDonald, Michael. "The Political Economy of Identity Politics." *The South Atlantic Quarterly* (special issue: *After the Thrill Is Gone: A Decade of Post-Apartheid South Africa*), 103, no. 4 (Fall 2004).

———. "Power Politics in South Africa." *Journal of Southern African Studies* 22, no. 2 (June 1996).

———. "The Siren's Song: The Political Logic of Power-Sharing in South Africa." *Journal of Southern African Studies* 18, no. 4 (1992): 709–725.

Mamdani, Mahmood. *Citizen and Subject: Contemporary Africa and the Legacy of Late Colonialism.* Princeton, NJ: Princeton University Press, 1996.

Mandela, Nelson. *Long Walk to Freedom: The Autobiography of Nelson Mandela.* Boston: Little, Brown, 1994.

———. *Nelson Mandela Speaks: Forging a Democratic, Nonracial South Africa.* Edited by Steve Clark. Cape Town: David Philip, 1994.

———. "Report by the President of the ANC to the 50th National Conference of the African National Congress," 1997. www.anc.org.za/ancdocs/history/conf/conference50/presaddress.html.

———. *The Struggle Is My Life.* New York: Pathfinder Press, 1990.

Manganyi, N. Chabani, and André du Toit, eds. *Political Violence and the Struggle in South Africa.* Halfway House, South Africa: Southern Book Publishers, 1990.

Marais, Hein. *South Africa: Limits to Change: The Political Economy of Transition.* Cape Town: University of Cape Town Press, 1998.

Maré, Gerhard, and Georgina Hamilton. *An Appetite for Power: Buthelezi's Inkatha and the Politics of "Loyal Resistance."* Braamfontein, South Africa: Ravan Press, 1987.

Marks, Shula. *The Ambiguities of Dependence in South Africa.* Johannesburg: Ravan Press, 1986.

Marks, Shula, and Anthony Atmore, eds. *Economy and Society in Pre-Industrial South Africa.* London: Longman, 1980.

Marks, Shula, and Richard Rathbone, eds. *Industrialisation and Social Change in South Africa.* New York: Longman, 1982.

Marks, Shula, and Stanley Trapido, eds. *The Politics of Race, Class, and Nationalism in Twentieth-Century South Africa.* London: Longman, 1988.

Marquard, Leo. *The Peoples and Policies of South Africa.* London: Oxford University Press, 1952.

Marx, Anthony W. *Lessons of Struggle: South African Internal Opposition, 1960–1990.* New York: Oxford University Press, 1992.

———. *Making Race and Nation: A Comparison of South Africa, the United States, and Brazil.* Cambridge: Cambridge University Press, 1998.

Marx, Karl, and Frederick Engels. *The Communist Manifesto.* New York: International Publishers, 1982.

Maseko, Sipho, and Peter Vale. "South Africa and African Renaissance." *International Affairs* (April 1998).

Mathabane, Mark. *Kaffir Boy.* New York: Signet Books, 1986.

Mattes, Robert. "South Africa: Democracy Without the People?" *Journal of Democracy* 13, no. 1 (2002).

Mattes, Robert, and Jessica Piombo. "Opposition Parties and the Voters in South Africa's 1999 Election." *Democratization* 8, no. 13 (Autumn 2001).

May, Julian, I. Woolard, and S. Klasen. "Input Paper: Poverty and Inequality

Report—The Measurement and Nature of Poverty and Inequality," August 1997. www.info.gov.za/otherdocs/1998/poverty/nature.pdf, accessed September 12, 2005.

Mbeki, Govan. *South Africa: The Peasants' Revolt.* London: International Defence and Aid Fund for Southern Africa, 1984.

———. *The Struggle for Liberation in South Africa: A Short History.* Cape Town: David Philip, 1992.

Mbeki, Thabo. "Address by the President of South Africa, Thabo Mbeki on the Occasion of His Inauguration and the 10th Anniversary of Freedom." Pretoria, April 27, 2004. www.dfa.gov.za/docs/speeches/2004/mbek0427.htm.

———. "Address of the President, Thabo Mbeki, at the Opening of the 51st National Conference of the African National Congress." Stellenbosch, December 16, 2002. www.anc.org.za/ancdocs/history/mbeki/2002/tm1216.html.

———. "Address of the President of South Africa, Thabo Mbeki, at the Second Joint Sitting of the Third Democratic Parliament." Cape Town, February 11, 2005. www.dfa.gov.za/docs/speeches/2005/mbeki0211.htm.

———. "Speech at the Annual National Conference of the Black Management Forum." November 20, 1999. www.anc.org.za/ancdocs/history/mbeki/1999/tm1120.html.

———. "State of the Nation Address." February 14, 2003. www.anc.org.za/ancdocs/history/mbeki/2003/tm0214.html.

———. "State of the Nation Address by the President of South Africa, Thabo Mbeki, to the Joint Sitting of the Houses of Parliament." Cape Town, February 8, 2002. www.info.gov.za/speeches/2002/0202281146a1001.htm.

———. "State of the Nation Address of the President of South Africa, Thabo Mbeki." House of Parliament, Cape Town, February 6, 2004. www.anc.org.za/ancdocs/history/mbeki/2004/tm0206.html.

———. "State of the Nation Address of the President of South Africa at the Opening of Parliament." Cape Town, February 9, 2001. www.dfa.gov.za/docs/speeches/2001/mbek0209.htm.

———. "Statement of Deputy President Thabo Mbeki at the Opening of the Debate in the National Assembly, on 'Reconciliation and Nation Building,' " National Assembly, Cape Town, May 29, 1998. www.dfa.gov.za/docs/speeches/1998/mbek0529.htm.

McDonald, David A., and John Pape, eds. *Cost Recovery and the Crisis of Service Delivery in South Africa.* Cape Town: HSRC Publishers, 2002.

McGregor's Who Owns Whom in South Africa. 21st ed. Westgate, South Africa: PSG Online, 2001.

McKinley, Dale T. *The ANC and the Liberation Struggle: A Critical Political Biography.* London: Pluto Press, 1997.

Miliband, Ralph. *The State in Capitalist Society: The Analysis of the Western System of Power.* London: Quartet Books, 1976.

Mill, John Stuart. *Utilitarianism, Liberty, and Representative Government.* London: J. M. Dent & Sons; New York: E. P. Dutton, 1910.

Miller, David, ed. *The Blackwell Encyclopedia of Political Thought.* New York: Basil Blackwell, 1987.

Miller, Roberta Balstad. "Science and Society in the Early Career of H. F. Verwoerd." *Journal of Southern African Studies* 19, no. 4 (December 1993): 634–661.

Mohr, P. J. et al. *The Practical Guide to South African Economic Indicators.* Johannesburg: Lexicon Publishers, 1995.

Moll, Peter. "Discrimination Is Declining in South Africa but Inequality Is Not." *Journal for Studies in Economics and Econometrics* 24, no. 3 (2000).

Moodie, T. Dunbar. *The Rise of Afrikanerdom: Power, Apartheid, and the Afrikaner Civil Religion.* Berkeley: University of California Press, 1980.

Murray, Martin. *Revolution Deferred: The Painful Birth of Post-Apartheid South Africa.* London: Verso, 1994.

Myers, Jason. "Fancy Dress: Concealment and Ideology in South Africa." *Transformation* 30 (1996): 30–46.

———. "The Spontaneous Ideology of Tradition in Post-Apartheid South Africa." *Politikon* 26, no. 1 (1999): 33–56.

Nattrass, Nicoli, and Jeremy Seekings. " 'Two Nations'? Race and Economic Inequality in South Africa Today." *Daedalus—Journal of the American Academy of Arts and Sciences,* 130, no. 1 (Winter 2001), "Why South Africa Matters." Special issue.

Nolutshungu, Sam C. *Changing South Africa: Political Considerations.* New York: Africana, 1982.

Norval, Aletta J. *Deconstructing Apartheid Discourse.* London: Verso, 1996.

O'Donnell, Guillermo, and Philippe C. Schmitter. *Transitions from Authoritarian Rule: Tentative Conclusions about Uncertain Democracies.* Baltimore: The Johns Hopkins University Press, 1991.

O'Meara, Dan. *Forty Lost Years: The Apartheid State and the Politics of the National Party, 1948–1994.* Randburg, South Africa: Ravan Press, 1996.

———. *Volkskapitalisme: Class, Capital and Ideology in the Development of Afrikaner Nationalism, 1934–1948.* New York: Cambridge University Press, 1983.

Peires, J. B. *The Dead Will Arise: Nongqawuse and the Great Xhosa Cattle-Killing Movement of 1856–7.* Bloomington: Indiana University Press, 1989.

———. *The House of Phalo: A History of the Xhosa People in the Days of Their Independence.* Berkeley: University of California Press, 1982.

Posel, Deborah. *The Making of Apartheid, 1948–1961: Conflict and Compromise.* Oxford: Oxford University Press, 1997.

Price, Robert M. *The Apartheid State in Crisis: Political Transformation in South Africa, 1975–1990.* New York: Oxford University Press, 1991.

Ramphele, Mamphela. *A Bed Called Home: Life in the Migrant Labour Hostels of Cape Town.* Cape Town: David Philip, 1993.

Rawls, John. *Political Liberalism.* New York: Columbia University Press, 1993.

Raz, Joseph. *Ethics in the Public Domain: Essays in the Morality of Law and Politics.* Oxford: Clarendon Press, 1994.

Reddy, E. S., ed. *Luthuli: Speeches of Chief Albert John Luthuli.* Durban: Madiba Publishers, 1991.

Relly, Gavin. "The Costs of Disinvestment." *Foreign Policy* 63 (Summer 1986).

Republic of South Africa. *Constitution of the Republic of South Africa.* Pretoria: Government Printer, 1996. www.polity.org.za/html/govdocs/constitution/saconst.html?rebookmark=1.

———. *Report of the Commission of Inquiry into the Riots at Soweto and Elsewhere* (Cillie Commission Report). Pretoria: Government Printing Office, 1980.

———. Central Statistics. *Statistics in Brief.* Pretoria, 1997.

———. Department of Finance. "Growth, Employment and Redistribution: A Macroeconomic Strategy (GEAR)." Pretoria, 1996. www.gov.za/documents/otherdocs/1996.htm.

———. Department of Trade and Industry. "The Evolution of Policy in SA: Proposed Guidelines for Competition Policy: A Framework for Competition, Competitiveness and Development." Pretoria, November 27, 1997. www.polity.org.za/html/govdocs/policy/competition.html.

———. Office of the Presidency. "White Paper on Reconstruction and Development: Government's Strategy for Fundamental Transformation." Cape Town, November 1994. www.info.gov.za/documents/whitepapers/index.htm.

———. Policy Co-ordinating and Advisory Services. *The Presidency. Towards a Ten Year Review: Synthesis Report on Implementation of Government Programmes, Discussion Document,* October 2003. www.gcis.gov.za/docs/publications/10years.htm.

Reynolds, Andrew, ed. *Election '99: South Africa from Mandela to Mbeki,* New York: St. Martin's Press, 1999.

Rich, Paul. *White Power and the Liberal Conscience: Racial Segregation and South African Liberalism, 1921–60.* Dover, NH: Manchester University Press, 1984.

Rousseau, Jean-Jacques *On the Social Contract.* Edited by Roger D. Masters. Translated by Judith R. Masters. New York: St. Martin's Press, 1978.

Roux, Edward. *S. P. Bunting: A Political Biography.* Bellville, South Africa: Mayibuye Books, 1993.

Seegers, Annette. *The Military in the Making of Modern South Africa.* Tauris Academic Studies, London: I. B. Tauris Publishers, 1996.

Seekings, Jeremy. *The UDF: A History of the United Democratic Front in South Africa, 1983–1991.* Oxford: James Currey, 2000.

Shubin, Vladimir. *ANC: A View from Moscow.* Bellville, South Africa: Mayibuye Books, 1999.

Sisk, Timothy D. *Democratization in South Africa: The Elusive Social Contract.* Princeton, NJ: Princeton University Press, 1994.

Slabbert, F. Van Zyl, and David Welsh. *South Africa's Options: Strategies for Sharing Power.* Cape Town: David Philip, 1981.

Smith, Anthony D. *The Ethnic Origins of Nations.* Oxford: Blackwell, 1986.

———. *National Identity.* Reno: University of Nevada Press, 1991.

Smuts, J. C. *Africa and Some World Problems.* Oxford: Clarendon Press, 1930.

South African Communist Party. "The Path to Power: Programme of the South African Communist Party." Johannesburg: South African Communist Party, 1990.

Southall, Roger. *Opposition and Democracy in South Africa.* London: Frank Cass, 2001.

Sparks, Allister. *Beyond the Miracle: Inside the New South Africa.* Chicago: University of Chicago Press, 2003.

———. *The Mind of South Africa: The Story of the Rise and Fall of Apartheid.* London: Mandarin Paperbacks, 1991.

———. *Tomorrow Is Another Country: The Inside Story of South Africa's Road to Change.* New York: Hill and Wang, 1995.

Stiglitz, Joseph E. *Globalization and Its Discontents.* New York: W. W. Norton, 2002.

Stultz, Newell. *Transkei's Half Loaf: Race Separatism in South Africa.* New Haven, CT: Yale University Press, 1979.

Suttner, Raymond. " 'It Is Your Mother Who Is the Enemy Now!' An Account of the Imprint of African National Congress Underground Activity in the 'Lull' after Rivonia." Paper presented to the International Political Science Association Conference, Durban, July 2003.

Tambo, Adelaide, ed. *Oliver Tambo Speaks: Preparing for Power.* London: Heinemann, 1987.

Tambo, Oliver. *Apartheid and the International Community: Addresses to United Nations Committees and Conferences.* Edited by E. S. Reddy. London: Kliptown Books, 1991.

Tamir, Tael. *Liberal Nationalism.* Princeton, NJ: Princeton University Press, 1993.

Taylor, Charles. *Multiculturalism and "The Politics of Recognition."* Princeton, NJ: Princeton University Press, 1992.

Taylor, Rupert. "South Africa: From 'Race' to 'Non-Racialism.' " In *Race, Ethnicity and Nation: International Perspectives on Social Conflict,* edited by Peter Ratcliffe. London: UCL Press, 1994.

———, ed. *Creating a Better World: Interpreting Global Civil Society.* Bloomfield, CT: Kumarian Press, 2004.

Taylor, Rupert, and Don Foster. "Advancing Non-Racialism in Post-Apartheid South Africa." In *National Identity and Democracy in Africa,* edited by Mai Palmberg. Bellville: Mayibuye Centre of the University of the Western Cape, Nordic Africa Institute, 1999.

Taylor, Rupert, and Mark Orkin. "The Racialisation of Social Scientific Research on South Africa." In *The Politics of Social Science Research: "Race," Ethnicity and Social Change,* edited by Peter Ratcliffe. New York: Palgrave, 2001.

Terreblanche, Sampie. *A History of Inequality in South Africa, 1652–2002.* Pietermaritzburg: University of Natal Press, 2002.

Thompson, Leonard M. *The Unification of South Africa, 1902–1910.* Oxford: Oxford University Press, 1960.

Tilly, Charles, ed. *The Formation of National States in Western Europe*. Princeton, NJ: Princeton University Press, 1975.

Tully, James. *Strange Multiplicity: Constitutionalism in an Age of Diversity*. Cambridge: Cambridge University Press, 1995.

United Nations Development Programme. *South Africa Human Development Report: The Challenge of Sustainable Development: Unlocking People's Creativity*. HDR 2003. http://hdr.undp.org/reports/detail_reports.cfm?view-686.

United Nations Human Development Reports. "2 Human Development Index Trends." HDR 2004. hdr.undp.org/statistics/data/indic_16_1_1.html.

———. "13 Economic Performance." HDR 2004. hdr.undp.org/statistics/data/indic_123_1_1.html.

Vail, Leroy, ed. *The Creation of Tribalism in Southern Africa*. London: James Currey, 1989.

Van der Berg, Servaas, and Megan Loux. "Changing Patterns of South African Income Distribution: Towards Time Series Estimates of Distribution and Poverty." *South African Journal of Economics* 72, no. 3 (September 2004). Special Conference Issue.

Van Onselen, Charles. *The Seed Is Mine: The Life of Kas Maine, a South African Sharecropper, 1894–1985*. New York: Hill and Wang, 1996.

———. *Studies in the Social and Economic History of Witwatersrand, 1886–1914*. 2 vols. Harlow, Essex: Longman, 1982.

Walshe, Peter. *The Rise of African Nationalism in South Africa: The African National Congress, 1912–1952*. Berkeley: University of California Press, 1971.

Walzer, Michael. *On Toleration*. New Haven, CT: Yale University Press, 1997.

Weber, Max. *Economy and Society: An Outline of Interpretive Sociology*. Edited by Guenther Roth and Claus Wittich. 2 vols. Berkeley: University of California Press, 1978.

———. *From Max Weber: Essays in Sociology*. Edited by H. H. Gerth and C. Wright Mills. New York: Oxford University Press, 1960.

Wilson, Monica, and Leonard Thompson, eds. *The Oxford History of South Africa*, vol. 2: *South Africa, 1870–1966*. New York: Oxford University Press, 1971.

Wolpe, Harold. "Capitalism and Cheap Labour-Power in South Africa: From Segregation to Apartheid." *Economy & Society* 1, no. 4. Also published in William Beinart and Saul Dubow, eds., *Segregation and Apartheid in Twentieth-Century South Africa*. London: Routledge, 1995.

———. *Class, Race and the Apartheid State*. London: James Currey, 1989.

Wood, Elisabeth Jean. *Forging Democracy from Below: Insurgent Transitions in South Africa and El Salvador*. Cambridge: Cambridge University Press, 2000.

World Bank. "Key Indicators of Poverty in South Africa." Analysis prepared for the Office of Reconstruction and Development Programme. Pretoria: South African Communication Service, 1995.

———. *Social Indicators of Development*. Baltimore: The Johns Hopkins University Press, 1995.

Wylie, Diana. *Starving on a Full Stomach: Hunger and the Triumph of Cultural Racism in Modern South Africa.* Charlottesville: University of Virginia Press, 2001.

Young, Iris Marion. *Inclusion and Democracy.* New York: Oxford University Press, 2002.

———. *Justice and the Politics of Difference.* Princeton, NJ: Princeton University Press, 1990.

Yudelman, David. *The Emergence of Modern South Africa: State, Capital and the Incorporation of Organized Labor on the South African Gold Fields, 1902–1939.* Westport, CT: Greenwood Press, 1983.

Zuern, Elke. "The Changing Roles of Civil Society in African Democratization Process." In *Consolidation of Democracy in Africa: A View from the South.* Edited by Solomon Hussein and Ian Liebenberg. Aldershot: Ashgate, 2000.

———. "Formal Democracy and the Fate of Participatory Governance: Contentious South Africans." International Political Science Association, Durban, July 2, 2003.

Index